CHARLOTTE GERE

Nineteenth-Century Decoration

THE ART OF THE INTERIOR

HARRY N. ABRAMS, INC., *Publishers, New York*

Library of Congress Cataloging-in-Publication Data

Gere, Charlotte.
    Nineteenth-century decoration/Charlotte Gere.
        p.   cm.
    Includes index.
    ISBN 0–8109–1382–8
    1. Interior decoration—Great Britain—History—19th
century. 2. Decoration and ornament—Great Britain—
History—19th century. 3. Decoration and ornament,
Architectural—Great Britain—History—19th
century. I. Title.   II. Title: 19th-century decoration.
NK2043.G45 1989
747.2′048—dc 19   89–158

Published in 1989 by Harry N. Abrams, Incorporated, New
York.

A Times Mirror Company

Designed by Trevor Vincent
Printed and bound in Italy

CONTENTS

Portrait of James and Sarah Tuttle by Joseph H. Davis, 1883
Courtesy of The New-York Historical Society

From the old German time, the conversation turned upon the Gothic. We spoke of a bookcase that had a Gothic character; and from this we were led to discuss the late fashion of arranging entire apartments in the old German and Gothic style, and thus living under the influences of a bygone time. 'In a house,' said Goethe, 'where there are so many rooms that some are entered three or four times a year, such a fancy may pass; and I think it a pretty notion of Madame Pankouke at Paris that she has a Chinese apartment. But I cannot praise the man who fits out the rooms in which he lives with these strange old-fashioned objects. It is a sort of masquerade; which can in the long run do no good in any respect, but must on the contrary have an unfavourable influence on the man adopting it. Such a fashion is in contradiction to the age in which we live, and will only confirm the empty and hollow way of thinking and feeling in which it originates. It is well enough, on a merry winter's evening, to go to a masquerade as a Turk; but what should we think of a man who wore such a mask all the year round? That he was either crazy, or in a fair way to become so before long.' (January 1827)

(Eckermann's *Conversations with Goethe*.)

ACKNOWLEDGEMENTS

Everyone attempting any study of this subject must acknowledge a debt to Mario Praz. A quarter of a century has gone by since the publication of his *Illustrated History of Interior Decoration*, in which for the first time the subject was studied in contemporary images. This book brought together a large body of examples of a charming minor art – hitherto largely ignored but now widely appreciated and collected – and played an important part in the revival of interest in interior decoration. Since 1964 others have added their own rich findings: John Cornforth's *English Interiors 1790–1848* (1978) followed his study of the eighteenth century undertaken with the celebrated decorator John Fowler; then in 1984 Peter Thornton published his masterly survey of four centuries, *Authentic Decor*. I have depended very greatly on the foundations laid by these distinguished predecessors, and can only hope that this opportunity to fill out the story of the nineteenth century in greater detail has been used to some advantage. I have been generously assisted in this task by many friends and colleagues.

I offer my grateful thanks to Princess Margaret of Hesse; Lady Abdy; Charles Alabaster of Hazlitt, Gooden & Fox, London; Mrs E. Aquilina of the Hammersmith Central Library, London; Jack Baer of Hazlitt, Gooden & Fox, London; Vicomte et Vicomtesse de Baritault du Carpia, Château de Roquetaillade, France; Mrs Elizabeth Bonython; Sir Walter Bromley Davenport, Bt.; Mrs Frances Collard of the Victoria and Albert Museum, London; James D. Draper of the Metropolitan Museum of Art, New York; Mrs Roger Dutnall; Mme Sonia Edard of the Musée des Arts Décoratifs, Paris; Eric Fischer of the Statens Museum for Kunst, Copenhagen; Sir Brinsley Ford; Dr Celina Fox of the Museum of London; Hildegard Fritz Denneville; Albert Gallichen; Richard Green of York City Art Gallery; Francis Greenacre of Bristol City Art Gallery; Rollin Hadley of the Isabella Stewart Gardner Museum, Boston; John and Eileen Harris; the late Francis Hawcroft; Mrs Michael Heseltine; Robert Isaacson; Mrs Stephanie Laing; the Hon. David Lytton Cobbold; Nicholas Maddex, archivist at Knebworth; the late Lady Mander; M. and Mme. Emanuel de Margerie; Charles Nugent of Christie's, London; the Hon. Mrs Roberts of the Royal Library, Windsor Castle; Peter Rose; the Countess of Rosebery; Mrs James de Rothschild; Peyton Skipwith of the Fine Art Society, London; Mrs Angela Steiner; Mrs Virginia Surtees; Patricia Tang; Miss Nancy Tennant; Mr and Mrs Eugene Victor Thaw; Peter Thornton of the Sir John Soane Museum, London; Mrs C.A. Trelogan, Abbot Hall, Cumbria; Clive Wainwright of the Victoria and Albert Museum, London.

My special thanks are due to Nicholas Merchant who brought my attention to Bedford Lemere's *Intérieurs anglais* and the album for Wickham Hall, and to Michael Whiteway for the unrestricted use of his incomparable library. I would like to thank the helpful members of staff at the Bridgeman Art Library, the Guildhall Library, the Lambeth Archive, the National Monuments Record and the Saffron Walden Library. Francis Graham accepted the task of researching *Intérieurs anglais* and then went on to interpret his brief so widely that I owe him gratitude for a host of interesting ideas and suggestions. Equally Mrs Jacqui Vincent brought to the mammoth job of researching and organizing the illustrations an inspiration far beyond the usual interpretation of this role. At Weidenfeld & Nicolson I have received constant encouragement from Michael Dover and Denny Hemming, with editorial assistance from Alice Williams. Trevor Vincent, the designer of this book, has been involved from the very begining. Having worked with him for many years on other projects, I have learned not to ignore his views, however discreetly put forward. The sensitive visual interpretation of this material is due to his long experience and impeccable taste in book design. The thankless task of interpreting and typing my manuscript was a team effort; my thanks to Francis Graham, Miss Sally Cooper and Miss Amanda Pask.

A century is an arbitrary division of time; it is not always possible to deal with a subject within its strict confines. I have strayed a little into the eighteenth century and the twentieth. However, Stephen Calloway's *Twentieth-Century Decoration* was well advanced by the time this book began to take shape so it was possible to take his treatment of the early years of the century into account when defining the scope of this book.

Charlotte Gere, London, 1989

INTRODUCTION

You remember our dear little house in Curzon Street; when we furnished it, nothing would please us but watered paper on the walls, garlands of roses tied with blue bows! Glazed chintzes with bunches of roses, so natural they looked, I thought, as if they had just been gathered (between you and me, I still think it was very pretty), and most lovely ornaments we had in perfect harmony, gilt pelicans or swans or candlesticks, Minton's imitation of Sèvres, and gilt bows everywhere. One day Mr Rossetti was dining alone with us, and instead of admiring my room and decorations, as I expected, he evidently could hardly sit at ease with them. I began then to ask if it were possible to suggest improvements! 'Well,' he said, frankly, 'I should begin by burning everything you have got.'

So remembered Lady Mount Temple in her *Memorials*, published in 1890. Having achieved a charming, unexceptionable result, utterly easy to live with, she was rudely awakened to the unguessed-at demands that the art of decoration makes on those who embark on a search for perfection in this difficult area. Painter and poet, Dante Gabriel Rossetti himself was a supremely successful exponent of the apparently effortless assemblage of furniture, fabrics, hangings, pictures, curiosities and *objets d'art* that is the hallmark of the 'artistic' style; in any case it was a matter to which he was prepared to devote much thought and effort. His fellow Pre-Raphaelite Holman Hunt recalled an occasion in the early years of their friendship:

My past experience in pattern-designing, and my criticisms upon the base and vulgar forms and incoherent curves in contemporary furniture, to which I drew Rossetti's attention on his first visit to me, encouraged visions of reform in these particulars, and we speculated on improvement in all household objects, furniture, fabrics and other interior decorations. Nor did we pause till Rossetti enlarged upon the devising of ladies' dresses and the improvement of men's costume, determining to follow the example of early artists not in one branch of taste only, but in all.
(*Pre-Raphaelitism and the Pre-Raphaelite Brotherhood*, 1908, vol. 1, p. 151.)

1

Pattern-book ornament 1869

Detail from the design entitled 'Chinois-Japonais', reproduced in Racinet's *Dictionnaire de l'Ornement* (1869), a widely used source book.

Michael Whiteway, London

In the event it was a latecomer to the Pre-Raphaelite circle, William Morris, who was to achieve the transformation in taste dreamt of by Holman Hunt and Rossetti. Through his firm Morris & Co., founded in 1861, he made the decoration and furnishings of the 'artistic' house available to the general public. Morris wallpapers and fabrics became the hallmark of sensibility and good taste. Edward Carpenter, in Morris's obituary, written for the anarchist publication *Freedom*, said of him, 'He hated with a good loyal hatred all insincerity; but most he hated, and with his very soul, the ugliness and meanness of modern life. I believe that was the great inspiring hatred of his life.'

Morris was a disappointed man at the end of his life and it is not likely to have been sufficient consolation that houses throughout the land, in the pursuit of 'sweetness and light', were furnished with Morris chairs, hung with Morris tapestries, curtained with Morris fabrics and carpeted with Hammersmith rugs. He had declared, 'We wouldn't procure the luxuries of life in a socialist society even if we could. We don't want them and we won't have them.' The patrons for whom he had mainly worked were either rich or aristocratic; in conflict with his political ideals, he beautified their environment rather than improving the lot of the masses. For the Manchester Museum he designed and furnished two model rooms which were intended to show the local working men how they might furnish cheaply but with taste, yet he was twice to provide enormously costly schemes for the State Rooms in St James's Palace. For the later scheme of 1881, in the Throne Room and Ante-Room the estimate for the curtains with their hand-worked borders and pelmets was £750 for each room. This was too much even for a royal patron.

Morris may have been unhappy with the results of his endeavours from the ideological point of view, but his influence, stylistically, was out of all proportion to the originality – or otherwise – of his decorative innovations. He was a pattern-maker of genius, and he understood the objections to what Ruskin called 'the fictitious idea of relief'. He never indulged in that nadir of artifice, suggesting cast shadows in a pattern of flower bouquets.

However, the later products of the Morris firm were to include furniture designs of eighteenth-century derivation which could equally well have come from Waring and Gillow or even the great Oetzmann emporium, neither of which made any claim to an avant-garde design policy. This change of direction came after the firm's acquisition

2

by Holland & Sons, the Pimlico workshops which brought to Morris & Co. the skills in cabinet-making that had been conspicuously absent in the joiner-made pieces of the earlier period. It is, nonetheless, with the simple, un-adorned lines of the famous Sussex chair and the artless daisy-patterned wallpaper that Morris was, and still is, identified.

Through his writings and teaching Morris's influence reached far beyond his native shores. Traces of Morrisian stylistic ideas are apparent on the Continent, particularly as the products of his firm were seen as essential elements in the development of the Modern style, and were collected early on by design-conscious museum directors. But it was in the United States that his ideas were most eagerly examined and applied. The extent of his influence is not surprising, since the elements that comprise the

2
The drawing room at
41 Cadogan Square 1890

This is the kind of room that Lady Mount Temple had devised.

Photograph by H. Bedford Lemere
National Monuments Record, London

3
Wightwick Manor, Wolverhampton 1898

This house dates from 1887. Morris & Co. materials and papers of the period survive; additional pictures, furnishings and objects appropriate to it have also been collected by subsequent owners. In 1937 it was given to the National Trust.

Private collection

4
The drawing room at
Draycott Lodge, Fulham 1893

The photograph shows one of the rooms in Holman Hunt's house filled with the fruits of nearly a half century of art collecting. The Morris-papered walls are hung with a miscellany of paintings, prints, sculptures, ceramics and metalwork. Interspersed among the severely plain furnishings from Morris & Co. are *cassoni*, Moorish tables inlaid with ivory and mother-of-pearl, carved ebony Javanese thrones, a Tyrolese milking stool and – entirely appropriate to this eclectic setting – the Egyptian-style chair inlaid with ivory made to Hunt's own design by J.G. Crace. The works of art and the furnishings in this room have been itemized and discussed in fascinating detail by the artist's granddaughter (Diana Holman Hunt, 'The Holman Hunt Collection' in *Pre-Raphaelite Papers*, ed. Leslie Parris, 1984, pp. 206–25). The individual pieces have, in many cases, proved to be less important than their owner believed, but the whole effect is an expression of the Aesthetic approach to interior decoration of this period. The ensemble is reminiscent of Leighton's studio (but not at all like the drawing room at Leighton House, which does not share the same eclectic mix of furniture and objects) and Rossetti's rooms in the Cheyne Walk house.

Private collection

4

3

5

5

Morris & Co. decorative scheme *c.* 1900

This dining room scheme is from the later phase of the firm's activities. Panelled in English oak, it is decorated with a painted frieze and furnished with a chair, table and sideboard from Morris & Co.

From the Morris & Co. catalogue

6

Rossetti's sitting room at 16 Cheyne Walk 1882

Rossetti is shown here among his lovingly amassed possessions, reading to his friend Theodore Watts Dunton. On the wall behind the sofa are family portraits flanking a large mirror in a chinoiserie frame. The use of mirrors gives the room an extra dimension of mystery, especially in the oblique and fragmented views that can be glimpsed in the Regency overmantel with its convex centre. Henry Treffry Dunn in his *Recollections* recalled his first visit in 1863 to the house in Cheyne Walk:

I was ushered into one of the prettiest, and one of the most curiously-furnished and old-fashioned sitting-rooms that had ever been my lot to see. Mirrors of all shapes, sizes and designs, lined the walls, so that whichever way I gazed I saw myself looking at myself. What space remained was occupied by pictures, chiefly old, and all of a most interesting character. The mantelpiece was a most original compound of Chinese black-lacquered panels, bearing designs of birds, animals, flowers and fruit in gold relief, which had a very good effect, and on either side of the grate a series of old Dutch tiles, mostly displaying Biblical subjects treated in a serio-comic fashion that existed at the period, were inlaid. . . . I sat down on a cosy little sofa, with landscapes and figures of the Cipriani period painted on the panels; whilst admiring this curious collection of things the door opened behind me, and turning around I found myself face to face with Dante Gabriel Rossetti.

H. Treffry Dunn, watercolour
National Portrait Gallery, London

Morris look are extremely simple: traditional furniture combined with tapestries and woven or printed fabrics, based on early naturalistic designs from medieval sources. The combination of these artistic aspirations with a political philosophy very much in tune with American ideals of equality and self-determination made Morris a natural exemplar for the craft movement which flourished in the late nineteenth century.

Walter Crane, himself one of the designers most closely identified with the Aesthetic movement, wrote:

The great advantage and charm of the Morrisian method is that it lends itself to either simplicity or splendour. You might almost be as plain as Thoreau, with a rush-bottomed chair, a piece of matting, and oaken trestle table; or you might have gold and lustre (the choice ware of William De Morgan) gleaming from the sideboard, and jewelled light in the windows, and walls hung with arras tapestry.
(The English Revival in Decorative Art; William Morris to Whistler, 1911, p. 54.)

The attraction of such a method is obvious; it is the epitome of the artistic revival with its blend of romanticism and rugged simplicity, plain craftsmen's values with richly coloured and elaborate medievalizing. Out of the frenzied eclecticism of the mid-nineteenth century Morris and his associates had forged a recognizable decorative aesthetic.

In Rossetti's own rooms in the house in Cheyne Walk there were examples of furniture to his own design mixed in with a great variety of interesting objects and works of art, antique and oriental, with papers, fabrics and furniture from the workshops of Morris & Co. J. Comyns Carr, a director of the Grosvenor Gallery, remembered Rossetti's Cheyne Walk house in the 1870's:

The room ... offered few or none of the ordinary features of a studio, and in its array of books around the walls spoke rather of the man of letters than of the painter; and the careless disposition of the simple furniture, though it bore some tokens of the newer fashion introduced by William Morris and by Rossetti himself, made no very serious appeal on the scope of deliberate decoration.'
(Coasting Bohemia, 1914, p. 47.)

The result was that 'picturesqueness which swell studios have taught to rich and aesthetic houses', to quote Vernon Lee's rather derisive description of the style (from the ghost story 'Oke of Okehurst' in *Hauntings*, 1890).

'Swell studios' there certainly were; artists' houses designed by some of the most eminent architects of the period are an important feature in the history of nineteenth-century interior decoration. The houses of Leighton and Alma-Tadema were celebrated examples of 'the house beautiful' and many others, particularly in Paris, were furnished and decorated with a grandeur not nowadays associated with the artistic milieu.

7

7
The drawing room at 16 Cheyne Walk 1882

The room is filled with the familiar mixture of exotic and antique arranged in a manner typical of the 'artistic' approach to interiors and appropriate to Rossetti's exotic style of living, which included keeping a small menagerie in the back garden. In this room overlooking the river Rossetti held his large dinner parties, and the room was arranged around such events with the care of a Hollywood art director. The five-panelled glass at one end of the room fragmentedly reflected the scene lit by the candles of the great Flemish candelabra. Heavy patterned curtains extended almost the whole length of the room. Rossetti, who was temperamentally midway between a neurotic and a showman, arranged his life and house accordingly. Mrs Haweis admired the result in *Artistic Interiors* (see *Beautiful Houses*, 1882).

George Robinson, watercolour
Private collection

Comyns Carr most succinctly summed up the elements of the studio style:

There are studios which seem deliberately fashioned for an effect of beauty – rooms so ornate and so adorned, that the picture in progress upon the easel seems the last thing calculated to arrest the gaze of the spectator. And there are others again, so completely barren of all decoration, and so deliberately stripped of every incident in the way of bric-à-brac or collected treasures, of carven furniture or woven tissue, that were it not for the half-finished canvas, it would be impossible to guess the vocation of its inhabitant. Between these two extremes there is room for every degree of careless or conscious environment...
(*Coasting Bohemia*, 1914, p. 80.)

From this description it can be seen that the artist and the art collector were often striving after the same effects. The

9

'Une visite à l'atelier' 1868

This painting perfectly embodies the romantic idea of the studio: a treasure house of beautiful objects in charming disarray used, with no regard for their value or antiquity, for such mundane purposes as holding brushes.

A. Ternisien, oil
Photograph Clarendon Gallery, London

8

8

The sculptor and his model 1890s

This photograph is almost literary in its powerfully evocative impression of *fin-de-siècle* French studio life. Its staginess might suggest an illustration to a story such as *Trilby*, yet the bust on the right would seem to portray the seated model.

Museum of Modern Art, New York
(Promised gift of Paul F. Walter)

9

10

10
Benjamin Constant in his studio, Paris 1893

French artists' studios displayed much the same taste as those of their English contemporaries, but the effect is usually more contrived and deliberate, less the happy accident of unity that comes with the haphazard but consistently interesting accumulation of an individual with artistic flair. However, this was the type of *mise-en-scène* expected of such a fashionable salon painter or noted orientalist as Constant had become. The public received in this room would be able to enjoy proximity to the exotic props and backgrounds used in the paintings. Many of the hangings, the suits of ancient armour, the pieces of metalwork and ceramics that were picked up by artists and their friends were of great value and rarity, matching the very similar acquisitions made by art collectors at the same date. A studio arranged by an artist with aesthete leanings and the installation of his possessions by the diligent art collector produce a similar result, and there was, no doubt, some cross-fertilization between the two. Constant's studio in the Impasse Hélène is described by Shirley Fox in the *Reminiscences of an Art Student in Paris of the 1880s* (1909, p. 202):

He possessed a choice collection of Moorish rugs and curtains and ornaments of all sorts, and with the aid of these, had transformed the place into quite a suggestion of the Alhambra itself. The block of buildings in which his place was situated consisted entirely of studios, some with and some without rooms belonging to them. It was in fact a veritable artist's colony, and was inhabited by quite a number of well-known men, as well as others less advanced in their profession.

Etching from *The Picture Magazine*, 1893, vol. 1

'carven furniture and woven tissue', acting as a foil for pictures and other works of art, could be found in the second half of the century in the houses of such celebrated art lovers as the Rothschilds, John Bowes and his wife who built the Bowes Museum, Sir Richard Wallace or Isabella Stewart Gardner of Boston, to name but a few. The austere magnificence of a grand gallery devoted to paintings or sculpture seems by the mid-nineteenth century to have lost its appeal. The contrast with the picture galleries of the past is very striking. In Lord Northwick's gallery at Thirlstain House as depicted in 1847 by Robert Huskisson, the pictures dominate in all their glory; a little dog prances in the foreground of a room almost bare of occasional furniture. However, the trend towards furnishing the picture gallery had begun, and by the mid-century was clearly irreversible. The picture gallery at Grosvenor House, depicted in 1866, was almost crowded with furniture.

The richly ornamented collector's ambience of the later nineteenth century is the real exemplar of which the 'splendid' version of the Morrisian method of Walter Crane's description is a sort of pastiche. Here would have been found the jewelled windows of the Middle Ages, Persian lustre and majolica of the Renaissance, the 'carven' furniture of the Tudor period and the tapestries and damasks of the seventeenth century; for the collector and the antiquary shared with the artist a common taste for the artefacts of the past as well as its art.

In soliciting Rossetti's opinion of her garlands and bows, Lady Mount Temple must surely have been aware of the ferocity of the lion into whose mouth she was so negligently sticking her head. The publication in 1869 of Matthew Arnold's *Culture and Anarchy* demarcated with brutal simplicity the cultural battle lines, identifying as 'Barbarians' and 'Philistines' the members of the upper and middle classes. In particular Lord Elcho was singled out for his resistance to new ideas; an unjust thrust at a man with an extraordinarily wide-ranging mind, who assembled in his ancestral home in Scotland a picture collection of considerable interest, and who took to sculpture in his old age with no little success.

One member at least of the aristocracy was wounded by the injustice of this attack. Before her first meeting with William Morris in 1870, Rosalind Howard, wife of the artist and patron of the Pre-Raphaelites George Howard (later Lord Carlisle), expected that he would take her for one of the 'Barbarians', but she hoped that 'if he puts up with me we shall job along all right'. In the event the friendship prospered, and the Howards' magnificent London house at 1 Palace Green, which was designed by Philip Webb, had Morris interiors. Rosalind Howard could not wholly approve of the house, which she stigmatized as being 'built for parties'. Space that should have been used for the sitting room was 'sacrificed to a fine arrival staircase. Not very sensible.' (Dorothy Henley,

Rosalind Howard, Countess of Carlisle, 1958, p. 45.) It is interesting to find that the early nineteenth-century ideal of rationalizing and simplifying the reception rooms was still frequently ignored, even for the newly built house of clients of supposedly Bohemian propensities.

In Philip Webb's Palace Green house the richly patterned Morris & Co. schemes were adorned with paintings and wall decorations by Burne-Jones, a team effort that was to be repeated many more times in the houses of artistic patrons. Webb and Morris had a number of rich middle-class patrons, such as Alexander Ionides, a member of the Greek community in London and a considerable collector, and William Knox d'Arcy, for whom an immensely ornate and richly gilded scheme was created at Stanmore Hall. More surprisingly, the partnership had a considerable success with a certain section of the 'Barbarian' aristocracy, the artistically inclined coterie known as the 'Souls', who enlivened society in the 1880s and 1890s.

The Souls' houses

At the centre of this circle of friends was Arthur Balfour, a leading politician later to be Prime Minister. Balfour commissioned from Burne-Jones an elaborate scheme of decoration for his London house in Carlton Gardens, a series of panels illustrating the legend of Perseus to be set in borders of acanthus pattern designed by Morris. The scheme was never completed as the panels were still unfinished at the time of Burne-Jones's death in 1898, but other commissions from the Souls' circle were brought successfully to fruition. Morris was responsible for such little redecoration as was undertaken at Stanway, the beautiful house in Gloucestershire inhabited by the Elchos. It is said that he hung the willow wallpaper that still survives in one of the bedrooms himself. Lady Elcho was Balfour's intimate friend and lifelong confidante, and might have been expected to share his artistic tastes. In any case she was brought up in the circle of Pre-Raphaelite patronage, for she was the daughter of the Hon. Percy Wyndham and his wife Madeline, who built Clouds, one of the most celebrated of the great artistic houses of the nineteenth century.

Clouds is regarded by many as Philip Webb's masterpiece. It was completed in 1885, having cost the vast sum of £80,000. It was cunningly contrived to look as if it had been built and added to over the centuries, and the same theme is pursued in the interior, where Madeline Wyndham mixed fine furniture of earlier dates with Morris carpets and covers, still at this date a pioneering decorative idea. The Wyndhams' London house at 44 Belgrave Square was decorated by George Aitchison, architect of Frederic Leighton's house and studio, and had on the stairs five panels painted by Leighton himself; at Clouds

11

the staircase was hung with great painted cartoons of angels by Burne-Jones. There is no doubt that Clouds was the more purely Aesthetic of the two.

In contrast, the other great Souls' project, Hewell Grange, built by Thomas Garner for Lord and Lady Plymouth, is a Renaissance palace, and reputedly cost a quarter of a million pounds; it comes near to being one of the most expensive houses of the age. Much of the interior was decorated with heavy panelling in the Tudor and Jacobean styles, though plasterwork of seventeenth-century inspiration ornamented with swags of flowers and fruit was used in some of the rooms. The small dining room was decorated in this way, and here also a paper with flowers like French chintz complemented a beautiful French commode inset with flowered plaques of Sèvres porcelain of the greatest delicacy. One of the bedrooms had a dado covered with blue and straw-coloured matting, a device much favoured by Morris, and one of the few traces of his influence to be found at Hewell.

Other Souls' commissions include the small-scale Beauvale Lodge of 1872, designed for Lord and Lady Cowper by E. W. Godwin. It cost less than £6,000 and is not very distinguished, particularly when it is compared with the sort of thing that Godwin could achieve for a truly audacious patron like Oscar Wilde; but it was very homogeneous, even having papers designed by Godwin.

12

11, 12

The White Drawing Room and Boudoir at Clouds 1910

I am glad indeed that you find your house fairly satisfactory, as in these days of rottenness in the arts, that is as much as can be reasonably hoped for. . . . When you decide on doing any whitewashing as advised by William Morris, please let me know, as there is a way of doing even this properly. I will give my advice as an amateur in the whitewasher's art.

So wrote Philip Webb to his client the Hon. Percy Wyndham. The interior of Clouds was remarkable in being almost free from the overbearing assemblage of patterns that dominate schemes of this period. The walls and woodwork in the drawing room (below) are white, even the decorative details being emphasized only by relief or openwork pattern. The curtains are plain and hang straight. The famous carpet by Morris & Co. dominates the room, the only other pattern being the upholstery. Much of the furniture is English of the eighteenth century, an advanced taste for the 1880s, which makes it easy to mistake the style of these rooms for Georgian revival of two decades later. Unusually for this date, only the upstairs rooms were papered.

Private collection

13

13
The Great Hall, Hewell Grange 1892

Hewell Grange was designed by Thomas Garner, of Bodley & Garner for Lord Windsor (later Earl of Plymouth). The Great

Hall was decorated by Tutnall & Cobley and was notable for its Italianate style and marble columns.

Photograph by H. Bedford Lemere
National Monuments Record, London

14, 15
Lord Leighton's studio,
Kensington *1866–c. 1880*

In the first phase, the most conspicuous feature of Aitchison's scheme for Leighton's house was the woodwork, door architraves, lintels, panels, window frames, balustrade and stairs, all in shiny black lacquer decorated with incised gilt leaf sprays and rosettes. The hallway, lit from above by a skylight, has a floor of black-and-white mosaic. Some ten years after he had moved in, Leighton added patterned wall tiles of a deep blue, especially made for him by De Morgan. Between the two great columns is a seat halfway up the first flight of stairs, fashioned from a Persian inlaid chest or *cassone* brought by Leighton from Rhodes. The silk upholstery of the seat was embroidered by Gertrude Jekyll, a noted needleworker before failing eyesight caused her to give it up for gardening. Antique chairs, oriental pots and a stuffed peacock (see plate 17) set the scene for the exotic delights of the adjoining Arab Hall (see plate 16) and the eclectic assemblage in the studio on the floor above. Visitors to Leighton's house on Sundays were as fascinated by his marvellously contrived living quarters as by his works. In the Great Studio a cast of the Parthenon frieze runs along the upper part of the south wall and, below it, set into the wall itself, is a cast of the Michelangelo Tondo of the Virgin and Child with the infant St John (the original of which is at the Royal Academy). The small landscape paintings, hung densely in the corner of the room, were kept by the artist and only exhibited and sold after his death. Julian Hawthorne, the son of Nathaniel Hawthorne, remembered Leighton's house in the 1870s:

The walls of the studio were a dull Egyptian red; around the base were luminous Oriental tiles; the door and woodwork were dense black, and there were scores of jewel-like sketches of Eastern scenes, in broad gold frames, ranged along the walls. The frieze was cast in brown plaster of the Parthenon series. At the end of the room was a wide semi-circular recess roofed with a semi-dome; at the end a high gallery with draperies pendent from the railing. The semi-dome was gilded, like the music room at Tadema's; a delicate winding stairway ascended to the gallery. Broad and rich rugs covered the floor. To the right were large pictures on easels, and beyond them a deep recess partitioned off by a screen of carved woodwork painted peacock blue, partly draped by a rug hanging like a curtain; light entered from a narrow window in the side. More than a score of chairs, each of a different design, offered repose from this gorgeousness; busts and casts from the antique occupied corners and niches; a writing-table, without writing materials, but a copy of the London Observer lying on it, stood somewhere in the middle distance.
(*Shapes that Pass*, 1928, pp. 176–7.)

Photogravure of Sir Frederic Leighton
Clarendon Gallery, London
Photograph of Leighton's studio
Royal Borough of Kensington and Chelsea, London

14

16
The Arab Hall at Leighton House 1879

The Hall was a later addition to Leighton House. It is one of the most successful of exotic tile-hung schemes, and consists of a combination of very fine Islamic tiles collected by the artist, with William De Morgan's specially fired peacock blue tiles and a frieze executed in mosaic designed by Walter Crane. Tiles of Islamic inspiration had by this date superseded revived medieval designs in popularity. Middle Eastern-inspired schemes appeared in country houses, too, such as Norman Shaw's dining room for Sir William Armstrong at Cragside; the dining room at Adcote in Shropshire; and the Great Hall at Greenham Lodge near Newbury. J.C. Bentley used Islamic-pattern tiles at Carlton Towers in Yorkshire, but the most thoroughgoing tile-dominated domestic interior was Halsey Ricardo's 1904 Debenham House in Addison Road, a few hundred yards from Leighton House. The mosaics in the dome were added later, much to Ricardo's regret, since they move the hall away from Islamic elegance towards Byzantine over-elaboration. In *The Puppet Show of Memory* (1922), Maurice Baring describes 'an afternoon party at Sir Frederick [*sic*] Leighton's house with music. Every year he gave this party, and every year the same people were invited. The music was performed by the greatest artists . . . in a large Moorish room full of flowers. It was the most intimate of concerts . . . The Leighton party looked like a Du Maurier illustration' (p. 55). Pierre Loti achieved tiled schemes of comparable richness in his amazing house in Rochefort. The modest house with its family rooms also contains a fabulous Turkish sanctuary. This was Loti's favourite retreat: tile-hung, fashioned from an Arab mosque, it is reminiscent of Leighton's Arab Hall (see Eileen Harris, 'Irresistible union, la maison Pierre Loti in Rochefort', *Country Life*, 11 July 1985).

George Aitchison, *Design for Arab Hall, Leighton House*
The British Architectural Library, RIBA, London

16

17

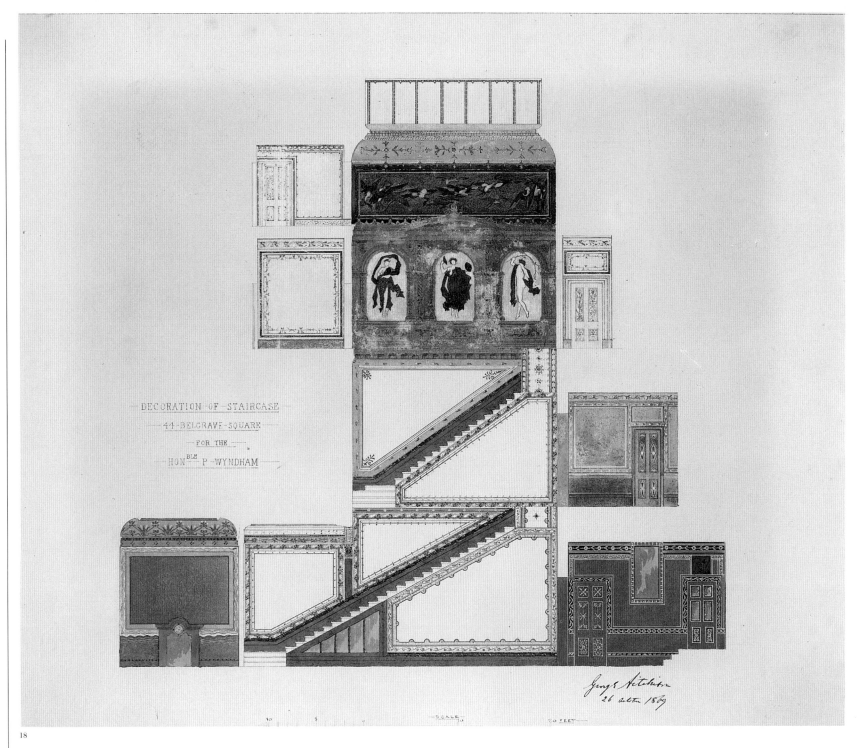

DECORATION OF STAIRCASE
44 BELGRAVE SQUARE
FOR THE
HON^BLE P WYNDHAM

18

17
The inner hall at Leighton House 1880s
From the *Magazine of Art*, 1904

18
Staircase hall, 44 Belgrave Square 1869
This decorative scheme was executed by George Aitchison for the Hon. Percy Wyndham.

The British Architectural Library, RIBA, London

More comparable with the achievement at Clouds or Hewell was Avon Tyrrell, designed for Lord and Lady Manners by W. R. Lethaby, a great admirer of Webb and subsequently his biographer. Avon Tyrrell is very much in the Souls' ethos, being large but deliberately unpretentious. The result is not entirely happy, the idea being to exploit the vernacular style in the manner of Richard Norman Shaw, Lethaby's master, but the house is too large for this to succeed and the rooms are awkwardly proportioned. The enlarged 'cottage' or manorial idea was to be employed more successfully by the next generation and for a different class of patron, who commissioned houses of a more appropriate scale. Full realization of the ideal of a truly classless architecture was hardly practicable for a mainly aristocratic clientèle.

The Souls' building and decorating activities were remarkable in the context of their time and within the larger social circle of which they were part. They seem to have been determined to overcome the 'Barbarian' stigma with which they had been so publicly branded, by a sustained record of distinguished patronage of art and architecture. No greater contrast could be found to the building activities of the merchant princes; the refinement of detail and the pale purity of colour, combined with the elegant but still unfashionable antique furniture (as opposed to antiquarian, which was admired more for quaintness than for elegance), was peculiar to England and to this particular set of people. This taste in interior decoration has no parallel elsewhere, though much the same effect was arrived at by casual accumulation in artists' studios abroad as well. Osbert Sitwell, wrote of a house rented in 1900 by his family from Mrs Morton Frewen, the sister of Lady Randolph Churchill:

It was 'done up' in the height of the fashion of the moment, for interior decoration had only just started as a mode and on its present professional basis, and Lady Randolph had been almost the first person to interest herself in it and may perhaps have had a hand in these colour schemes. Before 1900, the esthetes [sic] alone had shown an interest in the rooms in which they beautifully existed – ordinary rich people had been content to live in the houses in which they lived, with their possessions, ugly or beautiful, about them. They accepted that which fate had decreed, unless a fire, or new circumstances of one kind or another, imposed fresh surroundings upon them.
(Osbert Sitwell, *Left Hand, Right Hand*, 1945, p. 218.)

The twin developments of the Arts and Crafts movement and Art Nouveau were to see an extraordinary evolution in the artistic involvement in interior design. The work of, for example, Guimard or Tiffany for a middle-class clientèle created an ambience so powerful that it can only be compared with such exotic schemes as George IV's Pavilion at Brighton or the Byzantine fantasies of Ludwig II of Bavaria.

Britain and the Continent

In this book the vast subject of nineteenth-century decoration is necessarily approached from an English viewpoint. The environment that is known intimately is easier to interpret than that which is simply viewed from a distance as a visitor. But even if all the documentary references and all the illustrations came from English sources, the picture presented would not be insular. The most influential and innovative patrons and their architects and designers – not to be conterminous until well on into the century – traded in a fertile cross-breeding of taste and style. For example, the decorative works commissioned by George IV were eclectic to a fault. A great francophile with an important collection of French furniture, his most unforgettable contribution to nineteenth-century architecture and interior decoration is the exotic Brighton Pavilion, a flamboyant example of chinoiserie. At the other pole of contemporary taste, Thomas Hope was indebted to pioneering neo-classical publications by Giambattista Piranesi, the Italian architect; Winckelmann, the German antiquarian scholar; and the French scholar, the Comte de Caylus. He was a friend of Napoleon's architect Percier, and his style of drawing in outline was derived from the example of the German artist Tischbein.

A. W. N. Pugin, the influential architect of the Gothic Revival, was half French; his father was an *émigré* who had studied at the Academy Schools in London before being employed as a draughtsman by John Nash. Pugin himself was initially inspired by French Gothic architecture; later he travelled extensively in search of models, drawing both buildings and artefacts in Italy, Germany and the Low Countries. In the Palace of Westminster in London Pugin accomplished, with the architect Charles Barry, the most important non-religious neo-Gothic scheme of decoration ever attempted. The restoration of these interiors to their former brilliance has provided us with a touchstone by which we can judge the Victorian neo-Gothic achievement.

The next generation of neo-Gothic designers in Britain, with William Burges at their head, owed – and acknowledged – a great debt to Viollet-le-Duc. 'We all cribbed from Viollet,' remarked Burges.

'Victorian' taste was to a large extent the creation of a German collector and connoisseur with German mentors and advisors: Albert, Prince Consort, the Queen's husband, assisted by Ludwig Gruner and Gottfried Semper. Prince Albert's contribution to forming taste in the mid-nineteenth century merits, and has received, the assessment of a full-scale study (Winslow Ames, *Prince Albert and Victorian Taste*, 1968). His own taste, according to Queen Victoria, derived from the decorating and building projects of his father, Duke Ernst of Saxe-Coburg-Gotha, of which we have a visual record in the watercolours commissioned by the Queen (see plate 194). If it is difficult to reconcile these rather austere and sparingly furnished rooms with the popular notion of Victorian taste, it should perhaps be recollected that only after Prince Albert's death was the Queen's penchant for sentimental trivia allowed full expression and the generally overburdened look of many of the Royal rooms was due to this.

From a small volume entitled *The Private Life of the Queen*, first published in 1897 (and partially suppressed by Royal command so that until its re-publication in facsimile in 1979 it was extremely rare), comes the following description of the sitting room in the Queen's private apartments at Windsor:

Recalling the stiff primness which characterised the apartments of the later Georgian era, and the singular degree of discomfort that marked the furniture and decorations of the thirties, it is strange to note the lavish crowding of pretty things, and the orderly confusion of beautiful bric-à-brac *that make such a picturesque effect in the Queen's rooms. Even the grand piano, a very handsome instrument, which stands beyond the round table, and close to one of the many doors, is not saved from the crowd of* objets d'art *and dainty trifles that Her Majesty likes to have about her. The high-backed comfortable chair before the keyboard is a comparative innovation, for the Queen is essentially conservative in details, and the princesses had much difficulty in deposing the uncomfortable 'screw' music stool from its time-honoured position. At the end of the piano, and tucked away in a convenient corner, stands the* étagère *containing the bound musical works which Her Majesty loves so well and which are in frequent request during the short time that elapses between Her Majesty's dinner and the hour for retiring. To right and left of the fireplace are two large cabinets which are crowded with china, statuettes, models of favourite animals, flowers and photographs. Here I may remark that much as the Queen appreciates photographs, her most treasured mementoes of old friends and dumb pets always take the form of models. In clear Parian china, marble of all kinds, bronze, silver or gold, small busts, statuettes, and figures abound in profusion on all sides.*

Christopher Hibbert has painted an unforgettable picture of Edward VII at the time of his accession:

At Windsor Castle and Buckingham Palace he strode about with his hat on his head, his dog trotting after him, a walking stick in his hand, a cigar in his mouth, giving orders; opening cupboards; peering into cabinets; ransacking drawers; clearing rooms formerly used by the Prince Consort and not touched since his death; dispatching case-loads of relics and ornaments to a special room in the Round Tower at Windsor; destroying statues and busts of John Brown; burning the papers of his mother's pretentious and wily Indian attendant, the Munshi, whose letters from the Queen were eventually retrieved from his widow;

throwing out hundreds of 'rubbishy old coloured photographs' and useless bric-à-brac; *setting inventory clerks to work at listing the cluttered accumulations of half a century; rearranging pictures ... He would brook no opposition to his plans, overcoming any resistance with good-natured firmness, determined not to allow inconvenient sentiment to stand in the way of necessary overhaul. 'Alas!' Queen Alexandra lamented to her sister-in-law in Berlin, 'During my absence Bertie has had all your Mother's rooms dismantled and all her precious things removed.'*
(*Edward VII: A Portrait*, 1976, pp. 191–2.)

So passed the most authentic monument to Victorian taste.

Antique and exotic influences

English travellers to southern Italy were able to inspect the newly discovered ruins of Herculaneum and Pompeii which were to exert an undiminished influence on decoration for more than a hundred years. Pompeian-style schemes were carried out as late as the third quarter of the nineteenth century. Herculaneum had been rediscovered in 1709, sixteen centuries after the long-dormant Vesuvius had erupted, burying both Herculaneum and the neighbouring Pompeii in molten pumice and volcanic ash. Sporadic forays to the site dispersed some of the treasures, but no systematic excavations were undertaken until nearly thirty years later when the reigning Bourbon family furnished the first royal collections (now in the National Museum in Naples) by what Goethe disgustedly described as: 'haphazard, predatory grubbing'. Pompeii was discovered in 1748 and excavated from 1755 in rather the same way, with no regard for the archaeological value of the site. The earliest Pompeian-style schemes date from the first publication of the finds, but the continuing work on the sites ensured that public interest was repeatedly stimulated by new discoveries. It was only in the second half of the nineteenth century that the work of preserving the site with the finds *in situ* was put in hand in a properly organized manner.

The first account of Pompeii to appear in English was Sir William Gell's *Pompeiana. The Topography, Edifices and Ornaments of Pompeii*, published in two volumes in 1816–17. It was illustrated with engraved plates showing buildings reconstructed, and included detailed plans of the house and maps – Gell was an experienced cartographer – but, useful though these were, it was the colour of Pompeii that was to exert such a powerful fascination for the decorator. Examples of the architecture rendered in full colour were plentiful; indeed, this interest in the polychromy of antique architecture was perfectly in tune with the taste of the age. The effects can be traced from examples of full-scale re-creation to the nomenclature of colours – such as 'Pompeian' red – and to the unusually frequent use of black in decorative schemes

19

20

19
Visitors viewing the ruins of Pompeii
1877

Edwin Sherwood Calvert, watercolour
Photograph courtesy of the Fine Art Society, London

20
Pompeian decorative scheme *c.*1880

The Pompeian style proved enduringly popular, and although by the 1870s it had become comparatively unfashionable, J.D. Crace continued to produce such schemes. The Pompeian room at Ickworth in Suffolk is a late example, probably explained by the lengthy building history of the house which was begun in the eighteenth century, completed in 1830 and not finally decorated until 1879. The creator of the scheme illustrated, Frederick Marshall, worked for the Crace firm which carried out the work at Ickworth under the direction of J.D. Crace himself.

Frederick Marshall, pen and watercolour
Photograph courtesy of the Fine Art Society, London

that otherwise owe only a remote debt to classical antiquity.

The Pompeian Room in the Garden Pavilion at Buckingham Palace, dating from 1843, devised by Prince Albert and executed by Agostino Aglio, is an exquisite example of the genre. The Maison Pompéienne decorated by Alfred Normand for Prince Napoleon is much more ambitious; it did not survive for long and must have been very demanding to live in. At Ickworth in Suffolk the Pompeian Room, decorated by John Crace, was only completed in the 1870s when the classical taste had long been in the background of fashion, but this is some indication of the enduring nature of this style.

The greater possibilities for travel provided by the development of the railways and of steam navigation brought an increasing number of exotic influences to a much wider public, already prepared for the products of all nations by the recurring international exhibitions that were an important feature of Victorian cultural life.

Greece, Turkey, Spain, North Africa, India and the Islamic world were already known before the mid-century through the work of such journeying artists as William Alexander, Thomas Daniell, David Roberts, J. F. Lewis, Luigi Mayer and Thomas Allom, as well as through actual Indian and Chinese paintings and miniatures belonging to collectors.

Of great importance to the taste for the exotic in the nineteenth century is the knowledge of India that came through the activities of a number of British artists beginning with the visit of William Hodges, the landscape painter, in 1780. Thomas Daniell was the next artist of importance to work in India. The interior scenes by Daniell are full of charming incidental details: vessels, flowers in pots and textile hangings. Humphry Repton, writing in 1808 of his plans for Brighton Pavilion, acknowledged his debt to Daniell.

After the turn of the century, a new more intimate view of Indian life became popular in the hands of artists like Sir Charles D'Oyly and George Chinnery. D'Oyly's interior views are among the most charming ever painted of the surroundings of the British in India. It is ironic that when the time came in the later years of the century to re-create Indian interiors for European patrons, they should have been so oppressively over-ornamented. All that the British residents had learned about sparsely furnished, cool and relaxing surroundings was lost in a riot of intricate carving.

The 'Hareem' scenes by J. F. Lewis, painted with Pre-Raphaelite attention to detail, inspired many smoking rooms in the 'Arab' or Moorish style, fitted out with arched alcoves and fretted screens. The accuracy of the source is vouched for by Lewis's immensely detailed drawing of his own quarters in Cairo where he spent the ten years from 1841 to 1851.

One of the most important scholars in this area, Emile

21, 22, 23

'Scenes of Hareem Life' 1870s

John Frederick Lewis had direct experience of the East on which to base his popular harem subjects. His studio and living quarters in Cairo (right) were in a tall Arab house furnished with pierced screens which were a feature in his work. These paintings of the much admired orientalist genre were very influential in the field of interior decoration (below). The Arab and Moorish style was often used for smoking rooms or other male retreats, but the 'Arabian parlour' (see plate 23) would have been occupied by the lady of the house. Such exotic corners could be easily contrived out of very small spaces; the half landing on the turn of the staircase of a London terraced house, for instance, or at the end of a passage. Oscar Wilde had one such 'Moorish' cabinet in a small room at the top of his house in Tite Street. Suitable fabrics and furnishings, as well as authentic items such as brass trays, could be purchased from Liberty's in Regent Street.

J.F. Lewis, *The Artist's own Studio in Cairo*, watercolour
Victoria and Albert Museum, London
J.F. Lewis, *The Arab Scribe*, oil
Private collection (*Bridgeman Art Library*)
R.A. Briggs, *An Arabian Parlour in a London House*
From *The Magazine of Art*, 1904

21

22

23

Prisse d'Avennes, was born in 1807; at the age of nineteen he fought, like Byron, in the Greek War of Independence. He became an explorer, travelling off the beaten track, learning foreign languages – he even studied Egyptian hieroglyphs – and digging up the past. He made meticulous drawings of his discoveries, and became known as a considerable expert on the Orient. His great masterpiece, *Arab Art as Seen through the Monuments of Cairo* (1869–77), the result of his studies in the East, took ten years to prepare. Virtually every facet of Arab art, decoration and architecture is explored and the book contains more than three hundred illustrations. This immensely painstaking and scholarly undertaking has no rival in its thorough coverage of the subject.

The Egyptian style, like most of these exotic borrowings, has the origin of its revival in the eighteenth century (only the Turkish style was introduced to Europe before this, dating back at least to the sixteenth century). Interest was stimulated by the publication of the findings of the Institut de l'Egypte, set up by Napoleon at the time of his military campaign in Egypt in the 1790s. The twenty-three volumes of this great work, which appeared from 1809, together with Vivant Denon's *Voyages dans la basse et haute Egypte* (Paris 1802, London 1803), provided a vast body of material from which to draw inspiration for decoration in the Egyptian manner. The designs for Egyptian decoration and furniture by Thomas Hope and George Smith are archaeologically correct, but much of the proliferating Egyptian ornament simply exploits the recognizable motifs for popular consumption. 'You can have the Egyptian hieroglyphic paper with the ibis border to match. The only objection is that one sees it

24

24

A decorative scheme in the Moorish style 1873

This design for an arch-topped niche to house a looking-glass is six years earlier than Leighton's Arab Hall and represents the fanciful Moorish style that was popular in France. It is very much like the interior of the Moorish kiosk in the grounds of the Linderhof, the pavilion built for Ludwig II of Bavaria in the early 1870s. This kiosk was installed in the grounds in 1877; Ludwig had acquired it in the previous year from Schloss Zbirow in Bohemia, though it was thought to have been originally devised and constructed in Paris. In 1878 Ludwig acquired another 'Moorish House' from the Exposition Universelle held in Paris that year.

Alexandre-Eugène Prignot, watercolour
Niall Hobhouse, London

25

Project for a '*Salon Algérien*' 1870s

This project is by Tony Vergnolet, who described himself as '*artiste peintre décorateur, Paris*' in the inscription on the overmantel mirror of this 'Algerian Salon'. He was an exhibitor at the Paris Salon between 1870 and 1881.

Formerly Hazlitt, Gooden & Fox Limited, London

26

The Alhambra Court Early 1850s

This scheme by Owen Jones for the re-erected Crystal Palace, Sydenham, was completed in 1854.

Photograph, possibly by P. H. Delamotte for his *Photographic Views of the Progress of the Crystal Palace, Sydenham*, 1853 *Victoria and Albert Museum, London*

27

The 'Gold Room' at Townsend House

1880s

The decorations of Alma-Tadema's house were justly celebrated. Many of these individual elements appear in his pictures, and this evidence and the many descriptions of contemporaries permit a detailed reconstruction of the interior. With this depiction by the artist's daughter, herself an accomplished painter, we have an image which brings the fragments of information into focus. The silk-hung, gilded and lacquered room is as rich and exotic as the descriptions suggest. There are elements of the fashionable Alhambresque decoration, notably the ceiling, which is a painted version of the three-dimensional carved and gilded ones in Alfred Morrison's house at 16 Carlton House Terrace.

Anna Alma-Tadema, oil
Royal Academy of Arts, London

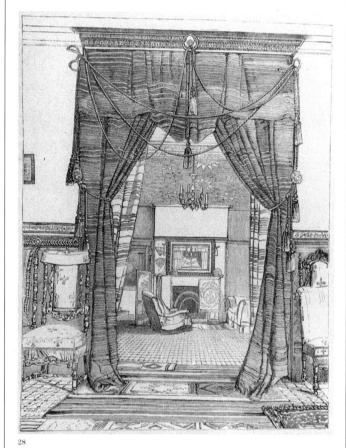

28

28

An entrance in the Moorish style   1882

The archway leading into the drawing room was hung with elaborately draped North African woven fabric of the kind so often found in artistic schemes of this date. The American writer Moncure Conway comments favourably:

Nothing is better understood than that no square angles should divide a drawing-room, and a curtain is more graceful than any arch or architraves for that purpose. The following sketch [above] may convey some idea of the effect which has been secured in Townsend House, residence of the distinguished artist Mr Alma-Tadema (p. 193).

Moncure Conway, sketch for *Travels in South Kensington*, 1882

30
Moorish art at the Alhambra

The Alhambra Court in 1851 was the fullest public exposure of
the Moorish style, which had been recently introduced with an
archaeological exactness by Owen Jones's *Plans, Details, Elevations and Sections of the Alhambra* (1836–45). Before that date
Moorish, Islamic and Turkish styles were a rather confused
presence in European decorative arts which reflected the
designer's attempts at an effect rather than authentic reproduction of Islamic patterns or features.

Unknown artist, *Perspective views of the Alhambra, Granada*,
mid-19th century, watercolour
Niall Hobhouse, London

29
Studies in Design   1874

In Christopher Dresser's ambitious and forceful work, of which
this is the third colour plate, he stressed that good design has
economic benefits; he prepared the plates 'with the hope of
assisting to bring about a better style of decoration for our
houses.' Dresser was influenced by Jones, but took the latter's
Islamic and Moorish patterns further towards abstraction.
Here, Dresser sought a new ornamental language which would
encapsulate 'the richness of the Arabian' and use 'the intricacy
of plot of the Moorish.'

Christopher Dresser, *Studies in Design*, plate III

30

everywhere – quite antediluvian – gone to the hotels even.' Thus did Maria Edgeworth dismiss the popular taste in 1809, in her novel *The Absentee*.

However much the arbiters might counsel against the popular interpretations of these exotic influences, the public interest was not likely to diminish when presented with the splendours of the Egyptian, Greek, Roman and

31

Japanese scroll painting   Late 18th century

This kind of highly purist Japanese interior caught the imagination of designers from about 1860 onwards.

Katsukawa Shunsō, *Moonlight*, ink and colours on silk
Kyūsei Atami Art Museum, Shizuoka, Japan

32

The Chinese junk *Keying*   1848

Smuggled out of Chinese waters by a consortium of British traders, the *Keying* sailed around the Cape of Good Hope and arrived in London, via New York, in early 1848. Reports in the *Illustrated London News* described it as a 'junk of the largest class', of which 'in accordance with the peculiar notions of Chinese navigators, each bow is decorated with an immense eye, with a view to enable the vessel to see her way across the ocean. Both interior and exterior . . . are gorgeously painted, after the most approved fashion of the Celestial Empire; and in decoration, as in all other respects, it presents a perfect contrast to the shipping of any other nation.'

Unknown artist, *Interior of Chinese Junk*, pencil and ink
Guildhall Library, London

31

32

Alhambra courts devised in 1851 for the Crystal Palace by Owen Jones and Joseph Bonomi. Jones had visited Egypt from 1832 to 1833, and the views that he painted there were published in a volume of lithographs in 1843, two years before the final completion of his most influential work on the architecture and decoration of the Alhambra in Spain. His collaborator on these two ambitious works was the French architect Jules Goury, who did not survive to see the completion of either. Goury and Jones met in Athens, where the Frenchman had been working with Gottfried Semper on polychromy in antique architecture, a subject on which Semper published a paper in 1834. A fascination with colour can often be seen to lie at the base of these investigations of antique and exotic sources, and the possibilities of colour reproduction which had been opened up by the development of chromolithography stimulated the public response.

Like Owen Jones, Thomas Allom was an architect, whose reputation was founded on his development of the area round Ladbroke Grove in Kensington. In his day, Allom was also one of the most prolific draughtsmen in the field of travel and topographical illustration. He visited Constantinople and Asia Minor in 1836, and his *Character and Costume in Turkey and Italy* appeared in 1845; his drawings of Constantinople were used to illustrate publications in collaboration with William Bartlett. The majority of his drawings were made with the engraver in mind and his work was used for a wide variety of publications, many concerned with travels in Britain and on the Continent, as well as Asia Minor and farther east: his *China, in a Series of Views* appeared in 1843.

By 1881 some of the glamour of the Orient seems to have faded. Col. Robert Edis was particularly emphatic on the subject in his *Decoration and Furniture of Town Houses*:

Nothing can be worse than art at second-hand, more especially when the associations and feelings of the two sets of workers, the original and the imitators, are totally different. In the study of all oriental art we can gain infinite knowledge of skill and grace of design and workmanship, and power and beauty of drawing and colouring, but the art-workers of this country are no more able to imitate these attributes, which we admire so much, than they can fly; and when we hear of rooms decorated with imitation Chinese bamboo work, and tinted sealing-wax red and gold, with splashes of blue and green, in imitation of Japanese lacquer, we can only request that the time and money thus wasted, in fruitless endeavour to obtain what at its best must be but a bad imitation, should not be applied to decoration.

The influence of Japan is of such crucial importance to the development of decoration after 1860 that it merits a separate section (see p. 279). The many facets of Japonisme in decoration may in part account for the widespread public response to the cult of Japan; whereas the Pompeian style or the Indian offer quite limited possibilities of

33

imaginative interpretation, the Japanese style could be employed at many levels, from the display of a few blue-and-white pots to the full-scale re-creation of a Japanese interior as realized by Mortimer Menpes in the 1890s. However, it is significant that one of the most influential Japanese-style schemes to be realized in England should have been carried out by an American artist – that is, James McNeil Whistler's celebrated 'Peacock Room', painted in the London house of his patron, F. R. Leyland.

33
Mortimer Menpes's Japanese interior
1893–95

The fittings for this room were all executed for Menpes in Japan. The house, designed by A.H. Mackmurdo, still stands, the daringly stylized Queen Anne exterior belying this astonishing room inside.

Photograph Royal Borough of Kensington and Chelsea, London

Nineteenth-century millionaires

The taste of the very rich has always tended to be international, transcending regional differences, since there is no necessity to consider the ready availability of materials. For most of the nineteenth century the prefererred style was based on the royal interiors of the seventeenth and eighteenth centuries in France, debased versions of which could even be found in many of the luxury hotels built around the turn of the century. Heinrich Heine, the German poet, wrote of Baron James de Rothschild's Paris house in the rue Lafitte; '... the palace ... unites everything which the spirit of the sixteenth century could conceive and the money of the nineteenth century could pay for. ... It is the Versailles of a financial potentate' (quoted in Virginia Cowles, *The Rothschilds*, 1973, p. 96).

The pattern of Rothschild patronage is a neat illustration of the internationalism of the taste of the very rich. Their commissioning of architects and artists did not take account of national boundaries. Once they started to build it was on a grand scale. After commissioning

34
The Great Hall, Mentmore 1863

Mentmore was built for Baron Meyer de Rothschild by Joseph Paxton, architect of the Crystal Palace, in the fashionable 'Jacobethan' style. Paxton's model was Wollaton Hall near Nottingham, the seat of the Willoughby family, but with features of a purely mid-nineteenth-century character, most notably the large plate-glass windows. The Great Hall at Mentmore is significant in being the first for which there is evidence of its having been designed as the main living room of the house (see Jill Franklin, *The Gentleman's Country House and its Plan*, 1981, p. 70). The transition from entrance hall, incorporating the main staircase, to living room had been going on since early in the century, the first indications that the hall might play a more useful role in the house being the setting up of a billiard table, some amusements for children and some chairs for onlookers. The hall at Mentmore was a source of much wonder, and a number of contemporary descriptions give a flavour of the effect that it had on visitors seeing it for the first time. Lady Eastlake wrote of a visit to the Rothschilds in 1872:

I arrived here yesterday, and it was like a fairyland when I entered the great hall – 40 ft by 50, and about 100 ft high – hung with tapestry, floored with parquet and Persian carpets: an open arcade above runs round and looks down through arches into the hall, which is filled with gorgeous masses of flowers and every sumptuous object that wealth can command. From the great centre hall, branch off lobbies floored with white marble; then three splendid drawing-rooms, two libraries, billiard-room – every place almost crammed with precious articles in enamel, bronze, gold, silver, amber, jewels &c. The house is a museum of everything, and not least of furniture, which is all marquetry, or pietra dura, or vermeille. I don't believe the Medici were so housed at the height of their glory.
(*Memoirs*, vol. II, p. 224.)

Rubens's enormous chimneypiece of black and white marble dominates even this vast space. The tapestries noted by Lady Eastlake were of Gobelins manufacture. Venice provided not only the great lanterns from the Doge's barge, but also the gilded parade chairs from the Palazzo Ducale. The hall at Mentmore does not look particularly conducive to social ease. There are no convenient groupings of chairs to encourage conversation, and the great archways giving on to the adjacent reception rooms must have discouraged any intimacies or relaxation. None the less, once established, the 'living hall' retained its popularity well into the present century.

H. Brewer, watercolour
The Earl of Rosebery, Rothschild-Rosebery Collection, Dalmeny House, Edinburgh

35
The Rothschilds at the Avenue de Marigny 1882

Barons Alphonse and Gustave with their families at 23 Avenue de Marigny, one of their Paris residences. This group portrait was painted by Eugène Lami, the Imperial favourite, who worked with Paxton on the French Rothschild houses, turning Old English rooms into Second Empire salons.

Eugène Lami, watercolour
Private collection

THE DRAWING ROOM, STRAND PALACE HOTEL

36

36
The Drawing Room of the Strand Palace Hotel Early 20th century

The taste of the rich adapted for a public room.

Postcard from a private collection

35

37

38

37, 38, 39

'You can't have too many Rothschilds'

1870s and 1880s

The houses of the Rothschilds have a similarity in their furnishings and décor whether they are in England, France or Austria. A love of finish and trimming, of velvet and damask, of ormulu and highly polished wood appears through all their rooms, as at Halton House (left). The finest works of art compete – and do not always win – against the most elaborate examples of the upholsterer's art. Gainsborough's *Morning Walk* can barely hold its own between the carved and columned bookcases that flank it on the dark panelled room of the library of Tring Park (right). Even in photographs the fine quality of the materials and many bibelots scattered about the rooms is apparent. This is one aspect of nineteenth-century decoration that is hard to relate to the present, since to re-create such interiors nowadays would be impossibly expensive even if the components and skills were available. Many Rothschild houses incorporate in the reception rooms examples of French craftsmanship of the eighteenth century, notably *boiseries* from the great *hôtels particuliers* of Paris that had been recently demolished to make way for Baron Haussmann's improvements. Waddesdon Manor had been built by Destailleur between 1874 and 1889. The breakfast-room panels were from the house of the Maréchal Duc de Richelieu at 27 rue de Richelieu; the dining room's mirror frames were from the Hôtel de Villars in rue Grenelle; the panelling of the Grey Drawing Room came from the Duchesse de Maine's house in rue de Varennes. Baron Ferdinand's study (above) is a conventional example of a comfortable male retreat. While working for the Rothschilds, Destailleur was rescuing other bits of Paris to re-install them at Courrances in Essonnes for the Berlin banker Baron de Haber.

Photograph of Baron Ferdinand in his study, Waddesdon
Mrs James de Rothschild, on loan to the National Trust
Photographs of Tring Park, Hertfordshire, and Halton House, Buckinghamshire, by H. Bedford Lemere
National Monuments Record, London

39

Paxton, architect of the Crystal Palace of 1851, to build the fantastic Mentmore Towers in Buckinghamshire, Baron Meyer de Rothschild proceeded to furnish it with a priceless collection of French tapestries, Limoges enamels, Sèvres porcelain, furniture which had once belonged to Marie Antoinette, fabulous gilt lanterns from the Doge's Bucentaur or state barge in Venice and a vast black and white marble chimneypiece from Rubens' house in Antwerp. Baron Meyer remarked that it was cheaper to buy antique French furniture than to patron-ize Maple's store in the Tottenham Court Road, London. Mentmore, like Highclere and Westonbirt, was based on Wollaton Hall, an Elizabethan house of great magnificence. It is perhaps significant that a secular model was chosen in preference to the Christian Gothic. The trend continued in later Rothschild commissions. Both the Continental and the English branch remained faithful to sixteenth- and seventeenth-century domestic architecture for their sources.

When Baron James saw Mentmore he immediately demanded from Paxton a similar palace, but twice as big. The result was Ferrières, twenty-five miles outside Paris, a vast, unwieldy French Renaissance edifice of which Wilhelm I of Prussia remarked, 'Kings couldn't afford this. It could only belong to a Rothschild.' Paxton built one more Rothschild house, the Château at Pregny near Geneva for Baron Alphonse, son of Baron James. Pregny had fabulous conservatories filled with rare plants arranged by country.

In the second wave of building in Buckinghamshire in the 1870s, Baron Ferdinand commissioned his magnificent French château, Waddesdon Manor, appropriately from a French architect, Gabriel-Hippolyte Destailleur. Incorporating elements from a positive medley of real French châteaux – Chambord, Maintenon, Anet and Blois – Waddesdon was almost entirely furnished from France, mostly with pieces bearing a royal provenance. Of this opulent ensemble, Gladstone's daughter Mary remarked: 'Felt much oppressed with the extreme gorgeousness and luxury. ... The pictures in his [Baron Ferdinand's] sitting room are too beautiful, but there is not a book in the house save 20 improper French novels.'

The next Rothschild château to rise in Buckinghamshire was Halton House, more *dix-huitième* than Waddesdon and dominated by an immense winter garden with a domed glass roof. By the 1880s the taste for the château style was in decline. Halton was incredibly luxurious, but this sort of taste was not universally admired. Lady Frances Balfour presents the conservative English attitude to this kind of opulence; she describes a visit to Halton with her husband who was a practising architect:

Yesterday we walked to see the new house that Alfred Rothschild is building for himself ... I have seldom seen anything more terribly vulgar. It is a large house holding about 25 guests. Outside it is a combination of a French château and a gambling house. Inside it is badly planned (except the servants' offices which are admirable) and gaudily decorated. There is a large central hall going through two stories. The walls of this are covered with white architectural plasterwork and crimson silk panels.
Oh! but the hideousness of everything, the showiness! the sense of lavish wealth thrust up your nose! the coarse mouldings, the heavy gilding in the wrong place, the colours of the silk hangings!
(Quoted in Jill Franklin, *The Gentleman's Country House and its plan*, 1981, p. 246.)

Our present-day perception of the nineteenth century is frequently stereotyped; far too little is made of the limitless inventiveness of successive periods. For example, the use of colour far surpassed in richness and audacity the somewhat circumscribed view of nineteenth-century practice held today. Much of this richness of

40

40, 41
Hamilton Place, London *c.* 1890

Here is a complete example of the Rothschild taste for French decoration, in the finest rococo style but set in an Italianate palazzo casing. It was built for Leopold at the bottom of Park Lane, behind Rothschild Row. Despite his nickname 'the Little Messiah', bestowed by Disraeli, Leopold was something of a disappointment to his family: a society figure, racehorse breeder and card player. Leopold's London house is the apogee of 1890s conspicuous consumption. He installed a hydraulic lift of legendary cost and also employed Italian carvers for two years on a staircase of sumptuous intricacy.

Photographs by H. Bedford Lemere for the decorators George Jackson & Sons
National Monuments Record, London

9384

41

effect was achieved by expensive and time-consuming techniques carried out by hand, such as the use of complex colour printing with a large number of different blocks for wallpapers and fabrics, or of very painstaking weaving techniques which restricted progress on a pattern of any complexity to only a few inches each day. The silk used for the bedroom decorated in 1805 for the Empress Josephine at Fontainebleau was one of the masterpieces of the great Lyons silk weaver Philippe de Lasalle, who died in 1805. The recently completed restoration of the room has taken twenty years and has involved the re-weaving of de Lasalle's immensely complex designs. The work was undertaken by Prelle, a firm renowned in the present day for the meticulous execution of hugely demanding eighteenth-century techniques. The sumptuous effect of the silk-hung bed and the walls behind is quite breathtaking. (See Barbara Scott, 'Rags and Riches', in *Country Life*, 18 June 1987.)

The re-created Victorian interior favoured today for room settings in period displays usually consists of a rather tasteless version of a middle-class urban scheme, all voluminous drapery, bobble edgings and crowded, over-stuffed furniture, garnished with some coarse pottery ornaments and stuffed birds in a glass case. Surviving interior views show that while this kind of re-creation does have some limited validity, in suggesting an approximation or lowest common denominator of a commonplace dwelling upon which no particular scheme has been imposed, there was a variety of influence and response to experimental ideas that is astonishing in range and width of application throughout the whole century.

While it is not possible in a general way to revive cripplingly expensive methods of manufacture – though it has been very successfully done for authentic restoration, for example at Versailles for the Trianons, and at Pavlovsk and Tsarskoe Selo outside Leningrad – it is surely feasible to emulate some of the decorative ingenuity of the designers. The nineteenth century might be seen as a sort of revivalist melting-pot. Every conceivable antique source was raided for models for furniture and decoration. Ancient Egypt and the newly revealed antiquities of Assyria, ancient Greece and Rome, Pompeii and Herculaneum, the splendours of Gothic architecture, the grandeur of the Renaissance, the richly ornamental taste of Tudor and Jacobean periods and the elegance of Queen Anne, all provided decorative motifs to be applied to the furnishing and decorating of houses. So, too, as we have seen, did the exotic cultures of the East. North Africa, India, Asia Minor, China and Japan came to be more widely accessible through the activities of the growing number of travelling artists, professional and amateur, whose architectural and topographical works fired the imaginations of the decorators and their patrons.

Some of the results of this eclecticism were disastrous and were perceived as such at the time. As early as 1853 a number of ornamental items were selected for exhibition at the Museum of Ornamental Art at Marlborough House in London, as examples of 'false principles of design': among these was a particularly elaborate wallpaper incorporating views of the Crystal Palace within an exuberant rococo framework. Now that this comic aspect of Victorian eclecticism is seen in the context of the revolution in taste that was an inevitable result of the enormous injection of new money into the consumer trades, it is beginning to be understood and re-evaluated. The rule of taste was no longer applied. Something more robust had taken its place. Our growing appreciation of the decorative achievements of the nineteenth century has slowed the destruction of much important art and architecture that was until recently dismissed.

The Victorians themselves were unappreciative of the achievements of their immediate predecessors, and much fine eighteenth-century furniture lay neglected in attics and outhouses until the revival of interest in the Adam style after 1876. Now in the late twentieth century the once despised Victorians are being revived in their turn.

The traffic in decorating ideas and influences was by no means all one way. For example, William Morris was revered in America and his example was the basis for many – if not all – of the Utopian craft communities that sprang up across the United States.

While for the first half – or even the first three-quarters – of the nineteenth century the main cultural influences on interior decorating in the United States came from England and France, the actual organization of the house and the level of comfort had for decades been well in advance of that in Europe. American visitors were entranced with the old buildings that they saw in Europe, but much less taken with the arrangements for the convenience of the inhabitants of the new buildings. In 1869 Stephen Fiske, the American drama critic, compared contemporary English house building with American to the detriment of the former:

I mean an average American house, such as those which are erected in all the cities of the United States for the residences of the middle-class population. Compared with a dwelling of this kind, the middle-class houses in England seem destitute equally of comfort and convenience, although those who have never been accustomed to anything different or better consider them quite comfortable and convenient enough for all practical purposes. But then different people have different minds. An Englishman absolutely believes that he can warm a room by building a grate-fire at one end of it. An American visiting this country is in a continual shiver, his face being scorched and his back cold, or vice-versa, until he becomes thoroughly acclimated, and learns that the most healthy warmth is that which exercise imparts to the blood.

(*English Photographs*, 1869, pp. 192–3.)

42

43

42, 43
The Gardner house at 152 Beacon Street, Boston 1890s

The impression created by these typically crowded interiors differs little from that of rooms filled with paintings and *objets d'art* of little or no consequence. Yet these rooms in the house of John and Isabella Gardner are filled with priceless works of art that are now displayed with full regard for their rarity and enormous value in a specially designed museum setting. It must have made a curious impression on the visitor to dine facing what appeared to be an altar, complete with candles (above). The whole ensemble from the dining room at Beacon Street is now in the Gothic Room at Fenway Court, Boston, standing under a rose window with Gothic tracery rather than the Raphael portrait of *Count Inghirami*. The *Virgin and Child* is placed on a French carved wood chest of about 1540, and the room is lined with tapestries. The inevitable enormous palm dominates an anteroom (below), where priceless paintings are stacked everywhere for want of wall space. Van Dyck's magnificent *Lady with a Rose* is propped up on two chairs; high on the wall above the writing table is the Pesellino *Madonna and Child with a Swallow*; on the same wall is Vermeer's *The Concert*. In another corner of the room serried ranks of photographs compete for attention with a motley but priceless collection of paintings, including Rembrandt's *Self-Portrait* and Botticelli's *Tragedy of Lucretia*; both clearly so highly prized as to merit the installation of rather primitive-looking picture lights. In 1875 a Boston journalist wrote: 'Mrs Jack Gardner is one of the seven wonders of Boston. There is nobody like her in any city in this country. She is a millionaire Bohemienne. She is eccentric and she has the courage of her eccentricity.' Mrs Gardner was interested in paintings, in music and in flowers, and although in theory her acquisitions were intended as furnishings for her home, in practice they were the beginnings of a museum collection. It is illuminating to read the description of Mrs Gardner's rooms written by Th. Bentzon in 1893. Of Boston in the 1890s he wrote:

A sober elegance is the distinctive trait of this society which wishes to show its refinement in all things. To be sure the splendours of luxury are not absent, but their éclat is muted, so to say tempered by good taste, which is not always the case. I could, for example, name a particularly opulent home which might all too easily have looked like some well furnished bric-à-brac shop or some pretentious museum of decorative arts. But with the greatest tact it succeeded precisely in avoiding this danger, so that nothing was de trop. From the altarpieces dislodged from Italian churches, bibelots from the eighteenth century, masterpieces of German and French painting, to the portrait of the lady of the house – the most beautiful Sargent ever painted – , everything was in its place, even the flag of Napoleon's Grenadier Guards which, by the corner of a Renaissance chimney, tells the glories of French armies. No clutter, no profusion, no show; it all fitted into a savant harmony; it was simply the exquisite frame for a charming woman.
(*Les Americaines chez elles*, Paris, 1893, p. 113.)

Photographs Isabella Stewart Gardner Museum, Boston

44

The dining room of the Villard House, New York *c.* 1900

The room was photographed after the house had been sold to the Whitelaw Reids. The new owners left the McKim, Mead & White scheme intact, and other alterations were comparatively minor. In 1897, the overmantel painting by Edwin Austin Abbey was added; entitled *La Pavanne*, it had been commissioned by Whitelaw Reid himself. Much of the elaborate woodwork was replaced by pilasters of marble with *bronze doré* capitals, equally sumptuous but representing the new 'French' fashion.

*Photograph McKim, Mead & White Collection,
Museum of the City of New York*

45

The Great Hall of the Villard House, New York Mid-1880s

The Villard House was contained in one wing of an impressive brownstone mansion on Madison Avenue, between 50th and 51st Street, commissioned by Henry Villard in 1882 from McKim, Mead & White. The architects chose the Roman High Renaissance as the source of inspiration for the building, which rose to five stories round three sides of a central courtyard. Six separate units were contained within this block; Henry Villard occupied the largest and most magnificent. The interiors were decorated by the Herter brothers in the style with which wealthy New York taste was to be increasingly identified. The fireplace and overmantel shown here were designed by Augustus Saint Gaudens. The Villard interiors are akin to those in W.K. Vanderbilt's house nearby on 52nd Street.

*Photograph McKim, Mead & White Collection,
Museum of the City of New York*

This high degree of comfort in American houses was, of course, achieved by a ducted hot air system. It was as available to British and Continental households as to the American, but Stephen Fiske was right in thinking the resistance to such convenience was a moral issue, at least in part.

Mrs Haweis, describing in 1882 for *Beautiful Houses* the Campden Hill residence of the American artist G. H. Boughton, has clearly been seduced by this American talent for providing warmth and comfort:

One of the most charming houses in London is that built, decorated and inhabited by G. H. Boughton. Mr Boughton has brought from America a certain elegance of style in living which has not yet become common on this side of the Atlantic; less posé than French taste, more subtle than English. The prevailing impression of the house is of softness, refinement, harmony. There is nothing bizarre or eccentric, to startle and not seldom annoy. The affectation of eccentricity is often founded on vanity and ill-nature; here we find no affectation, neither of gaiety nor of gloomy discomfort.

The house is described in great detail and seems at this distance of time to be very much in the same style as many other 'artistic' Queen Anne houses in London at that date. However, clearly some particular quality must have prompted the author into her superlatives. In spite of the claim that Boughton himself had designed and built the house, it was in fact the work of Norman Shaw, and resembles in style and use of materials – that is, brick with stone dressings and extensive tile hanging – a number of the other artists' houses for which this architect was responsible, including his own.

45

All notions of convenience and comfort are, after all, relative. If the country house in England seemed in a primitive state in this respect to an American observer, to Hippolyte Taine, writing his *Notes sur l'Angleterre* in 1861, one particular example seemed the epitome of well organized comfort:

Great attention has been given to comfort, notable in all that concerns sleeping, washing and dressing accommodation. In my own room there is a carpet covering the whole floor, oilcloth before the washstand, matting along the walls. Two dressing tables, both with two drawers, the first provided with an adjustable looking-glass, the second with a large pitcher, a small one, and a medium-sized one for the hot water, two porcelain basins, a brush rack, two soap dishes, a carafe and glass and a bowl and glass. Below this a third toilet table, very low, with a pail, another basin and a large shallow zinc basin for one's morning ablutions. In a cupboard, a towel rail with four different kinds of towel, one very thick and fluffy.

Taine's words echo those of Prince Pückler-Muskau almost forty years before; he too found the toilet arrangements admirably lavish and noted the generous proportions of the towels (entry for 7 October 1826, in *Pückler's Progress*, trans. Flora Bennan, 1987, p. 23).

In spite of a general impression that both central heating and adequate bathing arrangements were better managed in the United States throughout almost the whole of the nineteenth century, such ingenious pioneers of domestic comfort and efficiency as the first Duke of Wellington should not be overlooked. With a characteristic appreciation of such fundamentally desirable amenities as plumbing and heating, the Duke installed at Stratfield Saye a central heating system (two of the original radiators survive in working order and have recently been connected to a new system) and water closets in many of the rooms. There was also an efficient icehouse in the grounds that was so well constructed and insulated that it was capable of maintaining the temperature below freezing point for several years on end.

To give just two examples of the outward spread of British influence, the writings of Charles Eastlake, author of *Hints on Household Taste* (1868), inspired a decorative movement in America appropriately christened 'the Eastlake style', and the outstandingly original designs of the Glasgow architect Charles Rennie Mackintosh were far better appreciated in Vienna than in his native city. However, the forcible induction of British styles and methods elsewhere had the most deplorable effect, for example in India. It is to the credit of Lockwood Kipling that he understood the bad results of teaching our art and design practices to native craftsmen in the art schools there. The effect of promoting these alien methods may have been responsible for the undervaluation of Indian decorative art in this country.

In reaction to the erosion of national and regional stylistic distinctions that resulted from the international exhibitions, an interest in folk culture grew up at the turn of the century. For example, in Russia the Pan-Slavonic movement, encouraged by the Tsar himself as part of a complex package of ideals involving politics, culture and religion, promoted the almost forgotten decorative motifs and techniques of Russian peasant culture before the opening of the 'window on the West' in the seventeenth century. This Russian-Byzantine style, with its rich barbaric colouring and lavish use of gilding, had parallels in Scandinavia, where the national identity was seen to stem from the Viking period and found expression in the 'Dragon' style of ornament. This, in its turn, had distinct affinities with the Celtic revival in England, and more particularly in Scotland and Ireland. It was this cult of Scottish nationalism that the Glasgow artists, notably Mackintosh and his circle, were to draw upon in their development of a distinctive branch of Art Nouveau – distinctive enough, indeed, to merit its own label as the 'Glasgow' or 'Spook' style. At the same date another highly innovative designer, the Manxman Mackay Hugh Baillie Scott, was exploring much the same vein. The return to folk culture was one of the many paths that was to lead ultimately to the Modern movement.

In the United States the nationalistic tendency had been fostered by the 1876 Centennial Exhibition in Philadelphia. Celebrating as it did the successful outcome of the revolution against British rule, it was bound to promote a sense of national identity and to encourage the search for a style expressive of American culture. By 1893, at the great Chicago exhibition, the extent to which native architects and decorators had forged an individual identity was demonstrated by the work of Louis Sullivan, Augustus Saint Gaudens, Louis Comfort Tiffany and H. H. Richardson.

It is curious to reflect that this return to grass roots, this search for cultural continuity, was to emerge, transformed and refashioned by some of the greatest design talents of the age, as Art Nouveau in all its diverse manifestations.

The nineteenth century as an example for today

The decoration and furnishing of the interior in the nineteenth century is of particular relevance to our own time. The noble country house with its art collections and suites of fine furniture is the great achievement, in terms of interior decoration, of the eighteenth century. The prosperous middle-class, urban, 'artistic' or 'intellectual' house expresses the finest decorative aspirations of the nineteenth-century. Although the currently fashionable 'country-house style' has nostalgic and romantic inclinations towards the ideal of the eighteenth century, in practical terms it is much closer to certain aspects of nineteenth-century taste. Indeed, the feature of the eighteenth century most prized by the modern decorator is the ghostly, faded appearance that the fabrics and furnishings and wall colourings assumed in the nineteenth century. The brilliance of the original colours revealed by recent research have come as a not altogether pleasant surprise to many admirers of the period. Remembering Cockayne Hatley in the 1890s, Lady Diana Cooper confirmed that the taste for 'fine old faded things' was not new: 'The drawing-room had a palm and a draped grand piano and three big windows, whose blue curtains were seldom hung in the summer, as they had to be laid out on the lawn to get their inartistic brightness faded by the eternal Hatley sunshine' (*The Rainbow Comes and Goes*, 1958, p. 12). It is ironic that the ceaseless vigilance of the Miss Jenkynses was set at naught by future generations:

The greatest event was, that the Miss Jenkynses had purchased a new carpet for the drawing-room. Oh, the busy work Miss Matty and I had in chasing the sunbeams, as they fell in an afternoon right down on this carpet through the blindless window! We spread newspapers over the places, and sat down to our book or our work; and lo! in a quarter of an hour the sun had moved, and was blazing away on a fresh spot; and down again we went on our knees to alter the position of the newspapers. We were very busy, too, one whole morning, before Miss Jenkyns gave her party, in following her directions, and in cutting out and stitching together pieces of newspaper so as to form little paths to every chair set for the expected visitors, lest their shoes might dirty or defile the purity of the carpet. Do you make paper paths for every guest to walk upon in London? (Mrs Gaskell, *Cranford*, 1853, ch. 11.)

For the decorator of the present day, the neo-Victorian scheme does not need to be an approximation. Materials are increasingly available: wallpapers closely reproducing designs of the nineteenth century; tiles re-created from the designs of celebrated firms of the period; carpets and fabrics woven from old patterns; lace as elaborate as the work of a century ago; and furniture from models by the most eminent architects and decorators. It is somewhat disconcerting to see highly ornamented baths and other sanitary equipment returning to the primitive state of sitting on elaborate clawed feet instead of being neatly boxed in against the dirt.

Evidence as to how this material should be deployed is abundant. The practice of recording rooms with brush or pencil, whilst enjoying a limited revival, has been largely superceded by photography, but in the nineteenth century it reached the pinnacle of achievement. The quality of the early photographic interiors is perhaps even more remarkable than the range and variety of the graphic material. Here we have, then, the real exemplar, or such

approximation to reality as art – which by its nature deals in artifice – can achieve. No one has ever written more eloquently of this genre than Mario Praz:

Watercolours of interiors of which so many were painted, particularly in the first half of the nineteenth century, possess in a special manner, the virtue of bringing a place to life in the mind of the beholder, thanks to the diligence with which they reproduce every piece of furniture and every household object, every minute detail of carpets and curtains, and the feeling of light and shade in a room. It might be said that by means of this objective diligence they capture the soul of things, preserving them as a botanist preserves a flower in a herbarium, or an entomologist a butterfly. Like those Japanese paper flowers which, when put in water, disclose an exuberance unexpected in a piece of dry straw, or like the genie in the bottle of the Arabian tale who becomes gigantic when he emerges, so do these little pictures of interiors expand in the beholder's imagination. (*The House of Life*, 1964, p. 287.)

But more than this abundance of visual evidence, so nearly revealing, but in many ways so tantalizing, we have from this age so close to our own a rich hoard of survivals. Such complete examples as Calke Abbey and Erdigg have been identified as 'time capsules', giving the impression of actually permitting the visitor to travel in time, and to see through the eyes of his predecessors. This reality is, however, hazed over with decay, a faded picture of a period when taste was immensely robust. Perhaps we would have been startled by the vibrant reds and greens of buttoned leather upholstery when it was new, but the quality of the materials used in the past has ensured that those that survive have a magical insubstantiality in their slow decline, and it is this entrancing quality that lends the 'time capsule' an inimitable perfection.

The arrangement of the public or reception rooms in the eighteenth century is inappropriate for the present day; only in the nineteenth century did the grouping of furniture around tables and the source of light or heat come into general use.

Early in the century Humphry Repton was advocating the giving up of the large hallway which had been a common feature of all houses of any size, and in which the family often dined in considerable discomfort. He also urged a more rational arrangement of the rooms, and the abandonment of little-used state rooms, at any rate in country houses where they were only rarely required. His solution was to propose a flexible plan with rooms opening into one another, thus capable of providing a large space when needed. The following passage is taken from the chapter concerning 'Interiors' in his 1816 publication on architecture and landscape gardening:

... whether the house be Grecian or gothic, large or small, it will require nearly the same rooms for the present habits of life, viz. a dining-room, and two others, one of which may be

46

The Prophet in his Parlour 1878

The Carlyles moved into their London house in Cheyne Row in 1834. Carlyle speaks of the area as 'unfashionable', but he was taken with the historical associations of Chelsea. In a letter to his wife Jane, who had remained in Scotland, he described their future home in the early eighteenth-century terraced street in great detail:

The House itself is eminent, antique and wainscotted to the very ceiling, and has been all new-painted and repaired; broadish stair, with massive balustrade (in the old style) corniced and as thick as one's thigh; floors as firm as rock, wood of them here and there worm eaten yet capable of cleanliness, and still thrice the strength of a modern floor . . . there is a front dining-room (marble chimney-piece &c.); then a back dining-room (or breakfast room); a little narrower by reason of the kitchen stair; then out from this a china room or pantry, or I know not what, all shelved and fit to hold crockery for the whole street. Such is the ground area, which of course continues to the top, and furnishes every bedroom with a dressing room, or even a second bedroom. Red Bed will stand behind the drawing-room; might have a shower-bath beyond it. . . .

Thomas Carlyle sits in the first floor drawing room. Painted when the great prophet of early Victorian Britain was 83 years old, the room has hardly changed since the painstakingly detailed double portrait by Robert Tait of the Carlyles in the same room in 1857.

Helen Allingham, watercolour
National Portrait Gallery of Scotland, Edinburgh

called a drawing-room, and the other a book-room, if small, or the library, if large: to these is sometimes added a breakfast-room, but of late, especially since the central hall, or vestibule, has been in some degree given up, these rooms have been opened into each other, en suite, by large folding doors; the effect of this enfilade, or visto, through a modern house, is occasionally increased by a conservatory at one end, and repeated by a large mirror at the opposite end.*

After an interesting digression on the use of mirrors in interior design, Repton goes on to explain his reasoning more fully:

The most recent modern costume [sic] is, to use the library as the general living room; and that sort of state-room, formerly called the best parlour, and of late years the drawing-room, is now generally found a melancholy apartment, when entirely shut up, and only opened to give visitors a formal cold reception: but if such a room opens into one adjoining, and the two are fitted up with the same carpet, curtains ec. [sic], they become in some degree one room; and the comfort of that which has books, or musical instruments, is extended in its space to that which has only sophas [sic], chairs and card-tables; and thus the living-room is increased in dimensions, when required, with a power of keeping a certain portion detached, and not always used for common purposes.

These immensely practical observations can be seen to have been followed in all kinds of surviving modest dwellings, and their usefulness is only impaired when the essential folding doors are omitted or removed.

Many of our present-day decorative ideas which have been adapted from the decoration of the past, while conforming to eighteenth-century preferences in the colour schemes and general period style in design, in fact more nearly re-create the best of nineteenth-century middle-class inspiration. With hardly any exceptions the rooms depicted in the surviving visual documents – paintings, drawings, schemes for decoration and photographs – provide, either in part or in their entirety, easily realisable ideas for the house of today. Even the richly exotic, highly gilded decorative scheme at Castell Coch, devised by William Burges for his patron the Marquess of Bute, has provided inspiration in the transformation of a disused Presbyterian chapel in West Halkin Street, London (see *The World of Interiors*, March 1983, pp. 164–7).

On another level, contemporary drawings can be of enormous assistance in another kind of recreation, the restoring to its original state of a much altered or damaged interior. Drawings of Capesthorne, home of the Bromley-Davenport family, executed in 1844 by James Johnson, are so accurate in detail that they have allowed a full understanding of the complex decorating history of the house. The drawings of Gawthorpe have been used for the same purpose, to re-create the interiors from the time of Sir James Kay-Shuttleworth, Charlotte Brontë's friend and great admirer. With the help of drawings and photographs by Robert Tait dating from 1857, and a series of drawings and portraits executed by Helen Allingham in the 1880s, we can see that Thomas Carlyle's house in Cheyne Row has been decorated and re-furnished with minute accuracy.

The rise of interior decoration

It cannot be simply coincidence that the term 'interior decoration' was coined by Thomas Hope, the celebrated collector and scholar of the antique, at the very beginning of the century. Emulating the publication *Recueil de Décorations intérieures ...* of 1801 by the architects Percier and Fontaine who enjoyed the patronage of Napoleon I, and with whom Hope was acquainted, he produced a book of designs for furniture and 'interior decoration' in 1807. This gave a title and a framework to one of the most widely pervasive artistic achievements of the nineteenth century. But more important by far than the mere coining of a phrase was the circulation of these 'designer' ideas that publication afforded. The accessibility of these schemes for decoration was to inspire the growing middle-class population with hitherto undreamed-of aspirations for their personal surroundings. The importance of the development, at this same date, of practical colour reproduction for publications on interior design and decoration cannot be over-stressed.

In 1822 Walter Scott wrote to his friend, Daniel Terry, the architect turned actor: 'Pray is there not a tolerable book on upholstery – I mean plans for tables, chairs, commodes, and such like. If so I would be much obliged to you to get me a copy.' Terry replied some six weeks later: 'I have hunted London for a book on furniture and have ascertained that there is none of any character, Hope's is merely his own house which is entirely Grecian and there is a French one of Bonaparte's Palaces but not one of a style appertaining to your castle. ...' (Quoted by Clive Wainwright in 'Walter Scott and the furnishing of Abbotsford: or the gabions of Jonathan Oldbuck Esq.', *Connoisseur*, January 1977, pp. 3–15.)

Scott would have found Henry Shaw's *Specimens of Ancient Furniture* to be exactly the publication he was seeking. This handsome volume with its seventy-four plates appeared in 1836, and contained examples of mainly Gothic and Elizabethan furniture and metalwork. It was dedicated to the collector and antiquary Thomas Lister Parker, and indeed included illustrations of pieces belonging to him. Plates from this book were copied in a later French publication, Asselineau's *Objets du Moyen Age et de la Renaissance* (1844), and it was recommended by John Claudius Loudon in the later editions of his own immensely influential *Encyclopaedia of Cottage, Farm and Villa Architecture*, which first appeared in 1833. Shaw's

1847 *Encyclopaedia of Ornament* was to be the inspiration for the many pattern books of historical ornament that were produced in the nineteenth century.

Thomas Lister Parker was one of the very first to experiment with the Elizabethan style: his alterations to his house, Browsholme, date from before 1810. Parker was responsible for starting the architect Anthony Salvin on his Elizabethan enthusiasms, and thus for inspiring some of the finest nineteenth-century neo-Elizabethan schemes, for example at Harlaxton; but the focal point of antiquarian inspiration remains Walter Scott. To quote Clive Wainwright, 'The influence of the interior decoration and furnishings at Abbotsford was, I am convinced, widespread and international. Any serious study of the Gothic, Elizabethan or Tudor revivals and the antiquarian movement in the nineteenth century must start at Abbotsford.'

Proliferating publications set the seal of approval on a concern with the decoration of the home, which became increasingly widespread as the industrial middle classes became more prosperous. But the choices that so much information offered were almost overwhelming, and interior decoration came to be perceived as a complex operation only to be carried out with the help and advice of professionals. Such advice was to be forthcoming in bewildering profusion, much of it proffered with a high-handed disregard for the sensibility and the preferences of the patron, but much also of sensible and practical application.

Thomas Hope was a perfectionist and his counsel certainly verged on the high-handed. He believed that the Classical style was the only possible mode of decoration and would not even consider the claims of the Gothic taste. His attack, in 1804, on James Wyatt's neo-Gothic plans for Downing College, Cambridge, caused Wyatt's plans to be dropped, thus earning Hope an enemy for life. By no means everyone shared his rigorous design principles; after the publication of *Household Furniture and Interior Decoration* in 1807, Sydney Smith wrote in the *Edinburgh Review*:

Everything is to be adorned according to Mr Hope, with emblems and symbols connected with the uses to which it is applied, and all these emblems are to be derived from classical mythology. He has made a perfect hieroglyphic or enigma of most of his apartments by this means, and produced something so childishly complicated and fantastic as to be impenetrable without a paraphrase and ridiculous when it is interpreted.
(Vol. x, p. 478.)

Hope's treatise also advocated room settings that were planned down to the minutest detail to complement the works of art that they contained. The design of the furniture was meticulously researched and appropriate forms and ornament used to set off the extensive and

47

47

Sir Walter Scott's library, Abbotsford

1832

Prominent in the foreground is the pedestal supplied by George Bullock for the silver urn containing the ashes of Lord Byron.

William Allan, drawing
National Gallery of Scotland, Edinburgh

important collections of Greek and Egyptian antiquities housed in his London house in Duchess Street and at The Deepdene in Surrey.

Nevertheless, Hope's ideas were influential; and although there is little evidence of direct copying of specific examples from his designs, his ideas appear transformed but still quite recognizable in the work of some of his successors.

Half a century later the tone was very much altered. In Cassell's *Household Guide*, one of the many manuals of instruction that appeared with increasing frequency from the mid-century onwards, the didactic approach has been dropped. The following passage might have been written to refute Hope's view; it must surely have reassured the nervous amateur decorator:

It has long been a common practice . . . to adopt some general style, as Greek, or Gothic, or Renaissance; or some particular branch, as Elizabethan or Louis Quatorze; and to have the building and the furniture all designed in the one style; and by adopting this course, since each style of the past has its own peculiar spirit and characteristics, if these are not departed from uniformity will follow. . . . But in many cases it is not practicable to have the whole of the furniture and enrichments in one style; nor do we believe, as many do, in the desirability of adhering thus rigidly to some particular style, or period, of art, and of reproducing the characteristic details again and again with literal exactness.

Such imitation and repetition have already been overdone, and we much prefer to see uniformity which is not dependent upon the correctness with which ornaments of a past style have been copied but which arises from some similarity and congruity observable in the general character and treatment of the decoration throughout at least one apartment, or throughout the whole house.
(Vol. 3, 1869–71, pp. 77–8.)

It was no small achievement for the ordinary householder intent on decorating to thread his way through all the conflicting advice.

The core of this development is the achievement of the modest 'artistic' house, with all its implications of middle-class patronage of remarkable design talent and open-minded domestic innovation. It was in the ordinary prosperous family house that the greatest national and regional differences were retained. Local talent was often employed in preference to internationally celebrated 'names', and local traditions and building methods were respected, which ensured the continuance of a robust individuality. The momentum of this development was only checked by the rise of – to steal a phrase from John Betjeman, one of the most fervent apologists for the nineteenth century in all its many artistic manifestations – 'ghastly good taste'.

It is probably this same regard for good taste that is responsible for the purist approach to preservation in the present day. For example, Wightwick Manor, now the property of the National Trust, is much more authentically 'Morris & Co.' today than it was when decorated for the first owners in the 1890s. Interestingly, as evidence of the attraction of preconceived ideas, the re-created 'Victorian' room is more popular with the public than the Morris rooms; this might not have surprised Morris himself, always uncomfortably aware of being out of touch with the man in the street. The present-day austere orderliness of Keats's House in Hampstead has banished the ghost of poor Fanny Brawne; the accidents of chance acquisition or expediency cannot be reproduced convincingly. Century-old photographs of great architectural masterpieces of the seventeenth and eighteenth centuries, crammed with the proliferating nineteenth-century furniture and ornaments accumulated to meet the demands of family life and large-scale entertaining, somehow give a more convincing impression of family continuity than their present-day metamorphoses, furnished only with items appropriate to the date of the building of the house. The designers of the nineteenth century were less inhibited by reverence for antiquity and treated the great monuments of past centuries with ebullience, notably in the use of the most elaborate 'Elizabethan' carved interiors for the rehabilitation of perfectly genuine but more restrained Tudor houses, like Charlecote or Knebworth. Alice Fairfax-Lucy described her predecessor's activities at Charlecote:

He allowed his wife to root up the untidy plots in the court and replace them with a fair imitation of an Elizabethan knot garden. Less happily . . . he removed the organ gallery and the Tudor screen from the Great Hall and put a light oak dado round it. More unhappily still, he allowed Willement, on whose judgement he had come to depend, to flatten the ceiling of the hall (the Elizabethan gallery that ran the length of the top storey had been divided up into servants' attics). Willement's heavy barrel vaulting with its outsize Tudor roses robs the hall of impressiveness. Never

for a moment did the Lucys lose sight of Tudor England; even the door handles were carved with Tudor roses. Twisted pseudo-Jacobean chimneys gave the roof the richly fretted and pinnacled outline which our great-grandparents so much admired.
(*Charlecote and the Lucys*, 1958, p. 286.)

The first embellishments to Knebworth were carried out for Mrs Lytton Bulwer (as she was known) by Biagio Rebecca in 1816. The original fabric was clothed in crocketted and pinnacled adornments, presenting a fantastic silhouette. When Mrs Bulwer died in 1843 her son Edward Bulwer Lytton began on the further elaboration of his inheritance. Inside, a remarkable staircase imitates the magnificent carved Tudor example at Longleat. The state drawing room with its fine heraldic painted ceiling was decorated by Crace, and is as interesting an expression of the taste of the time as the noble carved screen in the dining hall is of the decade 1610–20.

In 1877 Lord and Lady Monkswell visited Knebworth:

Friday 18 June – We went down to the Grant-Duffs at Knebworth, Lord Lytton's house, which they have taken until they go to their own house at Twickenham. It is an enormous place, a brown stone and griphoned variety of Elizabethan. We slept in 'Falkland Room' Tudor Gallery, in an aged 4 poster. The room was full of old bureaux and had a dark oak mantel board up to the ceiling, carved with smitten hearts, flames, wreaths. The garden was cram full of vases, statues, fountains, ponds, ferneries. The dining-room was enormous, it had a great gallery for musicians, and a cupboard full of gold plate.
(*A Victorian Diarist*, 1944, p. 24.)

In his reconstruction of Knebworth, Bulwer Lytton was influenced by the rebuilding of Bayons by his friend Charles Tennyson d'Eyncourt, transformed from a plain Regency house in the 1830s into a fortified castle with moat and drawbridge. Another friend, the antiquary Thomas Baylis, also encouraged Bulwer Lytton in his baronial schemes for Knebworth. Baylis was responsible for the transformation of the modest Vine Cottage, on the River Thames by Fulham Church, into the Gothic treasure house which he called Pryor's Bank. Crofton Croker described the interiors in detail in his guidebook, *A Walk from London to Fulham*, and many of the architectural details were drawn by Fairholt. The house contained the astonishing mixture of objects and ornamental features, some of fine quality and some mere curiosities, that characterized the 'antiquarian' taste so prevalent in the 1830s and 1840s. Bulwer Lytton knew the house and its contents intimately – his views on some of the antiquities are quoted by Crofton Croker – and was in a position to visit frequently since, for the seven years before complication of the work on Knebworth (1839–46), he hired Craven Cottage (see plate 126), a short distance towards Hammersmith along the river.

48

48
A bedroom at Knebworth 1890s

In the 'Elizabethanization' of Knebworth Mrs Lytton Bulwer's elegant bedroom retained the lighter, Gothic character of an earlier period. Indeed, the delicate painted chairs are pure Regency. Edward Bulwer Lytton left the bedroom untouched as a gesture to the originator of Knebworth's nineteenth-century metamorphosis.

Photograph The Hon. David Lytton Cobbold of Knebworth House

Baylis left Pryor's Bank after he had been there for only four years, in 1841. The sale of the contents lasted for a week and detailed particulars were given in an article entitled 'Ancient domestic furniture' which appeared in the *Gentleman's Magazine* for January 1842. The florid style of the auctioneer gives an idea of the house:

It is erected in the GOTHIC ORDER OF ARCHITECTURE, *with a care and discernment that cannot be impugned, but it is to the fitting up within that the full force of the tasteful proprietor's judgement and knowledge has been directed; here the* EARLY TUDOR AND ELIZABETHAN PERIODS *reign triumphant; every object is in itself a beauty; there is a unity of purpose, and harmony of taste and execution, that are indeed admirable, and which it is fearlessly asserted never can be surpassed. The grand suite approaches in decoration and splendour to* REGAL MAGNIFICENCE.

ST GEORGE'S GALLERY, OR NOBLE ARMOURY, decorated in the truest style: a high classical tone pervades this noble appartment, and a large oriel window decorated with ancient stained glass looks out upon THE SILVERY THAMES; next is a splendid saloon which leads by noble plate glass and carved folding doors to THE GRAND DRAWING ROOM, with its splendid oriel window. It were vain to attempt to describe these appartments; suffice it here to observe, that an enormous expense has been encountered and a consummate taste exercised to effect so perfect an achievement. . . . The Hall, Library, and Refectory are all fitted up with selected specimens of fine English antique oak carvings, each with some history connected with the fifteenth century attached; there is a kitchen worthy of the abbots and pryor of old, besides all useful offices. The bedchamber department is commodious with TWO ANCIENT CARVED OAK CHAMBERS, worthy of the general character of this classical abode.

Pryor's Bank was demolished in 1897.

Baylis remained a close friend of Bulwer Lytton after both of them had left Fulham; he stayed frequently at Knebworth, sometimes for weeks, and is known to have advised over the alterations and additions to the house. The decorator was John Crace, and apart from the state drawing room and the staircase he created a library and another drawing room of which only photographs survive (plates 281, and 282).

Crace was also responsible for some of the decorating work undertaken by the sixth Duke of Devonshire at Chatsworth. The Duke had begun these works as early as 1818 with the assistance of Sir Jeffry Wyatville, who transformed the old Long Gallery into a library and restored the state rooms. The beautiful Yellow Drawing Room in the private apartments he designed in 1839. In the same year Crace devised the Lower Library (now the Duke's sitting room); the sixth Duke wrote of it in his *Hand Book of Chatsworth* of 1844:

Mr John Crace, the upholsterer, was the magician who transformed it into its present state, making it look something between an illuminated MS, and a café in the rue de Richelieu. I wished to have one room in the new style of decoration, and in a short time two or three bearded artists in blouses were imported from Paris, and completed the ceiling and pilasters.

The Duke also succumbed to the prevailing mania for an oak room; again from the *Hand Book* we learn:

One day, walking with a friend in Berners Street, we were tempted into the auction-room, and found carved oak being knocked down. I bought all that you see here, the fittings of some German Monastery, and the woodwork of an old-fashioned pew. So inconsiderate a purchase was never made – however, look at the result. Is it not charming?

49

49

The drawing room at Pryor's Bank 1860

A charming Residence, in the Gothic order of architecture, and arranged within after the early Tudor and Elizabethan periods. (Auctioneer's description of 1842.)

William Fairholt, drawn as an illustration to J. Croften Croker, *Walk from London to Fulham*
Guildhall Library, London

At Knebworth or Charlecote or Chatsworth the celebrated decorators Crace, Willement and Gillow reigned supreme. They designed and executed the scheme; they supplied the furnishings and fabrics. This is the pinnacle of the upholsterer's achievement, and this method of devising and realizing a decorative scheme was to continue in popularity throughout the nineteenth century, with the support of noble and wealthy patrons. For example, the decorative package, perhaps not particularly welcome, presented to the Duchess of York (later Queen Mary) at her marriage was the work of Mr Maple of the famous furniture emporium.

A contrast to this popular practice was provided by the patronage of the 'architect-designer' by the artistic middle-class client. The rise of the middle-class consumer in the wake of the Industrial Revolution has been conventionally perceived as the reason for a decline in taste, particularly taste in decoration and furnishing. While, broadly speaking, this is true – the catalogues of the international exhibitions held regularly throughout the second half of the nineteenth century are damning evidence enough – there is a considerable, and still undervalued, middle-class achievement which resulted from the collaboration between the cultivated patron and the talented, innovative architect.

Yet the patronage of a talented architect-designer was no guarantee against an excess of tasteful refinement. When Philip Webb remodelled Forthampton Court he seems to have misunderstood the limitations on his responsibilities in this respect. Having written to his patron, 'Practically with the fine roof, the wall hangings and the carpet, the room will be quite furnished, anything else added would be for convenience of use only; any other furniture could not be too scanty and should be I am sure, simple in the extreme', he seems to have been reminded of his presumption in setting up so dogmatically as an arbiter of taste: 'I had no wish to limit the moveable furniture for the Abbot's Hall to two cricket stools and a toasting fork. . . .'

One important innovation took place during this period; in many families, decisions about the decoration and furnishing of the home became the province, often the sole responsibility, of the wife. Whilst in the eighteenth century, the man of the household would have collaborated with his architect, in the nineteenth century it was the wife who collaborated with her decorator in such matters.

A certain dominating strain in character might be expected in a future monarch, but it was probably just insensitivity which led the Duke of York (later George v) to reverse this trend so completely at the time of his marriage in 1893. His bride, formerly Princess May of Teck, was determined to find her future home, York Cottage on the Sandringham estate, 'charming', but she was very taken aback to find that it had been entirely done up and equipped down to the last detail by her husband with the intention of 'saving her trouble'. She had been looking forward to the buying of furniture and choosing of colours and fabrics, an activity for which her interest in art, and in antiques in particular, and her good taste, equipped her most excellently. But at the end of 1892 Prince George had summoned 'Maple's man' and had chosen everything himself, assisted by his father and his sister Princess Louise, Duchess of Fife (Sir John Blundell Maple was an old friend of his father, Edward VII). But it is debatable whether the Duchess of York would have settled for this method of furnishing by ordering the entire scheme as a package, so to speak, a method calculated to deprive her of her favourite pastime, collecting.

York Cottage would hardly have provided a particularly rewarding object of the Duchess's attentions. It had originally been built as a guest annexe to the main house at Sandringham by the architect Col. Robert Edis, who was responsible for the addition of a second floor to Sandringham, after a fire in 1891 had damaged the upper part of the house. In his book on the decoration of town houses Edis claimed to give instruction on how to circumvent the disadvantages of urban living, but he seems to have managed to introduce a number of them, such as poky and restricted spaces and an absence of any vista, into this nondescript villa, which was originally christened 'Bachelor's Cottage'. Harold Nicolson described it thus:

It was, and remains, a glum little villa, encompassed by thickets of laurel and rhododendron, shadowed by huge Wellingtonias. . . . The rooms inside, with their fumed oak surrounds, their white overmantels framing oval mirrors, their Doulton tiles and stained glass fanlights, are indistinguishable from those of any Surbiton or Upper Norwood home. The Duke's own sitting-room, its north window blocked by heavy shrubberies, was rendered even darker by the red cloth covering which saddened the walls. Against this dismal monochrome (which was composed of the cloth used in those days for the trousers of the French army) hung excellent reproductions of some of the more popular pictures acquired by the Chantrey Bequest. This most undesirable residence remained his favourite home for thirty-three years.
(*King George v: His Life and Reign*, 1952, p. 51.)

It is perhaps worth noting that the manuscript of this book was submitted to Queen Mary for comment, and she seems to have found nothing to quarrel with in the above description. Disraeli reputedly found Queen Victoria's response to a situation a perfect gauge of the likely reaction of the most ordinary of her subjects. It seems that the taste of her grandson reflected that of the most unadventurous of his.

The great choice of inexpensive and impermanent materials such as machine-printed wallpaper and fabrics and veneered or machine-ornamented furniture permitted the indulgence of transitory fancies; the fitting-up of highly fashionable interiors could be speedily accomplished by a furnishing and decorating firm such as Maple's and would be superseded by some new 'range' in the near future. So went the indulgent but patronizing reasoning of the busy man. The result of feminine influence is apparent in the artless, seemingly uncontrived disposition of the frequently proliferating ornaments and accessories, which manages to stop just short of being untidy. Classical symmetry and order gave way early in the century to an encroaching 'boudoir' style (see Lady Mount Temple's description of her decorations in Curzon Street quoted p. 11), in all but the sacrosanct male preserves of library and smoking room. It is the proliferation of furnishings and ornaments, perfectly preserved in paintings of astonishingly minute accuracy of detail, which are so fascinating to the modern eye.

Fashion has relatively little to do with the way ordinary people furnish their homes. The enormous outlay needed to acquire and equip a house may mean that the owner and his family are realizing decorative ambitions that crystallized a decade or more before. Therefore the stock of a commercially successful furnishing and decorating supplier may reflect styles that are currently in demand, but are by no means fashionable or new. In the St Louis Exhibition in 1908, Waring and Gillow showed elaborately detailed Jacobean interiors of almost awe-inspiring banality. But these probably represent the most lavish and expensive realization of a widespread and persistent home-decorating dream. It should be emphasized that these exhibited schemes were light-years away from the Old English Manor House style featured in early issues of *Country Life*, where the taste for exposed beams, plain walls, oak furniture, copper, brass and pewter vessels and oriental rugs as used at Deanery Garden is given extensive coverage. This house, designed by Sir Edwin Lutyens for Edward Hudson, the founder of the magazine, was featured along with H. Avray Tipping's Mathern Palace, a restored medieval house carefully equipped with solid, plain oak furniture.

The historical style did not die with the opening of the new century and the advent of the Modern style; it simply retreated. The particular flavour of suburban architecture and decoration has only just begun to be appreciated, lagging far behind the other lost worlds in the recurring cycle of taste that long ago brought the merits of Art Deco and Aztec forms to the attention of a wider public. However, the 'Jacobean' of suburbia suffered from being produced for a mass-market taste and budget, and lacks the vigour that has enabled Victorian decoration to survive the hazards of mechanical reproduction.

The seemingly universal availability of cheap decorative materials underlines the enormous gulf that existed between even the smallest degree of steady prosperity and real poverty. As part of his efforts to improve the cottages of the labourers in his parish, the Rev. Whitwell Elwin, friend and correspondent of Lady Emily Lytton (who later married Lutyens), was happy to discover a source of pretty printed wallpaper to be had for only $2\frac{1}{2}$d (approximately 1 p) a roll; it might seem remarkable that the cottagers could not provide it for their own walls. The answer was, of course, that they could not afford it. Flora Thompson wrote of rural poverty in Oxfordshire in *Lark Rise to Candleford* (1939), describing the cottages in the village where she was born:

In nearly all the cottages there was but one room downstairs, and many of these were poor and bare, with only a table and a few chairs and stools for furniture and a superannuated potato-sack thrown down by way of hearthrug. . . . The interiors varied, according to the number of mouths to be fed and the thrift and skill of the housewife, or the lack of those qualities; but the income in all was precisely the same, for ten shillings a week was the standard wage of the farm labourer at that time in that district.

She recalls cutting pictures from the illustrated papers to stick all over the walls, a limitless resource for those who wished to embellish their surroundings but lacked the means to accomplish it.

50

50
Lamplight portrait of James Peale 1822

In this portrait by his octogenarian elder brother, James Peale is examining one of his own earlier works by the light of a colza-oil lamp. The introduction of efficient lighting, superseding candles, in the first decades of the nineteenth century transformed the evening life of the family home, a change that is marked in the number of representations of activities carried out by the light of a lamp. Most rooms are so arranged to make the most of daylight, and then lamplight as well as the heat of the fire in the evening.

Charles Willson Peale, oil
Detroit Institute of Arts (Gift of Dexter M. Ferry, Jr.)

Labour-saving devices

Alongside the technical and commercial decorative developments, which encompassed the adaptation of the most exotic inspiration to the convenience of the domestic consumer, went a simply breathtaking advance in the mechanics of the domestic routine. To take only one example, the century saw the progression from tinder box and candle – the striking match was not introduced until 1820 – to the immense convenience of instant illumination by the pressing of an electric light switch. In fact one of the great ironies of this aspect of nineteenth-century ingenuity, and one that certainly enhances the picturesque attraction of the period for us now, is the enormous reluctance with which many of these conveniences were adopted. Not until the final departure in 1939 of all but the most rudimentary domestic help from the majority of modestly prosperous households did the 'appliance revolution' really take off.

Lady Dorothy Nevill remembered the days of the oil lamps at Belvoir Castle:

The cumbersome oil lamps of pre-electric light days were a great source of trouble and expense, apart from the danger of fire which they sometimes caused owing to careless handling. In large houses men had to be specially told off to attend to the lamps. I remember the uncle of the present Duke of Rutland showing me the lamp-room at Belvoir full of gigantic barrels of oil; at the same time he told me that no less than six men were kept constantly employed at nothing else but looking after the lamps.
(*Leaves From a Notebook*, 1907, p. 96.)

Lady Diana Cooper's childhood memories of life at Belvoir included a regime which continued until the death of her grandfather in 1908. This account is in the first volume of her memoirs, *The Rainbow Comes and Goes* (1958, p. 35):

There were lamp-and-candle men, at least three of them, for there was no other form of lighting. Gas was despised, I forget why – vulgar, I think. They polished and scraped the wax off the candelabra, cut wicks, poured paraffin oil and unblackened glass chimneys all day long. After dark they were busy turning wicks up or down, snuffing candles, and de-waxing extinguishers. It was not a department we liked much to visit. It smelt disgusting and the lamp-men were too busy. . . . The water-men were difficult to believe in today. They seemed to me to belong to another day. They were the biggest people I had ever seen, much bigger than any of the men of the family, who were remarkable for their height. They had stubbly beards and a general Bill Sikes appearance. They wore brown clothes, no collars, and thick green baize aprons from chin to knee. On their shoulders they carried a wooden yoke from which hung two gigantic cans of water. They moved on a perpetual round. Above the

51
52

53

51, 52, 53
Bathrooms in the 1890s

The nineteenth-century luxury bathroom as it developed in England was not regarded as the room apart that it later became; it contained articles of furniture that might have been found in any room of the house. Many, indeed, had the bathroom fittings disguised within standard pieces of furniture that made the room appear undifferentiated in layout or décor from other rooms in the home. The bathroom of 1900 called for a spacious room possessing a number of windows. The expensive fixtures were placed at dignified distances from one another, leaving a central space ample enough for moving about and even for exercising (see Sigfried Giedion, *Mechanization takes command*, 1947). Moray Lodge in Kensington, London (above), was the home of Arthur Lewis, a successful silk mercer who also had literary and artistic interests. The house was altered in 1873–4. but the bathroom appears to date from later in the century. The bathroom at Ashley Place, London (above left), formed part of the exotic scheme carried out for Mrs Wallace Carpenter by H. & J. Cooper in 1893. Labour-saving convenience was spread patchily in Europe, and was not always luxurious, as can be seen from this bathroom in a villa near Helsinki (below left).

Photographs of Moray Lodge and Ashley Place, London, by H. Bedford Lemere
National Monuments Record, London
Photograph of a villa in Helsinki
National Board of Antiquities, Finland

ground floor there was not a drop of hot water and not one bath, so their job was to keep all jugs, cans and kettles full in the bedrooms, and morning or evening to bring the hot water to the hip-baths.

These two passages are illuminating on two fronts; it is hardly a revelation to be told that immense country seats were complicated and labour-intensive to run, but it is interesting to reflect on the strain that these dirty and demanding appliances put on smaller, less well served households.

However, the early days of electricity were not without almost comparable difficulties: the system at Hatfield House provided only very fitful illumination when it was first installed, and the fire hazard was still an ever present worry. The following account of an evening spent under the tyranny of this experimental system may be very amusing, but it was such indomitable persistence that ensured the extraordinary degree of domestic convenience that we now enjoy. While servants were still easily available it must have been very tempting to ignore the practical advantages of electricity, since the quality of the illumination, harsh and over-bright, was very much disliked. As late as 1891 Lady Monkswell was disgusted at being exposed to this unflattering glare; clearly there was still no appreciation of the inevitability of this innovation:

Fri 20 Feby [Lord and Lady Monkswell had been dining with Mr and Mrs Bryce at their house in Portland Place] . . . I was not much . . . pleased on arriving at the Bryces to be ushered into a drawingroom as cold as charity & lighted by some 8 or 10 electric lights so that it was considerably lighter than daylight and most unbecoming (tho' for that matter I was no worse off than the other women).
(*A Victorian Diarist*, 1944, p. 178.)

It is only with hindsight that the absence of bathrooms seems at all remarkable. When Clouds, the house built for the Wyndhams by Philip Webb, was burnt down only five years after it had been completed, the family spent the period of rebuilding in the large servants' wing which had survived undamaged. This accommodation was deemed very comfortable, owing, it was believed, to the fact that the socialist Webb had planned unusually lavishly for the servants; but among the twelve bedrooms in the wing there was not so much as one tap, let alone a bathroom – this in a house newly built on advanced lines in the 1880s.

It was thought to be vulgar to have handbasins in bedrooms, as such conveniences denoted a lack of sufficient domestic help. However, such innovations as were adopted were quickly hallowed by the sanctity of tradition: the magnificent lead-lined wooden bathtub installed at Longleat by the third Marchioness of Bath in 1840 was used until the death of the fifth Marquess in 1946.

A similar resistance to newly developed conveniences prevailed in many kitchens. In his memoirs *The Passing Years*, published in 1924, Lord Willoughby de Broke lamented the disappearance of the old order:

I have had the privilege of seeing the sirloin hanging by a chain, slowly turning round and round and being basted by the stout kitchen wench, whose face was quite as red and nearly as hot as the huge open fire in front of her. We did not bake the good joint in some patent, poverty-stricken, war-begotten, labour-saving monstrosity . . . as we do now.

Enthusiasm for mechanical assistance with the domestic tasks was obviously not going to be very noticeable in a society where even an income of £150 per annum was adequate to allow for the employment of a full-time maid-of-all-work, the lowest and most unenviable form of domestic service. In the great houses, where a truly enormous staff was considered essential, the introduction of time-saving appliances was regarded as an admission of encroaching poverty, a reduction in the lavish standards of living implicit in the requirement of a gentleman's family. To the domestic hierarchy, with its inviolable rules as to what should and should not be done by the mistress of the household, it would be instantly detectable that the domestic staff was inadequate.

In the present day the widespread availability of labour-saving devices has put an end to any inconvenience in an elaborately furnished and decorated interior, and thus to the practical attractions of a Corbusier-style '*machine à habiter*'. Only with a truly viable alternative to an adequate and skilled domestic staff has the fashion for a nostalgic re-creation of the decorative fancies of the past century become totally practicable, and therefore widely admired and emulated.

Pictures of the interior

However much a survey of the art of interior decoration in the nineteenth century contrives to be informative about fads and fancies, the development of an aesthetic, the harnessing of exotic fantasy and the practical structure of the living environment, it might be argued that all these facets of the subject are merely additional enticements to the appreciation of an art form of great refinement and subtlety. The art of depicting the interior has a long history, and the early nineteenth century marks one of its greatest peaks of achievement. Designs and interior views dating from the neo-classical period are now greatly appreciated and collected. The richly detailed and luxuriantly coloured paintings that reflect the taste of the later period are almost as eagerly sought. Their appeal is self-evident: among the most talented artists of the period many turned their attention, at one time or another, to making a record of their environment – a sort of interior landscape painting – fixing for posterity the fleeting effect of the interaction of light with the concentration of shapes and colours that result from recording the taste of one person at a moment in time. The drawings made for Queen Victoria seem to have been hung in the private apartments at Windsor: 'Of sketches of Balmoral, Rosenau [Prince Albert's birthplace], Osborne, and the favourite apartments of the Queen at her different residences, there are many scores' (from *The Private Life of the Queen*, published anonymously in 1897).

The industry of many of these amateur artists is almost incredible, the production equalling or even exceeding that of their professional counterparts. For example, the 300 drawings and watercolours by the Harden family in the Abbot Hall Art Gallery in Kendal are only a small proportion of the 1,600 or so once in the possession of Harden's daughter. The definition of 'amateur' needs some consideration here. Since painting was an accomplishment deemed essential in a well educated young lady, instruction was often given by a highly competent practitioner of the art. The Princess Royal, eldest child of Queen Victoria, painted the most exquisite interior views with almost professional skill. Her master was the watercolourist William Callow, who received as a gift from his distinguished pupil a painting in very much the same vein as the one illustrated here (plate 54).

Many of the painters who worked for Queen Victoria are otherwise little known – except of course Joseph Nash – but all deserve to be acknowledged for their mastery of this demanding genre. The Queen made a very remarkable contribution to social history in commissioning representations of so many of the royal interiors. She was not alone in the practice of this form of patronage. The drawings still retained by the Hesse family are also a record of the intimate quarters of many royal and princely relatives in different parts of Europe. By the middle of the nineteenth century the private rooms in royal palaces differed very little from those of the more prosperous subjects, and this invaluable record tells later generations a great deal about the taste of the past.

In his fascinating study of the home life of the Prince and Princess of Wales (later Edward VII and Queen Alexandra), *Marlborough House and its Occupants* (1896), Arthur H. Beavan, on being given access to the private apartments, remarked:

After looking into the plateroom, kitchen, wine cellar, linen-room and all the working part of the large household, I found myself within the sacred circle of the strictly private apartments. I saw the couch whereon an Empress reposes. I saw the antique bed where an Emperor sleeps like any other mortal. I saw the most beautiful of boudoirs. I saw the chambre à coucher *of more than one charming and accomplished princess; and I noticed on a dressing table – well, in fact, I noticed all that there is of refinement and fashion in this kind of apartment in the mansion of any well-bred lady throughout Great Britain; and – that is all!*

Even of a reigning monarch it was possible to remark:

The Queen's private sitting-room might well belong to any one of her wealthier subjects who possesses a simple taste in furniture and decorations, a large collection of pictures and sketches, and a full circle of friends. The general scheme of colour is crimson and cream and gold. Heavy damask draperies frame the windows, the lower panes of which are veiled with short curtains of snowy muslin. The blinds are of a dainty material called diaphene, in which is woven in a transparent pattern the insignia and motto of the Garter. The furniture is principally upholstered in the same flowered crimson and gold damask that drapes the windows. The walls are panelled in the same silk, and here, the constant recurrence of the pattern (a conventional bouquet of flowers) would become monotonous were it not for the number of pictures of every description which cover the walls from within a short distance of the ceiling of deep cream and gold, to within four feet of the rich crimson carpet, which is patterned with a delicate tracery of scrolls and garlands in pale yellow. The many doors are painted cream colour and decorated with floral panels and gold mouldings.
(*The Private Life of the Queen*, p. 15.)

There is no reason to suppose that the author is exaggerating the resemblance between this sumptuous room and those of many of Queen Victoria's well-to-do subjects at the end of the nineteenth century. Leaving aside the fabulously wealthy, such as the Rothschilds and the South African mining millionaires, many of the ordinary inhabitants of Mayfair and Belgravia had rooms of precisely this description, to which the vast accumulation of photographic views by Bedford Lemere bears witness.

The works of Camille Los Rios, executed in the early nineteenth century, must have provided a glimpse of the past of a rather different nature. He was a friend of the diarist Thomas Raikes, who wrote of him in his *Journal* published in 1858:

Oct. 1840 Saturday 3rd: Among the various eccentricities of men, the following trait of my friend Camille Los Rios, whose death occurred so lately, may be remarked. Though very attentive to his duties as a diplomatist when employed at London and at Berlin, he had few internal resources; he seldom took up a book and always led the dissipated life of what the French call a flâneur. *But he had a taste for drawing, and wherever he went always made a sketch of the interiors of the room which he inhabited; sometimes a mere etching, at others highly finished and coloured, according to the time he remained in it. As he had travelled much, and never omitted this ceremony at any inn where he slept during the last thirty-three years of his life, the collection in his portfolios found at his death was very surprising.*

54

54
Boudoir of the Crown Princess, Potsdam 1874

Like Queen Victoria, and many other members of her family, the Crown Princess had a taste for souvenir albums, assembling them from her own works and from commissioned drawings. She presented her maid of honour with a commemorative drawing, by herself, in an album with a covering note:

With the greatest of pleasure I painted the leaf which is to be a remembrance of both your weddings [Mary Lynar, another maid of honour, had also recently married] and of the time we lived together . . . . The other drawings, those of the Neue Palais and the room in which your engagement took place, are by the painter Schlegel and I hope they will give you a little pleasure.
(*Embassies of Other Days*, vol. I, 1923, p. 139.)

Walburga Paget, the maid of honour, recalls a curiosity of the Potsdam palace:

. . . the thing that fascinated me mysteriously was the window panes, which (as the palace had not been inhabited since the time of Frederick the Great) were all intact, and turned into the most lovely shades of pale amethyst, no two being alike.
(*Embassies of Other Days*, p. 113.)

Watercolour, signed 'Victoria' and dated
Private collection

Others also followed this admirable habit of depicting the places where they stayed on their travels, notably Mary Ellen Best and the Polish count Artur Potocki, who both had the impartiality that led them to record modest rented rooms as well as palaces.

Watercolour provided the perfect medium of expression for the amateur, and the late eighteenth century was to see a great increase in the numbers of these talented practitioners, many of them women. Watercolour painting was one of the polite accomplishments which formed part of the educational curriculum of a gentlewoman, and many were exceedingly well taught. The interior provided the perfect subject since it could be tackled without the need for chaperonage or any of the complicated special arrangements to which all outdoor expeditions were subject in the last century. A perfect mastery of technique and perspective is not essential for this branch of art since it is the incidental details which please, and the depiction of these is almost enhanced by some lack of technical facility.

From the end of the century comes the comprehensive and lovingly detailed record of a family environment provided by the Swedish artist Carl Larsson (plates 59, 125); it is of compelling interest. The preference shown by certain English artists and their patrons for the vernacular dwelling and its traditional furnishing and fittings was matched in Scandinavia, Central Europe – notably Hungary – and Russia by a similar revival of traditional folk ornament and decorative carving and patterning. These traditional forms and colours are used

55

55
A Viennese drawing room 1872

In this room, with its typical colour scheme and careful arrangement of furniture for social gatherings, the upholstered pieces are supplemented by classic bentwood chairs designed by the Viennese Michael Thonet in 1859. The notion of furnishing with lightweight, movable pieces had gained enormously in popularity in the nineteenth century, and although it is not usual to see Thonet's bentwood furniture in use in a rather formal reception room, chairs and tables in this material did represent the ultimate in portability.

Franz Alt, watercolour
Formerly Hazlitt, Gooden & Fox Limited, London

in all the furnishings, the decorative textiles and the choice of colours in Larsson's rooms. The details of design, ornament and domestic minutiae are revealed in the numerous drawings comprising *Ett Hem*, *Larssons* and *Åt Solsiden*, which are in a class of their own from the point of view of domestic history.

The advent of photography was to add an extraordinarily rich new dimension to the annals of interior views. From the first haunting images of Fox Talbot, the genre was to produce masters of this art form that have rarely been surpassed. They made of this still monochrome medium an art form of special quality in which the absence of colour is a positive advantage.

As to arriving at a completely authentic view of the taste of the past, the old adage 'the camera cannot lie' is as untrue in this as in any other area of subtle photographic contrivance, and the effects, albeit so contrasting, that were achieved by Henry Peach Robinson, Atget or Bedford Lemere are incredibly artful and manipulative. In contrast, apart from their value as a record of the much less easily investigated semi-suburban interior, the amateur photographs of college rooms in Cambridge (plates 350, 351, 352) are instructive in showing the results of total artlessness.

The art of depicting the interior reached its highest point of refinement in the nineteenth century; in the present day it is almost completely replaced by colour photography. Artists who are prepared to expend the immense labour required for such minutely detailed work are rare. Whether these few will suffice to satisfy the curiosity of future generations is open to question. For us there is the pleasure of an extraordinarily rich profusion of surviving material from which to form our vision of the past.

56

56

Interior, Berlin 1889

The art of photographing interiors reached extraordinary technical perfection in the late nineteenth century. The definition of detail and the depth of field still seem remarkable today. This subject, with its emphasis on atmosphere, is unusual in the interior photography genre. Here the play of light is captured with the same art that painters employed earlier in the century. The theatrical style of many early photographers' ignored light as a feature of a composition, and the length of exposure necessary to pick out a room's detail militated against anything more than neutral lighting.

Alfred Stieglitz, *Sun Rays, Paula, Berlin*
National Gallery of Art, Washington DC (Alfred Stieglitz Collection, 1949)

57

The Double Cube Room, Wilton

Late 19th century

Today the Double Cube Room is furnished with carved and gilt furniture attributed to William Kent and Thomas Chippendale. The sofa against the far wall, covered with carpet from the Wilton factory, is the single remaining nineteenth-century piece.

Photograph by H. Brooks
Royal Library, Windsor Castle; H M The Queen

57

58

Swedish peasant style   Early 20th century

A predictable result of Larsson's success was a renewed interest in traditional Swedish crafts by those who wished to achieve his style of interior. This illustration is an approximation of how Larsson's ideas might have been carried out.

Advertising photograph

59

Carl Larsson at home

Larsson made a sequence of twenty-six watercolours, collectively entitled *Ett Hem* (A Home). The first exhibition of part of the group was in 1897, there was another show in Berlin in 1898, and in 1899 an album of colour reproductions was issued that enjoyed remarkable success. Larsson intended that these drawings should provide 'a model for those who feel the need to furnish their homes agreeably'. The impact of Larsson's light-toned but distinctive style was the greater because of the dark and gloomy taste of Scandinavian interior decoration that it succeeded.

'Till en liten vira', watercolour for *Ett Hem*
Nationalmuseum, Stockholm (Statens Konstmuseer)

Evidence from inventories and literature

Even where we have whole series of rooms depicted in the greatest detail, the exact use of the rooms and how the accommodation was allotted remain uncertain. A room-by-room inventory of the entire contents of a large London residence, taken at the death of the owner, which is now in the Museum of London, provides a very illuminating picture of the organization of the household.

Number 4 Upper Belgrave Street belonged to the 'Rt. Hon. Charles, fourth Earl of Romney', who died in 1904. It seems likely from the comments about their condition ('much marked', 'scratched and discoloured', 'broken pane', 'chipped', etc.) that the decoration and furnishings had remained *in situ* for some time before the inventory was taken, so it is reasonable to accept this as a characteristic late nineteenth-century plan. The house consisted of six storeys: a basement, ground floor and four upper floors. Even with a fairly substantial house of this kind the vast quantity of its contents must have meant that it was crammed to bursting point. However, certain points emerge as rather unexpected. For the size of house there were few books, rather less than a thousand, of which a quite absurd number were different collections of the works of Shakespeare. Not one of the works of art sounds important or even particularly interesting, and there seems to have been no silver in evidence, even in the dining room. Five plate chests are listed in the butler's pantry but the contents are not specified. There is understandably no nursery accommodation; but in a very similar household, that of Lord Ronaldshay, inventoried for a valuation very shortly after Lord Romney's, the nurseries seem to have been equipped with superannuated furniture from other parts of the house, the only special equipment being china with patterns designed to appeal to young children.

On entering the hall in Upper Belgrave Street, the visitor would have been faced with a tiger-skin rug, pairs of antlers, hall chairs with shield-shaped backs, a table and chest of drawers and some rather forbidding portraits. One intriguing piece of equipment in the inner hall, otherwise furnished in the same way as the outer hall, is a bicycle. If this was not used by the owners, perhaps it was a convenient way for a manservant to take messages and run errands.

Visible on the first landing would have been the pier glasses, *jardinières*, *torchères*, pedestals and large blue-and-white vases which feature in the lists. For the first three flights the stairs were carpeted with amber-coloured, patterned-border Axminster fixed with brass rods.

On the ground floor, as well as a study and smoking room, both clearly masculine preserves, was a 'WC apparatus', one of only two for the whole of this large household. The smoking room was equipped with upholstered furniture, tables with a complete letter-writing set with letter scales, inkstand, blotter and so on, but no smoking equipment, though the ceiling was said, with a masterly grasp of the obvious, to be 'smoked'. Otherwise the room was supplied with novels and sporting books, 'portfolios of sketches by amateurs', and a *Times* encyclopedia in a special case.

The front room, on the ground floor, with its crimson plush curtains tied back with cord and muslin half-curtains, was lavishly equipped for writing with a bureau bookcase and two writing tables all in mahogany and all furnished with stationery cases, blotters, letter scales and inkstands. In a rosewood open-front bookcase were a number of novels by Dickens, Thackeray, Surtees and Scott, the inevitable works of Shakespeare, *Fire and Sword in the Sudan*, the *Clergy List*, Burke's *Peerage*, Lodge's *Peerage* and twenty-nine volumes of the Badminton *Sportsman*'s Library. The nineteen framed pictures included portraits, photographs and engravings. As well as a Japanese screen and a walnut work table with a silk storage 'pocket', there was a chest of drawers and a satinwood cabinet with glass doors, a walnut-framed chesterfield upholstered in crimson morocco and five easy chairs. All the rooms had open grates with fenders, coal scuttles and a purdonium and a full set of fire irons. Most of the rooms had elaborate overmantels, usually white-painted and inset with mirror glass, upon which a large number of ornaments must have been disposed. The carpets extended over the whole room in the accommodation occupied by the householders, supplemented in some instances by oriental rugs, and all these family rooms had illumination by both gas and electricity.

Also on the ground floor was the dining room, equipped for twelve covers, with a large round inlaid mahogany dining table, a Sheraton sideboard, a Chippendale side table, two butler's tray tables, a number of portraits and eleven large oriental bowls and vases. The carved overmantel was painted white and the curtains were of maroon plush lined with terracotta-coloured linen.

On the first floor were the drawing room and a rather masculine bedroom, plainly furnished.

The front drawing room was the most elaborately furnished room of all, with a suite of Louis Quinze-style seat furniture, *fauteuils* and single chairs, carved and gilded with upholstered backs and seats. The writing table and a further suite of upholstered furniture in walnut, a lacquered Japanese cabinet, a breakfront cabinet, an inlaid Dutch chest, an oblong parquetry-inlaid mahogany table mounted with ormulu, a revolving bookcase, a mahogany whatnot and a rosewood-case Erard boudoir grand piano with matching stool must have contributed to a rather miscellaneous appearance in what might otherwise have been a conventional Louis

THE NINETEENTH-CENTURY HOUSE

THE TOWN HOUSE

. . . the architect's house . . . is a most gorgeous affair of gilding, ultra-marine, and the newly invented . . . mosaic gold . . . in the richest Parisian style imaginable. Mr Nash seems to have emulated . . . the laboured elaborations of finish that characterises the works of M. Percier.
(Description of John Nash's house in Regent Street from J. Elmes, *Metropolitan Improvements*, 1827.)

The town house as we know it today, uniform and terraced, was an eighteenth-century invention. Many examples survive and are much admired as a rational and appropriate solution to the problem of high-density housing. The pattern of urban development established in the second half of the eighteenth century carried on with little alteration to the fundamental conception well into the second half of the next century.

Oct 29. 25.

View of the North and East sides of the Library.

60

London's classical character was fully established by 1830. Rows of narrow brick, or often stuccoed houses, their plain façades relieved with lacelike ironwork, radiated out in every direction from the City and Westminster. Later developments, as London extended to the outlying districts of Kensington, Bayswater, or Brompton, retained the terrace plan but the façades became heavier and ever more elaborate. The character of the Georgian interior, which had retained a simple elegance achieved with delicate classical plasterwork ceilings, mouldings and cornices in shallow relief, soon gave way to heavier ornamentation that was usually called 'Louis Quatorze' by the building trade. Grand developments of the 1830s, as at Carlton House Terrace, achieved lavish effects with vaulting and domed ceilings in the staircase wells and arched openings flanked by Corinthian columns. Mid-century terraces, however, have interiors that appear to be almost weighed down, sunk beneath ponderous swags of fruit and flowers and bold scrolling acanthus leaves.

London's nineteenth-century character was determined by a handful of distinguished architects and builders who expanded and varied the formula that had evolved since the mid-eighteenth century in places such as Bath or Edinburgh's New Town, as well as in London. John Nash and Decimus Burton between them set the precedent for prestigious but relatively inexpensive terrace development in the streets and crescents that surround Regent's Park. Thomas Cubitt was the contractor, and usually also the architect, who developed the Grosvenor estates of Pimlico and Belgravia. Less inventive architects and speculative builders followed in their footsteps.

While visual uniformity of London's streets and squares was assured, the scope for invention was limited. Sir John Soane's own house and office in Lincoln's Inn Fields occupied two plain brick terraced houses knocked into one, to which he gave a new identity with a façade of uncompromising modernity. The interior is no less remarkable for its complexity and ingenious use of space. Soane planned his house full of illusionist devices that effectively over-ride the traditional sense of space of a small London house. Mirrors placed as part of the wall seem to make the wall disappear and create vistas that repeat without ending. Soane's repertoire of visual tricks was too sophisticated for nineteenth-century taste, and it is only in the twentieth century that his imagination has been truly appreciated.

The enduring attraction of the Georgian house was its faultless sense of proportion. With the steadily growing wealth of London, the Georgian ideal succumbed to the pretensions and increase in scale that marked the aggrandizement of the Victorian era. In fact, the height of a 'first-rate', early-nineteenth-century house was often more than forty-six feet. Inside, a decidedly lavish

View of the front Drawing Room

61

60, 61

'A feverish dream' 1825

No. 13 Lincoln's Inn Fields, Sir John Soane's own house, is an almost unique survival of the neo-classical style of the 1820s. Its peers, Malmaison or Thomas Hope's Duchess Street house, were broken up by sales and later alterations, though we do have Percier-like illustrations of Duchess Street and Malmaison has been reconstructed as a *Musée nationale*. Nowhere is Soane's genius for spatial composition more effectively demonstrated than at Lincoln's Inn. Mirrors that are placed in ceiling spandrels and recesses confuse the viewer by multiplying spaces. The relatively confined interiors seem to expand into limitless vistas when in fact the volume of the rooms is further reduced by the construction of arcades, projecting piers and shallow domes below ceiling height. This play with space and vistas was not to everybody's taste. Dr Waagen visited the house and likened the experience to 'a feverish dream'. Soane's genius has a nervous quality of the Romantic age which belies the neo-classical poise of his style.

C. J. Richardson, *13 Lincoln's Inn Fields: Library* and *Drawing Room*, sketches
By courtesy of the Trustees of Sir John Soane's Museum, London

provision of space was contrived. Life on a palatial scale was quite feasible behind the discreet and impersonal façade.

The crucial difference in planning between a town house and a country house was the impossibility of removing the kitchen of a town house any distance from the reception rooms and the family's living quarters. Advice on the arrangement of houses usually included a recommendation about the serving of food from a lobby immediately adjacent to the dining room; here, equipment of varying ingenuity would be provided for keeping the dishes hot. In the absence of any real distance between the living quarters and the smells and noise of the kitchen quarters, the town housekeeper had to rely on well trained and meticulous staff to keep the area 'below-stairs' as unobtrusive as possible. According to Mary Carberry, writing of 2 Hamilton Place, the London house of the Curries of Glyn Mills, Currie & Co. (the Lombard Street bankers), the house was exceptionally quiet:

Thick carpets muffle the sound of steps; voices are low; no-one argues or shouts; the servants mumble. The quiet is so deep that one jumps when a clock strikes. Everywhere there is a scent of flowers and panelled walls. It would be shocking to smell beef being roasted or cabbage. When servants have shut themselves into the cellars, and Cousin Bertram has gone to the city, and Lawrence to his Mama's room to say prayers and learn his catechism which he hates, silence is like the quiet of night.
(*Happy World: The Story of a Victorian Childhood*, 1941, p. 112.)

By the mid-century, the *Journal of Design and Manufacture* had little to say in defence of the London town house:

A row of average-sized middle-class houses is simply a wall pierced with holes. Enter the house, and each room is the counterpart of the other. There are no other features than the four blank walls give, except in the kitchen, where stern utility compels the place to have a characteristic look that marks its purpose.

The article could see only one advantage in the plainness the builders' finish inside:

Certainly these bald materials have one advantage of leaving the decorator pretty free. He is not bound by any very stringent conditions. If the architecture furnishes him with no suggestions, it does not cramp his imagination. So far this present state of things may be viewed as an improvement on the age not long passed, where more precise and extensive affectations of Greek architectural ornaments necessitated similar affectations in all the furniture of the room, even in cups and saucers.
('Hints for the Decoration of Dwellings', vol. 2, 1849–50.)

An interesting London survival of a house decorated in the 'artistic' manner is the Linley Sambourne House in

Kensington. Stafford Terrace, where the Sambournes lived at No. 18, was completed in the 1870s as part of an estate developed for affluent professional people. The Sambournes took the house in 1874, shortly after it was built. It is apparent from the inventory, taken three years after they moved in, that the contents of the house today are still in the same place they occupied over a century ago.

62

62
The drawing room, 18 Stafford Terrace
1892

The photograph was taken by Edward Linley Sambourne himself; he was an enthusiastic amateur photographer. The flavour of the house is well conveyed even in this small corner which is packed with a profusion of objects and pictures. Details of the house are to be found as backgrounds to Linley Sambourne's own *Punch* cartoons. This picture tallies with the inventory made in the late 1870s, although it was taken several years later.

Victorian Society, London

The Linley Sambourne House appears on superficial acquaintance to be a copy-book Victorian survival, with its overwhelming profusion of furniture, ornaments and pictures. In fact it does have a strong stamp of individuality, which makes it more interesting in one way, but less typical. It is important because it affords us a complete picture of an 'artistic' house and milieu at a period in history when the artist and journalist were first accepted as members of Society. Linley Sambourne was a cartoonist of considerable repute on the staff of *Punch*, the humorous and satirical weekly; he ended his life as their chief political cartoonist. Evidence of his artistic preoccupations abound in the house; there are many works of art executed by his friends and colleagues. Unusually for the date, however, much of the furniture is eighteenth-century, or in an eighteenth-century style; these are mainly very plain brass-mounted French pieces and delicate Sheraton-style chairs and tables. The wallpapers, predictably, come from Morris & Co. The whole ensemble comes as something of a surprise after reading contemporary descriptions of the 'artistic' household. It is a corrective antidote to the eulogies of Mrs Haweis in *Beautiful Houses* (1882); her enthusiastic descriptions often obscure the sombre and oppressive character of the interiors she singles out for praise. Both she and Moncure Conway, the American writer, devote pages of great detail to the decoration of the house occupied by G.H. Boughton, an American artist, and though both insist on the delicacy and refinement of the interiors, it is apparent they were very similar to Sambourne's, with sage-green paper and imitation leather on the walls, and just as much furniture.

In spite of very typical Victorian touches in certain details, for instance the flounced and bobble-trimmed, velvet-covered mantel boards (surely made according to instructions in Cassell's *Household Guide*), or the window conservatory, visible from the street, as advocated in the gardening periodicals of the day, Sambourne's house does not quite comply with the descriptions and depictions of the typical mid-Victorian home.

Mary Cholmondeley, in her novel *Diana Tempest* (1900), ridicules the 'artistic' town house scheme as arranged by a pretentious hand:

Rooms seldom represent their inmates faithfully, any more than photographs their originals, and a poorly-furnished room, like a bad photograph, is, as a rule, a caricature. But there are fortunate persons who can weave for themselves out of apparently incongruous odds and ends of bric-à-brac, and china and cretonne, a habitation which is as peculiar to them as the moss-cocoon is to the long-tailed tit, or as the spillikins, in which she coldly cherishes the domestic affections, are to the water-hen.

Madelaine Thesiger's little boudoir looking over Park Lane was as like her as a translation is to an original.

Madelaine was one of the many girls who mistake eccentricity for originality. It is therefore to be expected that a life-sized china monkey should be suspended from the ceiling by a gilt chain, not even holding a lamp as an excuse for its presence. Her artistic tendencies required that scarlet pampas grass should stand in a high yellow jar on the piano, and that the piano itself should be festooned with terra-cotta Liberty silk. A little palm near by had its one slender leaf draped in an impromtu Turkish trouser, made out of an amber handkerchief. Even the flowers are leaving their garden of Eden now. They require clothing, just as chrysanthemums must have their hair curled. We shall put the lily in corsets next.

There was a faint scent of incense in the room. A low couch, covered with striped oriental rugs and cushions, was drawn near the fire. Beside it was a small carved table – everything was small – with a few devotional books on it, an open Bible and a hyacinth in water. A frame, on which elaborate Church embroidery was stretched, kept the Bible in countenance. The walls were draped as only young ladies, defiant of all laws of taste or common sense, but determined on originality, can drape them. The portière alone fell its length to the ground. The other curtains were caught up or tweaked across, or furled like flags against the walls above chromos and engravings, over which it was quite unnecessary that they should ever be lowered. The pictures were mostly sentimental or religious.

The Linley Sambourne House is a less extreme example, but one can see the tendency at work. The house has added interest in that there are survivals at two levels. The reception rooms are astonishingly preserved, although colours have faded and darkened with time. However, for her own use Lady Rosse, Sambourne's granddaughter, created a bedroom in the 'Victorian style', as that elusive concept was understood in the mid-twentieth century. It is almost as interesting a time capsule as the rest of the house; as much a document of a particular aspect of twentieth-century taste as the rest of the house is of artistic nineteenth-century taste. The whole impression of the bedroom, though the decoration seems at first to be in keeping with the rest, is of a different era. All the tones are light and delicate, the use of pattern is restrained, the curtains are adequately full but not lavish in their use of fabric. The fabric itself is neutral in colour and texture, in self-effacing good taste quite uncharacteristic of the forthright nineteenth-century householder. At first there is a sense of relief at quitting the muffling gloom of the other rooms, but by comparison with the richness of the nineteenth-century scheme, there is something timid and bloodless in the twentieth-century pastiche.

In the surviving nineteenth-century decorative scheme, darkened as it is by the passage of time, one most noticeable lack is the glimmer of gold highlights that must

63
Second Empire in America 1894

The taste of this room is French, even to the absence of carpet on the parquet floor. The upholstered furniture with its deep, close buttoning recalls the chairs at Compiègne which belonged to the Empress Eugénie. The decorative panels in the manner of Boucher ape the tapestries that lined the walls of private apartments in the Tuileries Palace and the reception rooms of the great *hôtels particuliers*. The *portière* owes a debt to Aubusson. Through the connecting door, however, can be glimpsed an Indian hanging which assorts strangely with the French style of the two rooms.

Photograph by Joseph Byron
Byron Collection, Museum of the City of New York

64
Kitchen in the home of F.L. Loring, 811 Fifth Avenue 1899

This kitchen for a substantial New York mansion would be more than adequate for a hotel, and in such a household would have to be capable of catering for as many people as a modest hotel dining room. The highly ornamental lamps of pierced metal, which have presumably been cleaned ready to be rehung, suggest that there are Eastern schemes, possibly Moresque or Islamic, in the reception rooms of the house. There is a Turkish lamp of this kind in Mrs Schroeder's bedroom, also photographed by Byron (in 1902), which has many other exotic touches. Much more elaborate wrought and pierced metal light fittings in the 54th Street house, built for Dr. William A. Hammond in 1873, formed part of an Egyptian scheme. They survived the arrival of a new owner, Chauncey Deper, in 1898, and appear in the Byron photographs of 1899. Deper's furniture, including a very outmoded Eastlake-style desk, seems to fit uneasily with exotic lamps.

Photograph by Joseph Byron
Byron Collection, Museum of the City of New York

65
The parlor in the home of Frederick Wallingford Witridge, 16 East 11th Street 1900

Witridge has respected the Greek Revival architectural style of the room, with its door architecture formed of flat pilasters with Corinthian capitals. The same pattern is found in another, similar house also photographed by Byron, that of Albert Stevens at 13 East 9th Street. Other features are similar too, such as the ceiling moulding and depth of the frieze. The Stevens house is more grandiloquent in style, but many essentials of the arrangement of the room are the same. Tall pier glasses occupy the space between the windows and, since neither room is very large, the furniture, much of it in the eighteenth-century style, is on a modest scale, covered with light, patterned upholstery and loose covers, possibly chintz or cretonne. Neither room has a dado. The photographer himself appears in the looking-glass.

Photograph by Joseph Byron
Byron Collection, Museum of the City of New York

A scheme for a New York brownstone house 1854

The Italianate brownstone terrace houses built in New York in the 1850s reflected the solid and increasing prosperity of the potential purchasers. A broad, steep flight of stairs led to an imposing entrance; the houses had three or four stories above the basement. The first-floor parlour was the showpiece of the house and was decorated lavishly at disproportionate cost. Papier-mâché enrichments for the ceilings and walls could be bought and stuck on in profusion. Rarely were they painted white, but picked out with gilding and colours on a paler tinted ground. The reader of the periodical from which the picture is taken was clearly expected to have an insatiable appetite for the wildest excesses of the revived rococo style; there is hardly a straight line to be seen in any part of the room.

From Gleason, *Pictorial Drawing-Room Companion*, 11 November 1854

66

65

67

67
The dining room of Harold Peto's house, 7 Collingham Gardens *c.*1890

A certain connoisseur, as the outcome of frequent travels, filled his house in town with as choice a collection of antique furniture as wealth and special knowledge could amass. But unfortunately he had forgotten to allow for the vast difference there is between the clear air of Italy and the murk of London. He had selected nothing but what was a faultless work of art of its kind, but for all the rich and imposing effect of each individual piece, in their new environment the ensemble was only gloomy and depressing.

(Aymer Vallance, 'Good furnishing and the decoration of the home', part I, *Magazine of Art*, 1904.)

Vallance is not so indiscreet as to offer clues that would identify the house and its owner, but it is easy to apply the lesson to the interiors in the English Renaissance style in Collingham and Harrington Gardens. The monochrome of a photographic view does, of course, emphasize the sombreness, but even so the dining room of the house when Peto lived there must have had a 'gloomy and depressing' effect even on the brightest morning.

Photograph by H. Beford Lemere, *Intérieurs anglais*
Private collection

once have enlivened the stamped leather lining the walls of the first-floor drawing room. A scheme such as this is very dependent for its full impact on such details, and the meticulously polished brass and ormolu trimmings on the French furniture contribute, particularly by artificial light, to the effect intended by the original owners.

Such urban middle-class survivals are rare, particularly ones so complete and so untouched as the Linley Sambourne House. Most have to be brought back to some semblance of their nineteenth-century character by extensive renovation and re-creation. The Merchant's House in New York is being lovingly restored; its resemblance to surviving depictions of just such bourgeois interiors of the same date is fascinating, as if the pictures were a script and the Merchant's House a performance being gradually perfected for the benefit of the audience.

In the Gibson House Museum in Boston some of the furnishings and possessions survive from its original decoration to give an authentic idea of the life of a prosperous Back Bay family in the second half of the nineteenth century. The embossed and gilt wallpaper in the hallway is the same as that used at Castle Howard in Yorkshire in 1859 in preparation for a visit by Queen Victoria. The Gibson House is at 137 Beacon Street, and was built in 1860 by the architect Edward Cabot. No. 152, a little farther down the street, was completed in the same year for David Stewart, a well-to-do New Yorker who gave it to his daughter Isabella on her marriage to John Lowell (Jack) Gardner. This was eventually to house the sumptuous treasures that now make up the Isabella Stewart Gardner Museum at Fenway Court. Photographs of the interiors at the time of the Gardners' occupation show a fine, solidly built town house, with the mezzanine above the entrance filled with flowers and plants in fashionable profusion. However, the rooms are arranged without any regard for decorative style, acting simply as repositories for countless acquisitions.

Reaction against the monotony of the terraced façades was often easier to achieve than variations of the plan. When the modification of the frontages was undertaken with bravura by George and Peto in Harrington and Collingham Gardens on the Alexander Estate in London, the fact that the internal plan of all the houses was fairly uniform tended to be overlooked. The comment in *The Survey of London* is significant:

Harrington and Collingham Gardens hold a special place in the history of the London house. Here amidst acres of humdrum middle-class housing sprang up two small developments which represent the extreme point of late Victorian architectural development.
(Vol. xlii, ch. 12.)

68

One of the most celebrated residents of Harrington Gardens was W.S. Gilbert, who lived at No. 39. A dramatic stepped gable surmounted by a ship prepared the visitor for an interior richly ornamented in a style consistent with the Northern Renaissance character of the house. Much panelling was employed; the hall, like the drawing room, was dominated by an elaborately carved stone fireplace reaching right to the ceiling. The ceilings in all the houses were either decorated with plasterwork or beamed or coffered, creating a curiously oppressive effect in these rather spacious rooms. In Gilbert's house, two of the rooms (the billiard and dining rooms) were decorated by Howard & Sons; the panels of Holbeinesque stained glass came from Lavers and Westlake and the leather-paper panels from Jeffrey & Co. The repoussé brass radiator grilles were provided by Starkie Gardiner.

68

The drawing room at 24 Harrington Gardens *c.* 1890

This room was to be found in one of the Flemish Renaissance houses designed by Ernest George and Harold Peto in the 1880s. The owner was Harold's brother Samuel Arthur Peto; their father was Sir Samuel Morton Peto, a notable Victorian public works contractor. Samuel Arthur was one of the original lessees of the Alexander Estate development. Clearly he shared his brother's aesthetic interests. Harold himself lived first at No. 9, then No. 7 Collingham Gardens.

Photograph by H. Bedford Lemere, *Intérieurs anglais*
Private collection

69, 70

The Great Hall, Stafford House 1843/50

In the nineteenth century a large number of magnificent mansions survived in the cities; they were a hangover from the past when the royal court was an important source of power and influence. London had avoided the devastations of war and revolutions, and could, until the present century, boast numerous great town houses owned by old landed families. And after the 1830s, many commercial and banking families came to take sites in or near Piccadilly, the traditional location since it was close to St James's Palace. One of the grandest was Dorchester House, built by Lewis Vulliamy for R.S. Holford, a millionaire collector of paintings. In 1908 E. Beresford Chancellor wrote an account of these magnificent buildings: 'If we sought one particular feature distinguishing London from other capitals of Europe, apart from its immense proportions, it would probably be found in the number of large houses many of which are the private palaces that I have called them.' Their imposing grandeur was not only in their appearance from the street; Beresford Chancellor goes on to state that 'nearly every one of them contains such a wealth of beautiful objects – pictures, furniture, china, and a thousand and one *objets d'art* – that they may defy comparison with the châteaux of France and even with Venetian palazzi in their days of prosperity' (*The Private Palaces of London*, 1908). Completed in 1838, Stafford House was amongst the most splendid of these mansions. Queen Victoria is reputed to have said to the Duchess of Sutherland, 'I have come from my house to your palace', a joke that captures the public impression of Stafford House's place in society. The enormous receptions which were held at the Sutherlands' saw even this staircase crammed with arriving guests.

Lord Ronald Gower, the Duchess of Sutherland's brother, was infatuated by Stafford House:

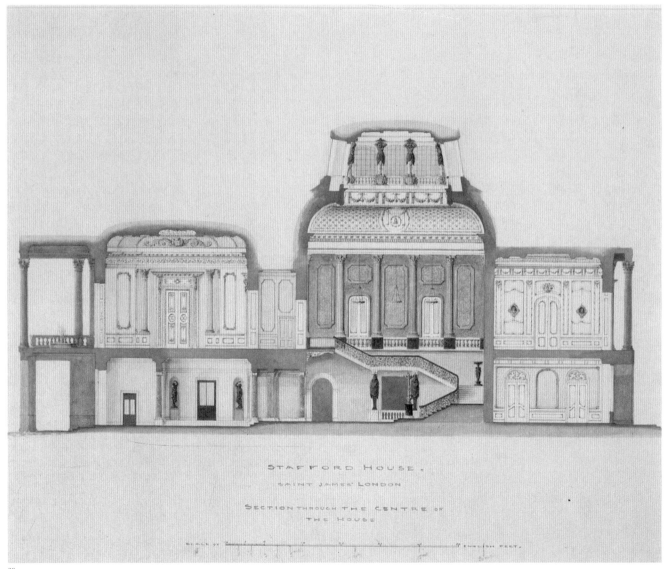

STAFFORD HOUSE.

SAINT JAMES' LONDON

SECTION THROUGH THE CENTRE OF THE HOUSE

69

70

Never was there a house equally magnificent and commodious. Every room in it, whatever the size, is comfortable as it is handsome. ... Unlike the palaces of Italy, which, although stately in appearance, resemble rather homes for the dead than dwellings for the living, at Stafford House the rooms, however vast, have a feeling of comfort about them. The great hall itself can, if needed, be converted into a most commodious sitting room. And so with the other galleries and chambers. In the great square banqueting room, so-called from its having been the scene of large dinners and ball suppers, and the adjoining gallery – the ball room – the wealth of decoration rivals Versailles itself.
(*Records and Reminiscences*, 1903.)

Lord Ronald claims that the Empress Eugénie had plans to build a replica of Stafford House on the site of the demolished Parisian house that once belonged to her sister the Duchess of Alba. She was deterred from this enterprise by the vast projected cost.

Scale section of Stafford House, watercolour, *c*. 1843
Joseph Nash, *Grand Hall and Staircase at Stafford House*, watercolour, *c*. 1850
Museum of London

Parallel to the search for external variety were attempts to alter the shape and proportions of the main rooms. A great choice of fretted woodwork for niches, alcoves, window cases, panels, fireplace surrounds and overmantels was obtainable from house-furnishers and decorators. By cutting corners off the rooms with alcoves and varying the flat surfaces with recessed panelling the proportions could be drastically altered; often, it must be admitted, not for the better. The oppressive 'Jacobethan' panelling of the 1880s was superseded in the next decade by white painted 'Adam' or trellised Louis Quinze woodwork. From the 1870s onwards there were also exotic 'Eastern' schemes which rivalled the heaviest 'Jacobethan' for sombre effect. Building a room within a room of Chinese or Japanese carved wood, with inset silks and paintings let into a lacquer or bamboo frame, was one means of achieving variety; usually, however, this was at the expense of light and convenience. In his house in Eaton Square J. Gennadius, the Greek minister, contrived an entire dado from overlapping Japanese fans. A mansion flat in Ashley Place was transformed by H. & J. Cooper into an Indian extravaganza full of carved wooden panelling and embroidered hangings. Mrs Wallace Carpenter's home was photographed by Bedford Lemere in 1893, recording a style of décor that had become very popular after the Indian Room went on exhibition at South Kensington; for a metropolitan audience it was even more influential than the Queen's celebrated Indian Room at Osborne.

72

71

A study in the Old English taste, Grosvenor Square *c.* 1890

Of all the problems which confronted the architect, the design of a town house affords one of the best opportunities to prove his skill, for every inch of space and every available outlook for light and air claim the most careful consideration. The most conspicuous ability is shown in the transformation of a narrow London house with its limited scope for outlook, light and air into an artistic and fairly comfortable dwelling.
(T. Raffles Davidson, 'The progress of recent architecture. Town houses', *Magazine of Art*, 1904.)

The enthusiasts who wanted their own houses to feature a Tudor or Jacobean scheme with carved ornament in dark wood and suitably 'historical' windows with stained glass or heraldic insets doubtless greatly taxed the architect's abilities. A house with rooms that were conceived to receive only relatively simple decoration became an awkward problem when it was altered to accommodate the often bulky and sombre features of the Old English style. And the penchant for old portraits did nothing to lighten the effect of such rooms, which were largely dependent on the advent of electric light to make them tolerably agreeable.

Photograph by H. Bedford Lemere, *Intérieurs anglais*
Private collection

71

72
A house in Palace Gardens *c.* 1890

The 'Jacobethan' style minstrel's gallery has been squeezed into a relatively cramped setting in this Kensington house.

Photograph by H. Bedford Lemere, *Intérieurs anglais*
Private collection

73, 74
The drawing room and study, 7 Brunswick Square 1825

A great number of London's modest terraced houses survive from the early nineteenth century. Brunswick Square was completed in the early decades; these drawings are dated 1 July 1825. The double doors dividing the two rooms are a standard and long-lasting feature of the London house, usually separating dining room and drawing room.

English School, pencil
Formerly Hazlitt, Gooden & Fox Limited, London

73

Given these cultural and historical aberrations and excesses in interior decoration, it is understandable that people of artistic sensibilities were drawn towards the experiments of Godwin, Whistler and Wilde. In her book *Beautiful Houses* (1882), Mrs Haweis lays considerable emphasis on the charm of artists' houses, describing in great detail those belonging to Frederic Leighton, William Burges, G.H. Boughton and Lawrence Alma-Tadema. She extolls the way in which, in the hands of these owners, both the Renaissance style and the Japanese influence were reinterpreted to produce an environment that expressed the personality of the inhabitant.

75

The 'Chelsea' bedroom 1890s

This was an early example of a style that would be popularized by Waring's Sloane Street showrooms under the name 'Chelsea'. The *Art Journal* for October 1898 described Waring's showpiece bedroom as:

. . . a most effective and charming little apartment, that, by virtue of ingenious fitments, though barely twelve feet square, gets plenty of floor space. The colour in this room is as fresh and gay as that of a piece of old Chelsea china. Its woodwork lining the walls, and most conveniently broken up with book shelves, cupboards, and fixed mirrors, is painted a green that is well-nigh white, so faint is its colour; and the chintzes are of bright design, such as William Morris loved.

Photograph by H. Bedford Lemere, *Intérieurs anglais*
Private collection

75

76

76
A Third Republic bedroom, Paris

Early 20th century

A suitably theatrical bedroom for the actress Mlle Sorel of the Comédie Française is in the revived Louis Seize manner. Her apartment at 99 avenue des Champs-Elysées was furnished and decorated in eighteenth-century style with fine *boiseries* and gilding.

Photograph by Eugène Atget
Museum of Modern Art, New York

77
American Louis Quinze 1905

This bedroom is in the mixed rococo manner like a French room of the same date, all white woodwork, canework, panelling and lace, relieved only by embroidered garlands and silk blooms on lace trimmed bed hangings. The cresting of the bed is ornamented with bunches of white ostrich feathers. Panels after Boucher are inset in the overdoors.

Photograph by Joseph Byron
Byron Collection, Museum of the City of New York

77

THE COUNTRY HOUSE

*It is a different matter with their dwellings, great machines,
with a touch of Italian or Gothic, without any real
character; one can see that they are spacious and well kept,
but nothing more.*
(Hippolyte Taine, *Notes sur l'Angleterre*, 1861.)

Apart from the popularity of the Italianate style so
rightly emphasized above by Taine, the most conspicuous
feature of the nineteenth-century country house was its
reliance on ecclesiastical models from the Middle Ages.
This use of precedents and the desire of patrons to re-
create the grandeur and solidity of a medieval castle had
its drawbacks in the design and planning of a practical
modern house. Repton had earlier noted this handicap in
his essay of 1808, *The Gothic Style*:

*The Castle Character requires massive walls, with very
small windows, if any are allowed to appear externally. The
correct imitation of this in modern times must produce the
effect of a prison. The Abbey Character requires lofty and
large apertures, almost equally inapplicable to a house,
although in some rooms the excess of light may be subdued
by coloured glass. But in the Abbey Character it is only the
chapel, the collegiate church, the Hall and the Library,
which furnish models for a Palace; all the subordinate parts
were the mean habitation of monks or students, built on so
small a scale, and with such low ceilings, that they cannot be
imitated in a modern Palace, without such mixture and
modification, as to tend to destroy the original character;
there it is necessary now (as it was in formerly) to adopt the
MIXED STYLE of Queen Elizabeth's Gothic for modern
Palaces, if they must be in any style of what is called
GOTHIC.*

Repton's ponderings on the impracticalities of adapt-
ing the Gothic and medieval style to domestic architecture already hint at the dilemma that was to exercise
Victorian architects and planners. How to choose the
appropriate historical precedent and context for a rail-
way station (as at Temple Meads in Bristol or St Pancras
in London), town hall, bank or warehouse, let alone a
town or country house, was a constant question in the
nineteenth century.

Some stylistic problems were resolved so satisfactorily
that they have hardly been questioned since, notably the
'reformed' Gothic rectory, the 'artistic' Queen Anne
family house, or the Greek Revival town terrace. Certain
architects, for example C.J. Richardson, whose book *The
Englishman's House* appeared in 1860, or William Burn,
were noted for their practical and workable plans for the
domestic adaptation of early styles. The Italianate and
Elizabethan styles were enduringly popular because they
lent themselves easily to a plan and circulation suitable to
large Victorian households. Considerations of cost and
practicality did not, however, deter ardent romantics who
admired the cult of the 'Abbey Character'. Jane Austen's
novel *Northanger Abbey* satirized the 'Gothic' sensations
of such places: 'And are you prepared to encounter all the
horrors that a building such as one reads about may
produce? Have you a stout heart? Nerves fit for sliding
panels and tapestry?' Henry Tilney asks Catherine
Morland.

A.W.N. Pugin, who was himself the arch-exponent of
Gothic Revival in England, made a satirical drawing of a
'modern castellated mansion', to which he added the
accompanying text:

*What absurdities, what anomalies, what utter
contradictions do the builders of modern castles perpetrate!
How many portcullises which will not lower down, and
drawbridges that will not draw up! ... On one side of the
house machicolated parapets, embrasures, bastions and all
show a strong defence, and round the corner of the building a
conservatory leading to the principal rooms through which a
whole company of horsemen might penetrate at one smash
into the very heart of the mansion! For who would hammer
against nailed portals when he could kick his way through
the greenhouse?*

Mocking the sham castle-builders, Pugin was equally
unimpressed with Gothic for the domestic interior. Commenting on a Gothic-style suburban house, he complains:

*Everything is crocketed with angular projections,
innumerable mitres, sharp ornaments, and turreted
extremities. A man who spends any length of time in a
modern room, and escapes without being wounded by some
of its minutiae, may consider himself extremely fortunate.*
(*True Principles of Pointed and Christian Architecture*,
1841.)

Perhaps significantly, Pugin's own domestic practice was
relatively small. Scarisbrick Hall in Lancashire (1837,
added to and altered by Pugin's son Edward in the 1860s),
a remarkable essay in Gothic, was built for a very rich
Catholic landowner whose life was a source of romantic
speculation about his large illegitimate family in Germany and his alleged ownership of a gambling house in
Paris (see Mark Girouard, *The Victorian Country House*,
1979, p.113). Neither argument nor satire could dissuade
the earnest abbey or castle devotees from building their
Gothic mansions. The historicism that runs like a thread
through nineteenth-century domestic architecture found
its most characteristic expression in a fantasy Gothic or
medieval pile, liberally supplied with towers, turrets and
battlements.

As late as 1910 the atavistic dream took hold of Julius
Drew, the then prosperous founder of Home and Colonial
Stores, who commissioned Edwin Lutyens to design
Castle Drogo, an ambitious and imposing medieval for-
tress perched on a Devonshire hill. The Castle Character
was maintained to an extent inside, with unplastered

78

78

The Carved Room, Petworth House 1844

The revivalist preoccupations of nineteenth-century interior designers gave depictions of earlier ensembles a particular relevance. The peopled views by Joseph Nash of 'olden times' were highly influential in the field of antiquarian taste; this painting by C.R. Leslie is quite different in being purely documentary. But it is also very interesting in showing, in its precise recording of the effects of light, and in the use of a viewpoint designed to include a diminishing vista of further rooms, the influence on the painter of the seventeenth-century Dutch masters. Many of his contemporaries were similarly influenced. After this view was painted the room was embellished with a mass of additional carved decoration. To the original scheme of Grinling Gibbons were added wood-carvings by Jonathan Ritson which almost covered the walls and part of the ceiling. After the second Lord Leconfield succeeded to the title in 1869 these were removed, and the white paint covering the seventeenth-century panelling which is shown in this painting was stripped off, returning the room to its earlier appearance, and indirectly reflecting the antiquarian taste of the mid-nineteenth century. The numerous English country houses that still have their contents intact and their surroundings unchanged constitute a remarkable survival, the result of the settled political conditions in this country over the last three centuries. The turbulent history of wars and revolutions on the Continent has left a legacy of empty châteaux and landless, possessionless noble families, with only rare exceptions. Many royal collections were dispersed or are now the property of the state. The distribution of property under the Napoleonic code fragmented great historic estates, whereas in Britain the law of primogeniture has kept them intact. Those great neo-classical ensembles initiated at the end of the eighteenth century are considered by many to be some of the finest achievements of British decorative art. As a greater distance of time separates us from the most eminent of the nineteenth-century architects and decorators, their achievement is increasingly appreciated – more so than in France, where the nineteenth century is still generally scorned and ignored for the purpose of historic building legislation.

C. R. Leslie, oil
Tate Gallery, London

granite walls softened only by ancient tapestries, and wide polished boards bare but for antique Tabriz carpets.

The idea of restoring and adding to ruined castles or religious buildings continued to have great appeal. In England this had an honourable precedent in the sixteenth century when landowners who had benefited from Henry VIII's dissolution of the monasteries built themselves houses using either the site or the materials, or both, from these ancient religious establishments.

With the 'rediscovery' of Scotland by the Victorians, castles all over Scotland were restored and rebuilt in the 'Scottish Baronial' style, in which newly acquired com-

forts inside were offset with equally unhistorical warlike appendages on the outside.

Ironically, Abbotsford, which was perhaps the greatest impetus to the Scottish Baronial style, was intended by Sir Walter Scott to be 'somewhat like an old English hall', and certainly Scott borrowed from English pattern books for the details. However, with the publication of R.W. Billings's *The Baronial and Ecclesiastical Antiquities of Scotland* in 1845–52, architects and clients had an archaeologically accurate basis for the Scottish Baronial style. Some Scottish architects of the eighteenth century had attempted an historic Scottish style, Robert Adam at

79

A property in Aberdeenshire 1860s

The attraction of Balmoral was privacy. Victoria commented favourably on the 'mountain solitude' of its location. Balmoral was originally a small Scottish Baronial-style house that the Royal Family rented. After some years of negotiations, the castle was bought outright and Albert proceeded to expand and alter the house in a mixture of German and Scottish idioms. Much of the charm of Balmoral for Albert was its similarity to his native Coburg: the scenery, the cold, the religion of his neighbours. Albert employed William Smith as architect and builder, but as with Cubitt at Osborne, the ideas were Albert's and the details of execution were Smith's. The interior again is Germano-Scottish. Tartans sit next to ash and pitchpine woodwork (this was given a coat of orange varnish only after Albert's death). The Prince Consort's study has the austere elegance of a Biedermeier room, the tartan carpet the only Scottish feature. The family cultivated local customs and pursuits with great enthusiasm. The royal pair learned to dance reels. The royal party went for excursions and picnics. This outdoor life was their annual break from political and court life, but also involved a re-creation of Albert's childhood and youth in Coburg. His great forestry plantations were presumably a part of the attempt to re-create Coburg's wooded scenery.

J. Roberts, watercolour
Royal Library, Windsor Castle; H M The Queen

Culzean (1777–92) for example, but by the mid-nineteenth century clients in need of country houses in Scotland were demanding more historical authenticity.

David Bryce (1803–76) was perhaps the most expert Victorian exponent of the style. Bryce's interiors contain many of the same features as would appear in a house of the same date south of the border designed in a revived 'historic' style: heavy strapwork ceilings, tall fireplaces with heraldic motifs, stairs and woodwork carved with a hotch-potch of detail. Antlers in quantity are perhaps the signal difference inside, as are high crow-step gables and pepper-pot turrets outside.

Robert Lorimer refined the style in tune with late nineteenth-century tastes for simplicity and a more roughcast finish. By the mid-century, when Queen Victoria and Prince Albert took Balmoral Castle as their Scottish residence, the threatening ghost of the Jacobite Highlanders had long been laid to rest, and the tartans, targes and trophies of the warlike Highlander were displayed on the walls in great numbers. By way of excuse for these assemblages of weaponry, which constitute the main decoration for the late nineteenth-century Scottish country house, the climate was never very hospitable to expensive paint finishes or wallpaper; all the more so because these houses were rarely lived in during the

80

80

Schloss Rosenau 1861

The Saxe-Coburg family were German princelings with great dynastic pretensions and only a moderate income. Prince Albert's birthplace, Rosenau, was a small country house outside Coburg. As in many country houses there was a degree of parlour-dressing and a skimpiness in the decoration of the private rooms. The rooms have a Viennese Biedermeier air, though some of the furniture was as likely as not made in Coburg. Duke Ernst also had a penchant for Empire-style objects, for example the clock with a Grecian figurine under glass.

F. Rothbart, watercolour
Royal Library, Windsor Castle; H M The Queen

coldest and dampest times of the year, and remained unheated.

In many latter-day castles, the absence of usable models from which to produce a house convenient to modern family requirements was simply solved by abandoning the pinnacled and beamed fantasies of the great hall and retreating to an added wing. Old photographs of Adare Manor in Ireland show that the Gothic style of the principal rooms was not matched in the far-flung regions where the children were housed; these quarters were conventional and somewhat featureless, but assuredly practical.

However impractical it may have been, re-created medieval splendour was impressive, and could provide the families who built castles with a spurious past and

pedigree. Penrhyn is an unusual essay in neo-Norman which mimicked the great Marcher castles that lined the Welsh border under the Normans and Plantagenents. Penrhyn is an ensemble of great grandeur: the hall has the air of an eleventh-century cathedral and Norman detail has been applied with consistent inventiveness to the interior and even the furniture. Such inventiveness was, as E.B. Lamb pointed out, essential for a 'conservatory is certainly the hardest thing to design in the Norman style' (*Architectural Magazine*, 1834, vol. I, p.340). Much of the ornament at Penrhyn was necessarily ecclesiastical in origin, as it was for Gothic Revival in general. If medieval domestic architecture had carried any decorative detailing, little had survived. William Beckford's Fonthill resembled the nearby Salisbury Cathedral. At Taplow House in Berkshire, William Burn was required to re-create the nave of St Magnus's Cathedral in Orkney for the great hall. Variations on the Octagon of Ely Cathedral are ubiquitous. In 1856, Salvin based his design for the kitchen at Alnwick Castle on the vaulted monks' kitchen at Durham. For the kitchen at Clouds, Philip Webb adapted the monks' kitchen from Glastonbury, an absurd conceit for a house built in the 1880s, and yet it demonstrates how very greatly the Victorians came to depend on medieval precedents both for intellectual justification and aesthetic satisfaction.

Antiquarian obsession retained its hold on the imagination of builders and decorators throughout the nineteenth century, not least encouraged by the vogue for establishing museums, which gathered enormous momentum in the second half of the century. When it first opened to the public, the Hôtel de Cluny in Paris was the subject of great fascination. A medieval building in the heart of Paris, the Hôtel was occupied for the ten years between 1832 and 1842 by the collector Alexander de Sommerard. De Sommerard installed his collection in the 'Romantic' style of his time, with the intention of evoking a feeling of a mysterious past rather than arranging a straightforward display of works of art. It was much visited by literary and artistic coteries during de Sommerard's lifetime; after his death in 1842 it became a museum. It exists still, but is now austerely furnished with only fine and rare medieval and Renaissance works. De Sommerard's collection was visited in 1834 by the diarist Thomas Raikes, who recorded his unfavourable impressions:

Went with Glengalls, Damers, and Lady Sandwich to see the Hôtel de Cluny, for the interior of which we had now a ticket of admission. The furniture, though collected at considerable expense, is more curious than valuable, more suited to an antiquarian than a man of taste. Every pawnbroker's shop in Paris seems to have been ransacked for the remnants of worm-eaten furniture, to complete the collection with which this old Gothic building is literally

81

81, 82, 83
The Vineyard, Saffron Walden, Essex
1860s

The Victorian Gothic Vineyard, built between 1863 and 1865, is a very well documented house, having been photographed while occupied by the man who had it built, William Murray Tuke, and then effectively inventoried for the sale catalogue when the house was sold following his death. Tuke employed an architect with a local reputation, William Beck. The house was completed in two years and alleged to have cost 1,000 guineas. It is a particularly consistent ensemble, never departing from the Gothic style – a Gothic derived from the Italian and French precedents illustrated in the works of Pugin or Burges. The hall (left) boasts an array of Ruskinian ornament inspired by *The Stones of Venice* (1853), carved in both the capitals of the columns supporting the pointed arches of the screen and again in the corbels supporting the roof beams and the ceiling mouldings. Although the house has passed through many hands since Tuke's death in 1908, many original fittings have survived. These include the massive six-panelled oak doors to all the principal rooms, and the stone mantelpieces which go through all phases of Gothic from relatively modest neo-Gothic (below) to full-blown attempts at a Burges fantasy (right). The tiled fireplace surrounds, of which those in the drawing room are by De Morgan, are still *in situ*. The floor of the main hall is of polished tiles with a decorative border. Castellated built-in cupboards survive in some of the rooms. The original water system was fed from a large tank beneath the kitchen floor. From the sale catalogue there is much to be learnt about the furniture and general style of the house. In the main, it was a mixture of antiques from the Tudor or Queen Anne period and modern Gothic or Old English-style pieces.

Saffron Walden Library, Essex

stuffed; and as the era of Francis I was not distinguished by much refinement in the arts of comfort or splendour, Hôtel Cluny is only remarkable as a contrast to modern improvements. There is a profusion of old carving in ebony, which does not enliven the picture; one fine cabinet in pietra dura, *evidently of Italian manufacture at that period; the bed of Francis I, carved in oak, with tapestry hangings; a chess-board and men in* cristal de roche, *at which two men in armour seem to have been puzzling themselves for the last few centuries; the chapel as it then existed, with a* mannequin *priest in* chasubel et etôle; *in the dining room, with the buffet, and laid with plates and dishes of Dutch* faience; *and in every room a profusion of ancient household furniture, from the massive* armoire *with carved pilasters, to the rusty snuffers or worm-eaten bellows which the indefatigible collector could discover in the garrets and lumber-rooms of the broker or antiquary. It is said that he has invested a considerable fortune in this burlesque exhibition, which the worms and moths hold in disputed possession with him.*
(*Journal of T. Raikes, Esq*, 1958, vol. I, p. 151.)

83

Raikes may not have appreciated the Cluny style, but others certainly did. The French obsession with Gothic attracted cartoonists: a lithograph by J.-J. Bourdet of 1837 showing a young man in his 'Gothic' room is captioned: '*Dieux, que je suis heureux depuis que j'ai ma chambre gothique. Je ne me rappelle pas m'être jamais autant amusé.*'

Not only did the visiting of ancient monuments and historic buildings promote revivalism in decoration, it also encouraged collecting – not that this perennially popular pastime needed much encouragement. Many of the prosperous middle-class homes of the late nineteenth century contained extensive art collections. The Vineyard, Saffron Walden, is exemplary in its combination of taste and intellect (see plates 81, 82, 83). Whereas eighteenth-century collectors had largely confined the

84

84, 85, 86
Three interior views of Roquetaillade
1868

The Château Neuf at Roquetaillade, near Bordeaux, is one of the most impressive early fourteenth-century structures surviving in France. Its restoration in the nineteenth century was prompted by the publication in 1865 of *La Guienne militaire*, a study of the castles of Aquitaine by the historian Leo Drouyn. It was on his recommendation that the owner, the Marquis Lodois de Mauresin, a nobleman of the Périgord with a substantial income from his vineyards, approached Viollet-le-Duc to undertake the rebuilding of the exterior of the Château and the creation of sumptuous Gothic-style interiors. Viollet-le-Duc was hardly in need of recommendation, even from such a distinguished source; since 1862 he had been busy with the ambitious transformation of Pierrefonds for the Emperor and Empress and was therefore the natural choice for this similar task. The designs for the Gothic rooms were prepared under Viollet's direction by his young assistant Edmond-Clément-Marie-Louis Duthoit, who exhibited these watercolours of the proposed schemes at the *Salon* in 1868. The *Grande Salle* or *Salle de Musée* (left) has as its focal point a magnificent (and more classical than medieval) fireplace, its design made up of elements from two fireplaces at the nearby Château de Cadillac, dating from 1606. Displayed are suits of armour, and an ingenious arrangement of rotating panels on a stand was intended to be used for the display of watercolours. This room was to suffer the fate of the unfinished interiors at Pierrefonds, as the Franco-Prussian War halted work in 1870. However, three of the planned interiors were completed, the dining room and these two bedrooms. Heavily under the influence of his master, Duthoit has borrowed extensively from the *Dictionnaire de Mobilier* for the architectural details of the doorcase and the panelling, as well as the astonishing lacquered furniture finished in an elaborate process by Tricot et Jeancourt of Paris. Some elements have crept in, as a reminder of Duthoit's travels in Syria and the Lebanon with the archaeologist Comte Melchoir de Vogué. This cross-cultural inspiration comes out particularly in the ceiling of the *Rose* bedroom, an eclectic combination that was also to characterize the work of William Burges. The interiors as achieved are astonishingly faithful to the watercolours, a very rare survival.

Vicomte et Vicomtesse de Baritault du Carpia
Château de Roquetaillade, Monument Historique

85

86

93

93, 94, 95

'Maison de Campagne de Prince Lopoukhine' 1850

The three views of this house confirm its perfect appropriateness to its country setting and the relaxed daily routine. The informal arrangement of old and new furniture, negligently disposed draperies and varied ornaments, would have been out of place in a town house where social life followed a more rigid pattern. In the Salon à Boiseries (above right), the shallow relief Gothic-style decoration is a sophisticated device, matched by the suite of furniture upholstered in yellow silk. The shades of the candelabrum are devised from panels of varnished paper 'transparencies', the making of which had been a popular pastime in the early years of the century. When the lamp was lit the painting glowed with brilliant colour.

Konstantin Ukhtomsky, oil
Musée des Arts Décoratifs, Paris (Sully-Jaulmes)

94

95

96

96, 97, 98
Hunsdon House: mid-century decoration 1860s

At the beginning of the 1860s Hippolyte Taine journeying in England, was greatly struck by the special character of the English country house. He captures minutely the flavour of the fashionable Italianate mansion of the period:

The house itself is a huge mansion, indifferently pleasing, massive, the interior modernized. The furniture of the ground and first floors, recently bought to replace the old furniture, cost £4,000. Three drawing rooms, sixty feet long and twenty high, are furnished with tall looking-glasses, good pictures, some excellent engravings, and bookcases. In front of the house is a conservatory where they spend the afternoons in bad weather and where, even in winter, there is an illusion of springtime. The rooms for any young girl among the house guests are fresh, light, virginal, papered white or blue, each with an assortment of pretty knick-knacks and delicate engravings, well suited to the amiable tenants of these rooms. For the rest, feeling for the picturesque in decoration and overall plan and arrangement are less developed than with us: for instance, less attention is paid to matching of colours and articles of furniture. But of grandeur and simplicity are not wanting, and there is no taste for overcrowding or bric-à-brac. They like large, bare surfaces and empty space, and the eyes are rested, there is room to breathe . . .
(*Notes sur l'Angleterre*, 1861.)

Private collection (National Monuments Record, London)

faintest traces remain of an elegant classical scheme in the Pompeian style, but the powdery fresco has all but vanished with the passing of time. Beyond, however, there is a much richer though sombre scheme typical of the taste of the period. In the hall (plate 97) there is a handsome Italianate damask-pattern paper in muted red and cream. Majestic marbleized pillars of green, yellow and porphyry red support an elaborate coffered ceiling in two stone colours. The ceiling mouldings are picked out in blue, buff and terracotta. Below the moulding there is an imitation plaster frieze of moulded embossed paper or

98

papier-mâché with a running foliate pattern on an orange ground. The grained pine staircase has a handsome banister with turned rails; the Lincrusta dado and the original turkey-pattern carpet complete the scheme.

In the drawing room (plate 98) the paper is printed with a diaper pattern in gold and three shades of grey on a white ground; the same colours are repeated in the ceiling mouldings and the doorcases. The monumental fireplace surrounds with tiled insets in the Japanese fashion are surmounted by enormous overmantel mirrors in heavily gilded and ornamented frames. The curtains are of heavy damask looped with tie-backs. The original patterned carpet survives, coloured predominantly in tones of blue and pinky-red; it covers the floor almost completely.

The survival of these decorations makes present-day Hunsdon a fascinating complement to contemporary photographs which show the rooms furnished. It is possible to glean a good idea of the original colours and textures, which are not always easy to make out from even the most meticulous of paintings since much of

99

100

99, 100
Two country drawing rooms in summer
1840s

Typical Biedermeier interiors are depicted here. The drawing room at Mauer has uncurtained windows and uncarpeted floors. The flowered decoration is enhanced by the pots of flowering plants. The wallpaper panels in the house at Lainz give a more formal effect, and the chairs are arranged in the old style against the walls.

Anon. Viennese artist, *In the Summer House at Lainz*, c. 1840
Louise Lodron and Octavia Merveldt, *A Drawing Room in Mauer*, 1848
Historisches Museum der Stadt Wien

101
The Library-Drawing Room at Bromley Hill, Kent   1816

The Library-Drawing Room at Bromley Hill exemplifies perfectly Repton's idea of a 'living room', with its combination of the functions of library, drawing room and repository of the treasures of a noted collector. Charles Long, later Lord Farnborough, was involved in politics and was a friend of Pitt and Addington, but the activities suggested in this charming room are those of a notable member of the artistic establishment. He was an advisor to both George III and George IV, and made many purchases on their behalf; he was a trustee of the National Gallery and of the British Museum. He was married to Amelia, daughter of Sir Abraham Hume, who was an artist of some repute, and was himself a collector of Oriental ceramics. Other aspects of this scheme invoke Repton, notably the use of great overmantel mirrors to reflect and enlarge the space. In his *Observations* (1816) Repton wrote:

The position of looking-glasses, with respect to the light and cheerfulness of rooms, was not well-understood in England during the last century, although on the Continent the effect of large mirrors had long been studied in certain palaces: great advantage was in some cases taken by placing them obliquely, and others by placing them opposite: thus new scenes and unexpected effects were often introduced. . . .

Further on in this same passage on the subject of the convenient arrangement of interiors Repton enlarges on the conservatory:

Of all the improvements in modern luxury, whether belonging to the Architect's or the Landscape Gardener's department, none is more delightful than the connection of the living-rooms with a green-house or conservatory; although they should always be separated by a small lobby, to prevent the damp and smell of earth. (See plate 107.)

J. Buckler, watercolour
Guildhall Library, London (Bridgeman Art Library)

101

102

Window wall of a library 1840s

The tall sash windows with their deep and boldly patterned shutter cases in this typical eighteenth-century country-house room are curtained in a voluminously swagged and gathered style which dates this picture. The furnishings, a mixture of both earlier and contemporary fashions, still have a severity of outline that would soon be replaced by the exuberant curves of the mid-century. The narrow red-and-white striped fabric covering the two sofas is to be found in rooms of this date both sides of the Channel. This scheme has some characteristics common to the Biedermeier style, a strain of English decorative taste – unpretentious and comfortable – that was encouraged in the writings of Repton.

English school, watercolour
Charles Saunders Antiques (photograph Spink & Sons)

102

112

113

The conservatory is highly ornamental from the style of its architecture, the free growth of the plants, the fine disposition of the climbers, the exterior approach through a terraced garden of orange trees and exotics, and above all, its connection with the galleries and cabinets of most exquisite sculpture, antique and modern. In front of the conservatory is a plantation of orange trees in pots sunk in the ground: and of different descriptions of green-house plants, chiefly from the Cape of Good Hope and New Holland, turned out of pots into the soil, in order to grow and flower during the mild season, and take their chance of standing during the winter. The effect in summer is excellent, and it has been found that several New Holland species, such as Acacia dealbata, and others, have survived several winters. We have repeatedly recommended this practice, both with hot-house and green-house plants, not only for the sake of the rare and splendid appearance produced during summer, but for the chance of finding some species hardy enough to stand the winter, thus adding to our acclimated trees.
(Quoted in Priscilla Boniface, *In Search of English Gardens: The travels of John Claudius Loudon and his wife Jane*, 1987, p. 47.)

W.H. Bartlett and Penry Williams, *A Series of Drawings, Illustrative of the Scenery and Architecture of The Deepdene, Surrey, made in the year 1825*, watercolours from an album *Borough of Lambeth Archives Department, London*

112, 113
The Round Conservatory at
The Deepdene 1825

J.C. Loudon greatly admired The Deepdene, Thomas Hope's house in Surrey. He visited the house in 1829 and particularly remarked on the conservatory:

114
A Russian Winter Garden Mid-19th century

This Russian Winter Garden is fully equipped with furniture and lighting and the arbour has surely been imported in a fully grown state to form the focal point of the display of flowering pot-plants. In his *Voyage en Russie* of 1865, Théophile Gautier wrote with admiration of the great displays of flowers in Russian salons, even in winter: 'Flowers, a true Russian luxury ... houses burst with them ... in the hall up the stairway. Magnolia and camellia trees flowering near the gilded ceiling, orchids fluttering around crystal or porcelain lamps, cornucopias of exotic flowers. As in a hothouse. Every apartment is a hothouse.'

Russian School, *A Conservatory*, watercolour
Eugene Victor Thaw Collection

115
A Russian flower trellis *c.* 1845

Théophile Gautier, again in his *Voyage en Russie*, noticed his hostess retiring with a few of her guests to sit, slightly screened from the rest of the room, behind a trellis of flowering climbers. Presumably these trellis arrangements, which are to be found in many Russian interiors, were sustained with tin containers for soil and water as described by Lady Londonderry in the diary of her visit to Russia in 1836 (see plate 268).

Russian School, *View of a Russian Drawing Room*, watercolour
Photograph courtesy of A la Vieille Russie

114

115

116, 117

An array of palms in Beacon Street 1890s

The house of Jack and Isabella Stewart Gardner at Beacon Street in Boston had a magnificent array of palms and aspidistras on a balcony above the entrance. The plants got light and air from this situation, though they would originally have been imported as mature plants from warmer climes.

Photographs Isabella Stewart Gardner Museum, Boston

117

luxuries were the prerogative of the very rich, since glass carried a punitive excise duty which was not removed until 1845. It was at this point that the possibility of having a winter garden or conservatory came within the means of any ordinarily prosperous house-owner. During the period of their greatest popularity considerable sums were expended on glasshouses of great size and sophistication. A record survives of the building costs of the magnificent glass and iron structure built for the second Earl of Harrowby at Sandon Hall in Staffordshire in 1866, by Messrs Stevens & Robinson of Derby. The total cost for the work and the materials was £7,396 6s 10d, which included a system of heating as it was to house tropical plants, and a basin and fountain, which when in play sent a jet of water almost to the roof (see *The English Garden Room*, ed. Elizabeth Dickson, 1986, pp. 25–30).

By the end of the Victorian era, the popularity of the conservatory was largely confined to the very wealthy; 'artistic' house-builders, who were discovering the beauties of nature *en plein air*, had no interest in the winter garden. At Cockayne Hatley in the 1890s, Lady Diana Cooper remembers: 'there was my father's study, well-lined with books and giving onto the garden, into which jutted a glass palm-filled bubble. Today we can admire a Victorian conservatory, but my pre-Raphaelite mother would have none of it' (*The Rainbow Comes and Goes*, 1958, p. 12). These glass appendages had no role to play in the Arts and Crafts manor house. The new fashion was for an open loggia furnished with rustic pieces, a dresser, a settle and some wooden rush-seated chairs, a style of semi-outdoor life that had its colonial counterpart in the verandah. An eighteenth-century precedent can be found in the open terraces that feature in some of Nash's villas and were called a 'viranda'. At Wilsford in Wiltshire, a country house built by Detmar Blow for the Tennants, the loggia was known as the Stone Parlour and in summer became another room of the house, used for meals and for reading aloud to the children.

As with the large country house in general, the luxuriant and extravagant conservatory needed a large staff of plantsmen to maintain it, and the running costs of heating apparatus were never cheap. The work of eighteenth- and nineteenth-century gardeners had succeeded in acclimatizing many new species of plant and shrub to the European climate, which to some extent made the conservatory as Loudon knew it superfluous. Finally, with the revolution pioneered by Gertrude Jekyll, the 'natural' garden turned its back on the conservatory and its artificiality.

119

118
Rivalry in the Winter Garden *c.*1878

In his painting entitled *In the Conservatory*, or *Rivals*, exhibited in 1879 at the Grosvenor Gallery, J.J. Tissot captures the delights of the conservatory as a secluded retreat where privacy and intimate conversations might be found. The distinction between a winter garden and conservatory is one of size; both were intended as places of display and entertainment, the actual business of raising the plants being carried out in adjacent greenhouses that were well out of sight.

J.J. Tissot, oil
Private collection (Bridgeman Art Library)

119
Sarah Bernhardt's Winter Garden 1879

Even more than Tissot's *Rivals*, this painting demonstrates the amenities of a winter garden. Like the very popular 'Moorish' or Arabian boudoirs and smoking rooms, it provided an informal retreat away from the rigidly organized public reception rooms.

Louise Abbema, oil
Formerly Hazlitt, Gooden & Fox Limited, London

THE WINTER GARDEN, GENERAL VIEW, STRAND PALACE HOTEL

120

120

Tea in the Winter Garden   Early 20th century

The Winter Garden at the Strand Palace Hotel is a fully realized example of the luxurious, French-influenced style that was the hallmark of grand hotel design in the early years of the twentieth century. An idiom identified with luxury and high life, it illustrates the chain of influence in taste. From the palaces of kings to the mansions of millionaires, and then to commercial buildings, the style can be traced to its final exploitation and degradation. So long as a room of this kind is perfectly maintained it can momentarily transport the occupants to an unaccustomed style of life.

Postcard from a private collection

121

121

The *jardin d'hiver* in a Parisian mansion 1860s

The *jardin d'hiver* of Princesse Mathilde's Paris house in the rue de Berry was used more as a place of entertainment than for conserving plants: sofas and chairs far outnumber the palms. Since exotic plants were grown in pots and led a peripatetic existence, they could be installed in any room of the house as easily as in the conservatory, or brought outside in summer as with Thomas Hope's orange trees, or buried to provide an avenue to a town house as at the de Retz Ball in Stendhal's *Le Rouge et Le Noir*. Princesse Mathilde's Paris house was fabulously decked with flowers for entertaining. Great banks of plants were set along the walls and around the bases of the columns in the handsome rooms. Although Taine spoke so admiringly of the English talent for flower arrangement, it is difficult to imagine the equal of such an impressive show as Princesse Mathilde's.

Musée des Arts Decoratifs, Paris (Sully-Jaulmes)

122

122

A veranda in Madras *c.* 1840

One feature of southern and colonial architecture that attracted house builders in northern countries was the veranda. Particularly appropriate to the Italianate style, it was, however, frequently adapted to designs in the Gothic or Old English taste. In default of suitable climatic conditions these light-denying additions to suburban houses often deteriorated into depositories for garden furniture and unused croquet sets, but the intention was that they should provide just such a charming feature, linking the house with the landscape, as is depicted in this view of the Adyar River in Madras.

F. J. Delafour, watercolour
Niall Hobhouse, London

123

The Garden House at Wickham Hall 1897

Rustic garden buildings had become popular in the early years of the nineteenth century as part of the vogue for the informal or 'Picturesque' garden. Many were perfectly useable labourers' cottages. This example, perched high up in the garden at Wickham Hall, was clearly intended as a rustic retreat for members of the family in search of solitude.

The rustic style is perfectly complemented by the wild garden setting. By this date formality of garden design so fashionable in the mid-century was giving way to the more naturalistic planting schemes promoted by William Robinson.

Private collection

123

THE COTTAGE

Don't you a little bit wish you lived in a little house – and it was all sweet and tiny, and didn't take any thought or waste any time, and were rather poor – only with pocket money for books and toys – and no visitors – all friends living in the same street, and the street long and narrow and ending in a city wall, and the wall opening with a gate on to cornfields in the south, and wild wood in the north – and no railways anywhere – all friends and all one's world tied up in the little city – and no news to come – only rumours and gossips at the city gate, telling things a month late and all wrong.
(Edward Burne-Jones to Lady Horner, quoted in her *Time Remembered*, 1933, p. 122.)

The longing of the Victorian householder to abdicate the responsibilities and social obligations of the day has surely never been more pathetically expressed than in this letter. Even such a relatively untramelled existence as Burne-Jones's was sufficiently constraining to make the idea of the simple life in a tiny cottage seem a mirage of happiness. The realities of rural poverty were ignored in the cult of the rose-bowered cottage. Indeed some remarkably successful conversions were effected by architects such as Gimson and Webb on the basis of simple stone-built village houses; they were often more successful than the 'cottage-style' designs of poky proportions and devoid of atmosphere or charm.

There was, of course, quite a wide divergence of opinion

124

125

125
Larsson's Country Retreat

All the elements of the new interest in the eighteenth century, in old peasant culture and in the austere side of neo-classicism, are present, as well as an awareness of Arts and Crafts culture that had enthusiastic adherents in Great Britain and the United States.

'Blomsterfönstret', watercolour for *Ett Hem*
Nationalmuseum, Stockholm (Statens Konstmuseer)

124
Kate Greenaway, Marigold Garden 1880

Like Walter Crane, Kate Greenaway through her illustrated books influenced taste as much as she followed it.

Private collection

about what constituted a cottage. The Royal Lodge in Windsor Great Park started off as modest dwelling called Lower Lodge where a Mr Frost once lived. John Nash was commissioned to transform it into a fashionable *cottage ornée*, very prettified and rustic, with many pointed dormer windows and a long veranda. Nash took great trouble to make the building appear as small as possible, but without, it seems, managing to fool the observant visitor. The resulting edifice was known ironically as the 'King's Cottage' and Lord Brougham remarked, 'Though called a cottage, because it happened to be thatched, it was still a very comfortable residence for a family.'

In 1836 Lady Londonderry visited the rustic cottage built for the amusement of the Russian Imperial family in Alexandria Park close to Tsarskoe Selo:

[We] were conducted by a beautiful drive coasting the Gulf of Finland to the cottage where the Emperor and Empress pass [a] great part of the summer. Here they live with their children in retirement. The cottage consists of three storeys. The Emperor and the children occupy the

SECTION OF ROYAL DAIRY.

GROUND PLAN.

LOOKING SOUTH.

Scale 1 in. to 4 feet.

128

The Royal Dairy, Windsor 1858

The tiles are from Minton and were designed by John Thomas, who also made this drawing. Prince Albert himself would probably have decided on the main features of this dairy. An American visitor, enchanted by this building, wrote:

It is no wonder that this is a favourite resort to the Queen, not only because it was the last work of her husband, but also because it best reflects the cherished features of his character. She visits it frequently with her children, who look with lively wonderment at all the processes that produce butter. I was told by the head dairy-woman that the youngest were delighted at permission to turn the crank of the barrel-churn, and would tug at it full fifteen minutes at a time, till their faces were hot and flushed with the exercise, and their hair flashed over their eyes at every round.

(Elihu Burritt, *A Walk from London to Land's End*, 1868.)

Royal Library, Windsor Castle; H M The Queen

The dairy . . . is surrounded by a deep veranda, the supports of which are festooned with climbers; this completely shades the wall, and its doors and windows, from the sun; except at mid-winter, and before and after that period until the sun at midday is 25° above the horizon. The roofs are thickly thatched . . . the walls [inside] are lined with glazed white tiles, the floor is paved with tessellated bricks, the shelves are of white marble, and the vessels in which the milk is kept are of white Wedgwood ware. . . . Large vases and jam jars of coloured china are placed as ornaments on the marble shelving round the walls.
(*Encyclopaedia*, 1836, pp. 974–5.)

This is, except for the floor, another example of a white dairy. Prince Albert's much grander conception pointed the way to the polychrome-tiled schemes of the later years of the century. The dairy was one of the first places to exploit ornamental tiles, and the usage spread to other places where food was handled or displayed, as noted in the *Art Journal* in 1887: 'Glazed earthenware or maiolica . . . is now the accepted method of decorating restaurants, buffets and the like' (p. 198). One complete and magnificent tiled interior survives in Harrods Food Hall in London.

Lord Ronald Gower believed himself to be very modestly housed at Gower Lodge. He compares it to a gate-lodge, by definition of similar status to a cottage, though designed to accommodate domestic retainers rather than agricultural labourers on the estate. The lodge and its contents are described in minute detail in *Bric-à-Brac* (1888):

[In 1878], I had purchased the little red-brick house now called 'Gower Lodge', tempted by its home-like and comfortable look, with its large gable, mullioned windows, and its creeper round the porch. The little house reminded me of some of the lodges at Cliveden designed for my mother by Devey; and what my mother liked has always been dear to me. The building, with the little plot of ground between it and the road, on which rests the defiant bronze of my 'Old Guard', would easily find room at the foot of the staircase of Stafford House.

The modest country retreat of this type, in this case a lodge, housing an accumulation of French furniture and fine paintings seems little in keeping with the spirit of the simple life. Lord Ronald enumerated the contents of one of the rooms on the ground floor:

Saloon: this saloon – although this is a vague term, which may apply to a ballroom or a small antechamber – was an afterthought, and not existent in the house when I first got it. It rejoices in armorial windows carried out by Mr Pace, and in a very successful chimney and fireplace designed by Mr A.Y. Nutt, Her Majesty's architect. In the upper central compartment is a medallion portrait of Constance, Duchess of Westminster, by the Scotch sculptor, Munro; beneath, casts by Brucciani of the angelic choir by Donatello at Padua. It is always a matter of surprise to me that such faithful reproductions of some of the most beautiful things in modern or ancient art are not more introduced into our homes. On the tables are books, bric-à-brac, and 'bibelots'.

Two more sitting rooms on this floor are described, both of them equally stocked with paintings and works of art. Illustrations suggest that the furniture was mainly French of the eighteenth century:

Ground floor sitting room: On the walls of this little room I have had the colour that Sir Edwin Landseer recommended as best for pictures hung – namely, a dull pale green, as like a grouse's egg as possible. The colour harmonizes admirably with the gilded cornice, door and mirror frames to the set of

English historical pictures relating to the seventeenth century, painted by Benjamin West, formerly at Grosvenor House, and which are now panelled in the library at Eaton Hall. Had I not rescued them, they would have been thrown away as useless lumber. The bas reliefs on either side of the fireplace are casts from Germain Pilon's works in the Louvre, known as 'La Force' and 'La Foi'. As in the case of the casts in the Saloon, they show how admirably such things can be adapted to harmonise even with the surroundings of a cottage.

129

129

Interior of a Wiltshire cottage 1849

William Morris, describing his plans for the equipping and furnishing of a working man's house as an exhibit for the Manchester Museum, enthused about the decorative effect that could be achieved with the arrangement of utilitarian objects on the wall and shelves in a living room. To recapture the uncomplicated naturalness of the artless peasant was an aim that was rarely achieved by the Arts and Crafts intellectuals. Note that this room contains a very fine array of the blue-and-white china which had attracted both Taine and the younger Hawthorne when visiting cottages later in the century. Elizabeth Pearson Dalby, who painted this picture at the age of sixteen, was the daughter of the rector of Compton Basset. Both her parents were keen amateur artists. She and her father moved to Compton Basset in 1840 after Mrs Dalby's death.

Interior at Compton Basset, Wiltshire, gouache
Salisbury and South Wiltshire Museum

130

A fireside in a cottage 1868

The perfectly arranged 'simplicity' of this cottage hearthside became the ideal of the middle-class world that read the works of Richard Jeffries and W.H. Hudson and subscribed to the comfortable myth of 'Merrie England'.

Plate from C.L. Eastlake, *Hints on Household Taste*

The effect of the gilded surrounds of the door, the fireplace and the cornice, with their classical picture frame mouldings, is extraordinarily rich in this otherwise rather modest room.

In his *Notes sur l'Angleterre* (1861), Hippolyte Taine compares the English workman's cottage to that of the French peasant – to the advantage of the former:

Yet his little house is clean; plates with bluish patterns are neatly arranged on a dresser, the iron chimneypiece is well laid out. I had already seen other cottages of this kind; almost always, at least in a main room, an old carpet covers the floor; there is often wallpaper, chairs of polished wood, little framed prints, always a Bible, sometimes some other volumes, devotional books, new novels, how to raise rabbits etc; in short, more useful objects than in our very poor cottages.

Taine was writing before the agricultural depression which reduced many rural communities to abject poverty. Twenty years later, Francis George Heath's *Peasant Life in the West of England* records a sadly changed picture:

Never have we witnessed so sad a sight as we saw in the that miserable garret of a hut. There was one bedstead, besides two other – we cannot say articles of furniture – things purporting to represent a table and chair, on a bare floor. On the bedstead, in the darkest corner of the room, which might have been some twelve or thirteen feet long, by some eight or nine feet wide, and perhaps seven feet high, lay the poor old bedridden grandmother, her poor wrinkled face looking the picture of patient and uncomplaining misery. Nothing on the floor besides the wretched bedstead and table and chair; no pictures, even of the rudest kind, on the walls.

Taine was further struck by the style of life enjoyed by farmers who held not particularly extensive farms and yet seemed prosperous to the eyes of a French visitor:

We went to see a fourth farm: six hundred acres, and about £600 a year rent. This time I was astounded: we were introduced into a cool and lofty drawing room. Long curtains held back by gilt loops; two elegantly framed looking-glasses; chairs in good taste. In the middle a table with a number of handsomely bound books. In short, the country drawing room of a Parisian with a private income of twenty-five thousand livres. Adjoining the rooms was [une espèce de serre, un parloir vitré garni de fleurs], giving on to a pretty countryside of sloping woods and distant meadows.
(Trans. Edward Hyams, *Notes*, 1957.)

The phrase retained in the original French is, in fact, translated by Mr Hyams as a 'conservatory', which is obviously correct, but it is intriguing to find that such an amenity was unfamiliar to Taine and there was no specific word for it in French. Although a new addition to the average British house, conservatories had been regarded as attainable luxuries since early in the century, and the design of a conservatory to adjoin the house had been discussed in detail in Repton's *Observations* of 1816.

When Taine turned his attention to the newly furnished and more pretentious habitations of the well-to-do, he was less impressed with their taste than with the native good taste of the century-old farmhouses which had preserved their simplicity against the tide of the Industrial Revolution. Particular scorn is reserved for the architect-designed cottage: 'Many of their stylish cottages, topped or overburdened with gables, look like toys or painted cardboard. All their imagination, all their native inventiveness has gone into their parks.'

Describing the cottage of his recently married host, Taine brings the interior into focus with his detailed observation:

Inside the house, pink or white wallpaper, light-coloured paint – lilac or creamy yellow; small-patterned tile or parquet floors, and a great many small-paned windows reminiscent of the Middle Ages. There is a good piano in the drawing room and several handsome books – wedding

THE McKINLEY OLD HOME, CONAGHER, DERVOCK.   R.W. 1186.   R.

131

presents – Tennyson, a prayer book, and others bound in blue velvet, in wood carved in gothic style, in tooled and gilt morocco leather, all carefully illustrated with neat pencil work peculiar to English artists and some of them decorated on every page with coloured paintings and arabesques. Not an article in the house but it bears witness to a studied and even meticulous taste. Everywhere are jardinières, filled with rare flowering plants; inside, as outside, a wealth of flowers. This is the prettiest element of English luxury, and one they understand as a gourmet understands food.

131
Living room in a house in County Antrim *c.* 1910

As in the Tayside souter's cottage (plate 132), this fireside is equipped with a spinning wheel, cooking pots, and traditional – not to say primitive – furniture. This house was once the home of President McKinley's family.

Ulster Folk and Transport Museum

132

132
Interior of a souter's cottage, Tayside
1840s

This cottage, as well as being the home of a souter, or cobbler, would also have been his workshop. A great number of traditional pieces of equipment remained in daily use, and it was this kind of artefact that southern cottage-owners sought for the sake of decoration. In Gertrude Jekyll's *Old English Household Life* (1926) these artefacts received the scholarly attention normally accorded to the fine furniture or *objets d'art* of the past. Indeed, these humble tools were to be treated as if works of art: both The Vineyard, Saffron Walden (plates 81, 82, 83) and Samuel Peto's house in Harrington Gardens (plate 68) have spinning wheels displayed as ornaments in the drawing room. The inglenook fireplace of the Surrey cottage was seldom without just such a boiling pot or gridiron as we see in this humble house. Roasting jacks, copper kettles and other largely obsolete items of household equipment were also transplanted into the cottages of the middle class.

Watercolour
Royal Museum of Scotland, Edinburgh

133

134

133

A cottage at Dulwich 1820

These living quarters seem to have been fashioned out of some kind of outbuilding. The open shutter reveals a window seemingly without glass; the floor is stone flags scantily covered with rugs or sacks. However, the rather elegantly proportioned table bears traces of painted decoration, and the chairs must once have graced a very different setting. It is not uncommon to find the good furniture of an earlier period demoted in this way, a fact not unknown to antique collectors of later periods who investigated cottages on the look-out for just such eighteenth-century pieces. W.G. Constable (1887–1976), curator of the National Gallery in London in the late 1920s, recounted that one of his duties:

. . . when estates were being broken up was to go and see if they contained anything of national importance. Often I went into rooms where the masters themselves never had been; it was not only my right but my function. One found the oddest things. In a great house where the top of a wing had been partitioned off for maids' rooms in the eighteenth century, I went along the corridor and found a complete dozen of Chippendale chairs, two in a room . . . where they had been apportioned perhaps a century before. Down below, in the mansion's rooms of state, was Victorian black walnut.
(*Dialogues of Alfred North Whitehead*, London, 1954, p. 103.)

Arthur Glennie, watercolour
Martyn Gregory Gallery, London

134

Pioneers at home 1884

The emotional subject matter of this Australian painting is highlighted by the carefully observed background detail. The woman's wearing of mourning implies that the returned husband has been given up as dead; she has been forced to take in laundry to support her home and infant son. Immigrants who made their way to Australia in the last century often left behind a very different life, of which the elegant silver tea and coffee pots would have been heirlooms brought over on the long voyage. A similar domestic drama is portrayed in Ada Cambridge's novel *The Three Miss Kings* (1891). The house where the eponymous heroines have lived all their lives is described minutely:

A pretty pathetic picture they made as they sat round the table, with the dim light of one kerosene lamp . . . discussing ways of getting their furniture to Melbourne. That time-honoured furniture, and their immediate surroundings generally, made a poor setting for such a group – a long canvas-lined room, papered with prints from The Illustrated London News *. . . from the ceiling to the floor, the floor being without a carpet, and the glass doors furnished only with a red baize curtain to draw against the sea winds of the winter nights.*

Frederick McCubbin, *Home Again*, oil
National Gallery of Victoria, Melbourne (Purchased through the Art Foundation of Victoria with funds provided by H.J. Coles Pty. Ltd., 1981)

144

ornamental wood-carving and plasterwork, would later come to serve, often in a more mannered form, for Arts and Crafts houses. The Arts and Crafts Movement had links with Continental art movements at the end of the nineteenth century, and then more directly with American architectural developments of the same period. The spare forms evolved by Voysey, Ashbee and Gimson, van de Velde, Hoffmann and Adolf Loos, Frank Lloyd Wright and Gustav Stickley are the immediate precursors of the Modern Movement's rectilinear designs which marked the final break with the nineteenth century's derivative historicism.

145

144
Democracy in America 1832

This family portrait was painted at a period when the United States was shedding its former colonial status and taking on nationhood. The interior combines the traditions of Protestant individualism and self-reliance – simple, unfussy furniture, home-made or locally made rugs – with wallpaper of red and green sprigs on a pale ground that had been fashionable in Paris a decade before.

Deborah Goldsmith, *The Talcot Family*, watercolour
Abby Aldrich Rockefeller Folk Art Center, Colonial Williamsburg, Virginia

145
A Textile Art c. 1845

In the far-flung communities of rural America textiles were scarce and highly prized. Every scrap was used and the quilting tradition thus relied heavily on patchwork and appliqué to utilize the pieces that could be salvaged from worn-out clothes and soft furnishings. The decorative potential of patchwork has never been more fully exploited than in nineteenth-century America. The finest achievement in patchwork is the 'album' quilt, prepared by friends for a bride. The many geometric repeating patterns based on diamonds, hexagons, squares and graded oblong pieces give a fascinating variety of tone and pattern.

Baltimore bride's quilt
The American Museum in Britain, Claverton Manor, Bath

146

146
A Quilting Party Mid-19th century

The lively occasion depicted here gives the flavour of self-reliance in decorating and equipping the home that is the hallmark of small, self-contained communities with limited access to mass-produced commodities. The patchwork quilt is a remarkable art object, with a set of traditional design rules that allow great freedom of interpretation as well as economy.

Anon., American school, oil
Abby Aldrich Rockefeller Folk Art Center, Colonial Williamsburg, Virginia

The house of Walter Pater in Oxford   1880s

The drawing room which runs the whole breadth of the house from the road to the garden behind was 'Paterian' in every line and ornament. There was a Morris paper; spindle-legged tables and chairs; a sparing allowance of blue plates and pots, bought, I think, in Holland, where Oxford residents in my day were always foraging, to return, often with treasures of which the very memory now stirs a half-amused envy of own past self that had such chances and lost them; framed embroidery of the most delicate design and colour, the work of Mr Pater's elder sister; engravings if I remember right, from Botticelli or Luini, or Mantegna; a few mirrors, and a few flowers, chosen and arranged with a simple yet conscious art. I see that room always with sun in it, touching the polished surfaces of wood and brass and china, and bringing out its pure, bright colour.

(Mrs Humphry Ward, *A Writer's Recollections 1856–1900*, 1918.)

The Art of the Interior
1800-1900

From Charles Dickens, *The Old Curiosity Shop*, 1841,
with engravings by George Cattermole

Part One
1800-1820

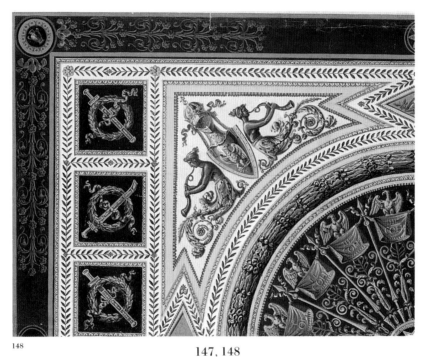

148

147, 148

Designs for carpets in the Imperial taste *c.*1800

The motifs on the design above indicate an imperial commission. With the
consolidation of his position and the establishment of the Tuileries and St-Cloud as his
residences, Napoleon was in need of extensive new furnishings for these palaces.
During the years of revolution production had all but ceased at the Gobelins and
Savonnerie factories. Most of the designs and cartoons had disappeared, and those
that survived were not in the taste of the period. Napoleon was eager to encourage
new manufacturers for two reasons: to stimulate profitable production for the benefit
of the economy, and also to contribute to the pomp and splendour of his own image.

Photographs Sotheby's

Very rarely does a new era in taste or fashion coincide conveniently with the beginning of a new century. In most respects the first two decades of the nineteenth century must be seen as a continuation of the development of decorative arts and architectural ideas that had started in 1795. Much of England remained untouched by the new century and the innovations of a rapidly industrializing country until after the Great Reform Bill had been passed in 1832. However, the first two decades saw developments in interior design that were to be of crucial importance to the art of interior decoration. For the first time copiously illustrated publications appeared that dealt with the subject as a stylistic whole rather than as an assemblage of parts (as with earlier pattern books for furniture and all manner of ornamental accessories compiled by, for example, Chippendale or Piranesi). The work of Napoleon's architects, Percier and Fontaine, entitled *Recueil de Décorations intérieures* ... (1801), was followed by Thomas Hope's *Household Furniture and Interior Decoration* (1807), and George Smith's *Collection of Designs for Household Furniture and Interior Decoration* (1808). From 1808 to 1828 Rudolf Ackermann's *Repository of the Arts* appeared with illustrations in full colour, providing an unflagging stream of inspiration for the embellishment of relatively modest houses. Similar periodicals dealing with designs for interiors had appeared on the Continent a few years earlier.

The introduction of colour illustrations of such fine quality was to transform the recording of the transient art of decoration and furnishing and ensured that the publications of the period had a most remarkable impact. W. H. Pyne's *History of the Royal Residences* (1817–19) has magnificently reproduced views of the interiors of Hampton Court, Buckingham House, Windsor Castle, Frogmore House, St James's Palace and Carlton House, which are as sumptuous as modern colour photographs. Pyne supplies an unrivalled source for lost or altered interiors, especially at Carlton House, an exquisite miniature palace, which contained schemes of consummate richness and elegance, but was demolished in 1826.

In Germany at this time, Karl Friedrich Schinkel (1781–1841), one of the greatest practitioners of the neo-classical style, was beginning his career. Working in Berlin, Schinkel used motifs reminiscent of Thomas Hope, but these never had quite the flamboyance of Percier and Fontaine in Empire Paris. As with his contemporaries in England, such as Sir John Soane (1753–1837), Schinkel experimented with the Gothic style, and a subtle mingling of the two sources is characteristic of his decorative work. A late example of this stylistic mix is found in the rebuilding of Fischbach in Silesia (plates 221, 222). Decorative ideas were augmented by a profusion of other historical styles, yet they always remained secondary to the main battle between neo-classical and Gothic Revival.

The terminology of styles in the early nineteenth century can be confused. Historically, the French Empire lasted from 1804 to 1814 and the British Regency from 1811 to 1820, but both terms are commonly employed to cover the whole quarter century up to 1825. It is more usual to describe French taste of the period from 1795 to 1825 as 'Napoleonic'. British taste of the same period, or even until the beginning of Queen Victoria's reign in the 1840s, is still loosely called 'Regency', probably for lack of a more evocative term to describe the elegance which is popularly considered the salient feature of the style. For historical reasons the Empire style had a more abrupt end. Politically, it was expedient to play down the memories of Napoleon's regime and eradicate the visible reminders that might evoke memories of the lost imperial grandeur.

However, war and the repressive regimes installed after 1815 could not suppress ideas that were common to the age rather than strictly national. Parallel thinking is evident in the stylistic vocabularies of the period, and ideas were exchanged via illustrated publications on every new architectural and decorative development. Sources common to all would have been the increasingly scholarly investigations and re-creations of Greek and Roman architecture.

For reasons of state, the Prince of Wales was prevented from adopting certain elements of the Napoleonic vocabulary that amounted to blatant imperial myth-making. This was a deprivation, since the supremacy of French taste in all areas of decoration was acknowledged throughout Europe. The influence of French cabinet-makers of the early nineteenth century is apparent in Scandinavia and Germany, as well as Spain and Italy, where members of the imperial family and French generals had been set up as kings and princes.

For a man of the Regent's cultural inclinations, it must have been a hard sacrifice to turn his back on the decorative novelties that were appearing across the Channel. He found a partial solution to this difficulty by employing Henry Holland, an architect whose work was distinctly 'Anglo-French'. Holland's interpretation and refinement of Continental neo-classical trends may be regarded as a major contribution to the taste of the period. However, much of the decorative detail of Carlton House was the work of craftsmen and designers who had worked at the court of the late Louis XVI, such as Gabriel, who carried out the sumptuous balustrade for the grand staircase; and Charles-André Boulle, for whose work the Regent had a continuing predilection, purchasing furniture in this style even for the oriental fantasy of Brighton Pavilion.

The gulf thus created was to have long-term effects. Examples of Empire furniture are rare in Britain in comparison to work of the *ancien régime*. There are even fewer survivals in British decoration schemes of the early century of the famous scenic wallpapers devised by the firm of Dufour et Cie. These were admired in the United States, and a number of rooms with such papers do survive there. In Britain, Chinese hand-painted wallpapers, which had been imported since the early eighteenth century, continued to be popular, even after the fall of Napoleon. However, French scenic papers found their way into some houses. Schemes survive at Doddington Hall, Lincolnshire and Ombersley Court, Worcestershire. Indeed, a description by Smithers of Liverpool notes:

A few years since every room in some houses and some rooms in all, were ornamented with paintings and prints . . . and now, we see the walls decorated with the glare of French or Swiss papers, in fresco, illustrative of glowing colours, unlike anything in nature. This fashion is in such bad taste that it cannot long continue.
(Quoted in John Cornforth, 'Vitality and variety. The Musée de Papier Peint at Reixheim, near Mulhouse, France', *Country Life*, 9 April 1987.)

It may well be that the taste for scenic papers came to this great seaport from the United States or with immigrants from the Continent.

The effects of being cut off from French cultural influences were not all negative. The emergence of a native school brought an idiosyncratic figure such as George Bullock into a prominence that might have been denied him had he been working in the shadow of the great French neo-classical cabinet-makers. His forms are bold and vigorous, almost crudely foursquare in the context of Henry Holland's elegant designs for Carlton House. Yet Bullock was an inspired ornamentalist: his bold Grecian-style inlay anticipates the work, using the same techniques, carried out by Lamb of Manchester to designs by Christopher Dresser. To acknowledge the originality of Bullock is, to some extent, to diminish the reputations of succeeding designers: Pugin, whose *Floriated Ornament* (1849) seems almost to echo some of Bullock's work; and Owen Jones and Dresser, who also exploit the decorative impact of bold inlay on severe architectonic forms. In the light of new discoveries relating to Bullock's most important commissions, a slight revision of the nineteenth-century chain of inspiration has become overdue (see *George Bullock, Cabinet-Maker*, catalogue, 1988).

Constraints of political expediency did not affect a mere subject, and, unlike the Prince Regent, Thomas Hope was able to absorb the influences of his friend Charles Percier without reservation. Hope was too uncompromising to attract a large following, but his importance to aspects of neo-classicism is marked. Surprisingly, the most faithful re-creation of a Hope interior was in a house by A. J. Davis, *c*. 1845 (see plate 297).

The roots of the Egyptian Revival go back beyond the year 1800. Napoleon's campaigns of the 1790s in Egypt gave enormous impetus to this aspect of antiquity, especially with the publication of Dominique-Vivant Denon's *Voyage dans la basse et la haute Egypte pendant les campagnes du Général Bonaparte* in 1802. Denon's topographical views supplanted Piranesi's fanciful Egyptian motifs in *Diverse maniere d'adornare i camini*, published over thirty years earlier. Egyptian elements occur frequently in furniture designs of the period, but in contrast to the popularity of 'Etruscan' or 'Pompeian' schemes, it is rare to find whole rooms in the Egyptian style. Thomas Hope's house in Duchess Street is one well recorded example. Another such scheme is the Hall and Library at Craven Cottage, a thatched *cottage ornée* purchased in 1805 by Walsh Porter, who was a friend of the Prince Regent and the hidden hand in the decorations of Carlton House. Porter employed the young Thomas Hopper, the future architect of the Carlton House conservatory, to remodel the interior in a variety of styles. Craven Cottage receives a very full account in Faulkner's *Historical and Topographical Account of Fulham* (1813):

The principal entrance from the lawn, is through the Egyptian Hall; which is fitted up in the Egyptian style, being an exact copy from one of the plates in Denon's Travels in Egypt, during the campaigns of Buonaparte in that country. The two great doors cost two thousand guineas; they are composed of wrought iron work, divided into various compartments filled with plate glass, and are the exact copies of the original represented in Denon's work. The interior is richly painted in the Egyptian style; it is supported by eight immense columns covered with hieroglyphics, and at each corner of the room is a palm-tree. A sphinx and a mummy are painted on each side of the door; the ceiling is painted with hieroglyphics; a female figure in bronze, as large as life, stands near the door, holding up a curtain painted in imitation of a tiger's skin; and a moveable camel, in bronze, stands near the entrance. The whole of this room is striking and characteristic.
(pp. 432–4.)

An important source for Percier and Fontaine's own style of ornate neo-classicism was the Villa Albani, built outside Rome by Cardinal Albani to house and display his unrivalled collection of classical antiquities. The antique sculptures are incorporated into the architecture as ornament; the reliefs provide distinctive and original surface ornament and the monumental figure sculptures are treated as parts of the fabric. Some indication of Percier and Fontaine's admiration for this unique ensemble is demonstrated by the space afforded to the Villa, both in text and illustrations, in their *Choix de plus célèbres Maisons de plaisance de Rome et des environs* of 1809. A number of their schemes, notably for the Tuileries dining room and the ceiling of the Salle de Vénus in the Louvre, incorporate elements of antique decoration

152

152
The *Salon de Musique* at Malmaison 1812

The interiors at Malmaison are the epitome of the Empire Style in decoration and furnishing. The property was the choice of the Empress Josephine, who bought it, without being in a position to pay for it, in 1799, even before Napoleon was made First Consul. The modernization of this charming manor house at Rueil, near Paris, was entrusted to the architect-decorators Percier and Fontaine. Many details of the early progress of this commission are given in their *Recueil de Décorations intérieures* (1802). The most intensive phase of the refurbishing of the house took place before 1804 when Percier and Fontaine directed the neo-classical decoration, in the Pompeian style, of many of the rooms. After Napoleon became emperor, the house was little used as it was too small to accommodate the Court; however, after 1809 the rejected Josephine lived there, free to follow her own decorating inclinations. The *Salon de Musique*, situated on the ground floor, has survived almost intact with many of the paintings and furnishings still *in situ*. The fine detail in this view allows many of the paintings to be identified: on the left, F.-M. Granet's *Stella Drawing on the Walls of his Prison*; on the right, *The Death of Raphael* by P.N. Bergeret. The room was completed in 1800, the furniture having been executed by Jacob Frères and the decorations by the painter Moench. The scheme of mahogany panelling with paired columns coming forward from the walls echoes that of Napoleon's library at the opposite end of the château. Through the glass at the end can be seen the *Grande Galerie*, an enlargement of the room undertaken for Josephine in 1809 to house her growing collections of Old Master paintings and antique sculptures. It was designed by L.-M. Berthault, by this date in charge of the works at Malmaison. Berthault was an architect of the old regime who had worked for Louis XVI, and was also responsible for the bedchamber of Madame Récamier. The extension was destroyed some time after 1840. This elegant bedroom was illustrated by Krafft and Ransonette in their *Plus belles Maisons et Hôtels construits à Paris* (1802). Robert Smirke did a drawing of the room from the same viewpoint, but differing in a number of details. Madame Récamier's portrait by David is the quintessential neo-classical icon: in a setting of exaggerated simplicity she reclines in her filmy classical robe on an antique couch. It is almost impossible to imagine how the cluttered profusion of the mid-century could possibly have succeeded such austere rooms.

Auguste Garneray, watercolour
Musée de Malmaison (Réunion des Musées Nationaux)

153, 154
Neo-classical carpet designs 1800

Carpets were by this date the established fashion in France, and there was no lack of expert manufacturers who could execute these complex and detailed designs. The finest carpets were made at the *Manufacture impériale de la Savonnerie*. From 1804, under the direction of the Intendant Général of the Emperor's household, carpets designed by Percier and Fontaine were supplied for the furnishing of the palaces. The vast carpets were decorated with emblems of war: helmets, breastplates and trophies intermingled with symbols of imperial majesty: laurel wreaths, stars, bees, eagles, and the Imperial crown (see plate 148). The carpet made in 1809 and given by Napoleon to the King of Saxony survives in the Musée de Malmaison. The Emperor's own carpet for his *Grand Cabinet* at the Tuileries is at the Château de Compiègne. The designs were often made with one or more borders that could be added or removed to vary the size of the carpet at very little cost. Designs consisting of a centre-piece in a large plain field, with a simple band of repeating motifs for the border, resemble the carpet made for the bedroom of the Empress at Compiègne. The design for the Emperor's bedroom, on the other hand, is nearly as complex and symbolic as that of the carpet for the *Grand Cabinet*. Both these bedroom carpets are now in the collection of the *Mobilier National*. The designs for the imperial commissions at the Savonnerie factory were made by the painter La Hamaydé de Saint-Ange, who continued to create carpet designs under the succeeding regimes, for Louis XVIII, Charles X and Louis-Philippe. The distinctive style of his work was influential throughout Europe, and echoes of it can be discerned in carpet manufactories throughout the nineteenth century.

Photographs Sotheby's, Monaco

153

154

155

155, 156

Imperial memories in Florence 1841

The Villa Demidoff was once in the possession of the Bonapartes and was sold by Jerome Bonaparte to his future son-in-law, Anatole Demidoff, in 1840. The painting above shows the library, the year after Anatole's marriage to Princesse Mathilde Bonaparte. Jerome had also managed to persuade Demidoff to buy the great Canova sculptures of Napoleon and his mother for 10,000 francs each. Here Napoleon, with his upraised arm, dominates the room, palatial in its formal arrangement.

The Salone at San Donato (right) has as its focal point Canova's *Madame Mère*. There are more Napoleonic treasures in this great domed state room: it is lined with Empire chairs in the style of Percier and Fontaine; the massively draped curtains are in velvet of imperial purple. Princesse Mathilde loved San Donato; ironically, her estranged husband was to retain a Napoleonic palace while she made for herself an ambience of fashionable Parisian luxury touched with Bohemianism.

In 1871, Walburga, Lady Paget was visiting Florence and confided to her diary the following observations:

Early in June the famous collection of San Donato, belonging to Prince Demidoff and made by his uncle, the husband of Princess Mathilde, is to be sold. . . . The place was perfectly empty, and I could at my leisure contemplate the wonderful riches huddled into this comparatively small and ugly house. The pictures and statues were of great value. . . . Tapestries and embroideries of every kind, tables of malachite and lapis, slabs of precious marbles and rare alabasters abounded there. I cannot say, however, that the whole was harmonious or agreeable to the eye.
(Walburga, Lady Paget, *The Linings of Life*, vol. I, 1928.)

Fortuné de Fournier: *The Library of the Villa Demidoff at Pratolino, near Florence*; *The Salone at the Villa di San Donato, near the Porta al Prato, Florence*
Photographs Sotheby's, Florence

157

Queen Charlotte's model villa 1817

In 1790 Queen Charlotte bought the lease of a small house with estate about a mile and a half from Windsor Castle, and employed James Wyatt to rebuild it as a model neo-classical villa (1792–5). The result was so eagerly admired that tickets-to-view would only be offered to 'respectable parties'. The library was furnished in a golden brown with woodwork grained to imitate satinwood; the doors were finished in black-edged panelling. Along the top of the bookcase were the plaster 'library' busts of the literary greats. The Queen was one of the first to have an example of the 'Davenport', a small and easily portable writing desk which remained a popular library item well into the second half of the nineteenth century. The tall windows reaching from ceiling to floor with their flower patterned green curtains mitigated the richness of the décor.

C. Wild, *The Library*, commissioned for W. H. Pyne's *Royal Residences*, 1819, watercolour
Royal Library, Windsor Castle; H M The Queen

158

158

Carlton House 1817

The Crimson Drawing Room was supplied in about 1810 with curtains and ornamental draperies that ran right around the wall beneath the gilded and stuccoed ceiling; the wall coverings and upholstery were of crimson satin damask. The effect of red and gold – with touches of emphasis in the black and gold doors, the black borders to the upholstery and the black marble fireplace with the massive bronze figures supporting the shelf – was set off by the light blue velvet pile carpet. The chandeliers in this room, in the Circular Drawing Room (see frontispiece) that led off it, the Ante-Chamber to the Throne Room and the Blue Velvet Room, and the Red Satin Drawing Room were all of equal splendour, and Pyne regarded them as amongst the finest in Europe.

C. Wild, *The Crimson Drawing Room*, commissioned for W. H. Pyne's *Royal Residences*, 1819, watercolour
Royal Library, Windsor Castle; H M The Queen

159

159

The Perfect Palace *c.* 1815

The Prince Regent's short-lived palace of Carlton House was the most important house of its time in Britain. Pyne accords no less than twenty-four plates of *Royal Residences* to its interiors, a mark of its influential role, and also fortunate for posterity since it was demolished in 1826. From 1783 until about 1814, when funds were being diverted to Brighton, Carlton House was altered and refurnished in an ever more opulent and sophisticated style. Thomas Hopper's conservatory of 1807 was on the same scale as the rest of the palace. Henry VII's chapel was the model for this fantasy. It was constructed of cast-iron which allowed for a high ratio of window to wall, yet its main function was not to grow plants but to serve as a dramatic approach to Nash's Gothic dining room.

From J. Britton, *Public Buildings of London*, 1828

Scholarly design versus innovation 1807/1828

The Duchess Street Mansion (right) was not really a private house for the peaceful occupation of a family. From the very beginning Hope admitted the public to the suite of museum rooms on the first floor, and he and his wife lived in a smaller suite of rooms upstairs. Tickets were issued on application, to 'persons of known character and taste', a precedent set by Horace Walpole, who permitted the public to inspect Strawberry Hill in just the same way. To go from the austerities of Thomas Hope's antique authenticity to the dazzling intricacies of Soane's celebrated ante-library at Lincoln's Inn Fields (below) is to span the gulf between the scholar and the innovator. Depictions of Soane's interiors, although minutely accurate in detail, imply a scale of magnificent proportions. The rooms themselves are surprisingly small in reality, but fascinating in their subtle and suggestive exploitation of space.

'The Egyptian Room', from Thomas Hope, *Household Furniture and Interior Decoration*, 1807
From J. Britton, *Public Buildings of London*, 1828

161

160

162

163

162, 163
Decorative schemes for the Royal Palace, Copenhagen 1790s

Nicholas Abildgaard (1743–1809), Denmark's best-known neo-classical painter, also produced designs for furniture, interior decoration and architecture, including these drawings for the Royal Palace at Amalienborg. The geometric simplicity and well-informed use of classical vocabulary refer back to the eighteenth-century stability of the *Ancien Régime* and reject the contemporary work of Percier and Fontaine's Empire exuberance, or the sculptural and the applied ornamentation of Masreliez's schemes for Gustav III of Sweden.

Statens Museum for Kunst, Copenhagen

164, 165
The neo-classical decoration of Swedish palaces Early 1800s

Louis-Jean Desprez (1743–1804) was born in France and trained as an architect; he won the Grand Prix de Rome in 1776. In Italy his career became dominated by stage design, and in that capacity he went to work for Gustav III in 1784. He remained in Sweden until his death. As court architect his designs were in the Romantic vein, an Egyptianizing scheme with life-size statues in heavily shadowed niches being typical of his work. Louis-Adrian Masreliez (1748–1810) was a native of Stockholm, the son of the painter Adrian Masreliez who was his teacher before he travelled to France and Italy, spending fifteen years working there before returning to Stockholm in 1783. He, too, was employed on many royal commissions.

Louis-Jean Desprez, *Wall Decoration for Gustav III's Palace*
Louis-Adrian Masreliez, *Wall Decoration for Gustav III's Haga Pavilion*
Statens Konstmuseer, Stockholm

164

165

166, 167

Federalist Boston 1820

No. 10 Franklin Street was the home of the painter Henry Sargent (1770–1845), and these pictures are by him. Franklin Street was a handsome curved row of sixteen town houses built in 1794 by Charles Bullfinch in the same style as John Wood the Younger's crescents and terraces in Bath. The rooms were decorated in the 'Federal' period taste. In *The Tea Party* the reception room is furnished in the French Empire style, with chairs in the manner of Percier and Fontaine's *Recueil* of 1802. The furniture in *The Dinner Party* is still of an English style. The Revolution of 1776 had diminished the influence of things British, but Sargent trained as a painter under Benjamin West in England and remained a close friend of John Copley, so that he presumably retained an affection for the England of his youth. The scale of both rooms is slightly exaggerated, which has the effect of dwarfing the guests and the handsome furniture at both functions; this may be due to the fact that the artist's sight was failing at the time.

Henry Sargent: *The Dinner Party* and *The Tea Party*, 1820
Museum of Fine Arts, Boston (Gift of Mrs Horatio Lamb in memory of Mrs Winthrop Sargent)

167

168

169

168, 169
Thomas Hope's country house 1825

Even at the more approachable Deepdene, Hope's country house in Surrey, the grandeur of his arrangements induced awe in the visitor. J.C. Loudon visited the house in 1829:

We do not speak of the sculpture gallery, because, greatly as we admire its contents, and respect the highly cultivated mind that selected and placed them there, we feel that we are incompetent to do it justice. Duly to appreciate works of art of such extraordinary rarity and excellence as are here assembled, would require more of the mind of the artist and the classical scholar than we can pretend to. All must feel the effect of sculptures and paintings to a certain extent; but this feeling, like every other, to be made the most of, must be highly cultivated.

(Quoted in Priscilla Boniface, *In Search of English Gardens, The travels of John Claudius Loudon and his wife Jane*, 1987.)

The Statue Gallery and The Amphitheatre from W.H. Bartlett and Penry Williams, *A Series of Drawings, Illustrative of the Scenery and Architecture of The Deepdene, Surrey, made in the year 1825*, watercolours
Borough of Lambeth Archives Department, London

170
Scheme for the library in a palace *c.*1800

In a scheme of great delicacy and subtlety, this library is decorated in tones of blue, grey and pale brown that give the fullest possible impact to the rows of books, the classical busts and sculptural reliefs and the magnificent full-length portrait let into the niche above the built-in *canapé*. No superfluous ornament detracts from this function. The chair is in the very elegant form that marks the transition between the styles of the late eighteenth century and the severity of strictly neo-classical taste. The top rail still has a slight scroll and the legs at the front are still of sabre shape. Only two pieces of furniture in the room are free-standing, but the built-in library shelves and the *canapé* are proportioned and finished with all the finesse of the cabinet-maker's art. This drawing is firmly attributed to Charles Percier, and is undeniably in the Percier and Fontaine manner, but the absence of surface ornament on the cabinet-work combined with the severity of the whole scheme makes this a somewhat uncharacteristic product of the partnership. It may simply mark the taste of an unusually austere patron, or perhaps suggest the work of a follower or close imitator.

Charles Percier, watercolour
Photograph Sotheby's, Monaco

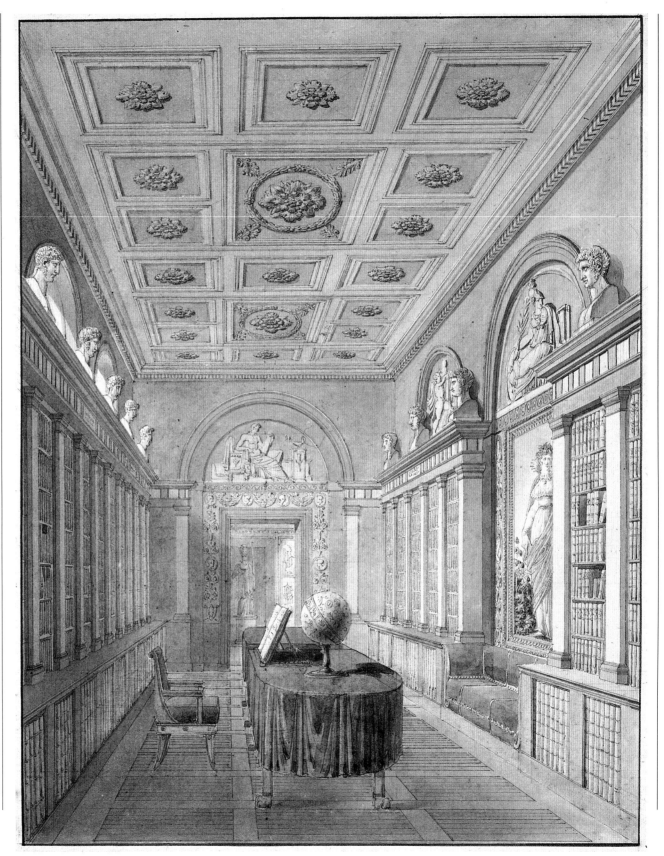

171

171
The Grand Drawing Room at Fonthill Abbey 1823

John Rutter describes the furnishings of this fine room thus: 'A suite of chairs, gold and purple damask. A circular table of *brèche universelle*, from Malmaison. Four boulle candelabras with candlesticks, with designs from Cellini.' Strangely, he does not mention the desk, a French royal secrétaire by Reisener with the most elaborate inlay and mounts of chased *bronze doré* which is now in the Wallace Collection, London. He does mention a 'carpet of extraordinary costliness'; it is Aubusson, also of Imperial provenance, having been made for Napoleon's refurbishment of the palace at St-Cloud. The walls were hung with deep blue silk damask. From the 1823 catalogue of the sale of the contents of William Beckford's Fonthill Abbey, it is apparent that the chairs, the sofa and the X-stools that can be seen in this illustration were upholstered in the same blue damask; another six chairs were covered in the purple damask described by Rutter. The Gothic style of the architecture makes a surprising framework for this French neo-classical taste, but the assurance with which Beckford creates his ensembles carries the eclectic mixture triumphantly.

Plate from John Rutter, *Delineations of Fonthill and its Abbey*, 1823

172
Scenic wallpaper in America 1876

This house was built in 1754; Wyllys Elliott called it 'one of the best examples of the best style of house built in New England in the last century of the colonial period'. He also notes its careful preservation since, which explains the survival of scenic wallpaper on the left-hand wall: 'This gives a gay tone to the whole house and cannot fail to impress whoever enters it.' However, the owners in the 1870s have been unable to resist 'a few antique chairs and cabinets', Japanese pots, busts on pedestals and a turkey stair carpet, all of which distract from the wallpaper. Eliott mentions a 'great head of spreading antlers', which is not visible in this picture; in a later photograph of this hall the antlers can be seen to have obliterated part of the scene at the far end (see Catherine Lynn, *Wallpaper in America*, 1980, p. 211). The subject of this particular scenic paper is identified as *Télémaque*, published between 1815 and 1820 by Dufour et Cie. The paper was available from American suppliers in the 1830s. President Andrew Jackson had two sets for his own house.

The Hall of Francis Peabody Esq., at Danvers, Massachusetts from C.W. Elliott, *American Interiors*

173

173, 174

A sort of portrait *c.* 1804

Soane's country house, Pitzhanger Manor in Ealing, has recently been restored. This house was created at the high point of Soane's life, when he was working on his greatest project – the re-building of the Bank of England. Many of the ideas for Pitzhanger were developed from those used for the Bank. The house was designed to accommodate and display the growing collection of sculpture and architectural fragments that were to reside finally in the Museum of Lincoln's Inn. The small physical size of the newly restored interiors come as a surprise after these views which imply great spaciousness.

J.M. Gandy, *Pitzhanger Manor: Front and Back Parlour*
By courtesy of the Trustees of Sir John Soane's Museum,
London

174

175

175
Breakfast at the Soanes' 1825

This was Soane's first house in Lincoln's Inn Fields, where he lived from 1794 to 1812; subsequently he acquired the adjacent Nos 13 and 14. Though the shallow arch is present in this design, Soane's style is not as overpowering as it was to become when developed to its extremes next door in the house and museum.

J.M. Gandy, *The Breakfast Room with the Soane family; 12, Lincoln's Inn Fields*
By courtesy of the Trustees of Sir John Soane's Museum, London

180

180
'Comfortable and ladylike' 1800s

Everything indoors and out was well kept – the house was well furnished, and it was altogether a comfortable and ladylike establishment, tho' I believe that the means that supported it but were small –
(Caroline Austen, *My Aunt, Jane Austen*, 1952.)

The small luxuries of English provincial life, such as Jane Austen and her heroines led, are here ready to hand: the well-furnished bookcase, the folding writing desk with sloping top and neatly contrived spaces for storing paper, pens and ink. The Hennell-style inkstand on the table would date the picture to the first decade of the nineteenth century. This artist has also depicted the garden of the house, modest but well planned and planted, with the same attention to detail as shown in this room. Simplicity and a tranquil tastefulness were the unavoidable hallmarks of such interiors where opportunities for acquisitions were restricted.

14 St James Square, Bristol, watercolour by a member of the Pole family
Bristol City Art Gallery

181
A painter's studio bedroom 1820

Jean-Baptiste Isabey was a celebrated Empire period miniaturist – the best known of the miniature portraits of Napoleon's second wife, the Empress Marie-Louise is by him – and the designer of the gold wreath of laurels with which the Emperor crowned himself in 1804. Napoleon presented Isabey with a single leaf from the wreath, set into the lid of a gold box, which is now in the Napoleonic Museum at Fontainebleau. This room, painted by Isabey himself, a workroom with sleeping quarters combined, is surprisingly modest in its decoration and furnishings. An earlier Parisian version, also combining these two elements of the artist's needs, is illustrated in detail in Percier and Fontaine's *Recueil* of 1802, there entitled *'Studio of Citizen I.'* (Isabey). In Percier and Fontaine's design the bed with its sculptural heading and draped screen behind dominates the scheme, which is otherwise devoid of useful furniture. The room at Plombières, on the other hand, is fitted in the most practical way with all the necessities for living and working. The decoration of the walls in this room is interesting. Between widely spaced stripes are individual motifs, not a repeating pattern, which may have been executed freehand. The trophies of helmets and arms are very like those in the bedroom of *'Monsieur T. Paris'*, also included in Percier and Fontaine's *Recueil*, and it might be speculated that Isabey wished to re-create something of the character of his splendid Parisian studio. Otherwise, the unornamented, severely plain furniture is a long way from the refined splendour of the full-blown Empire style, a style known in intimate detail by Isabey from his work on the paintings of *Napoleon in his Study* and *Napoleon Placing his Son in the Arms of Marie-Louise after his Baptism* (reproduced in Mario Praz, *An Illustrated History of Interior Decoration*, 1964, plates 156, 158).

Ma Chambre à Plombières en 1820, watercolour
Private collection (photograph Agnew's)

182
An artist's studio and living room, Northern Europe *c.* 1820

The great charm of this rather austere room is in contrast to Isabey's practised rendering of his quarters at Plombières. The artist's works in uniform frames line the walls. At the conclusion of the working day, music-making is the main activity of the artist's leisure.

German or Russian school, *The Artist's Room*
Private collection

181

182

183

183
'Interior with a young woman tracing a flower' 1824

This genre painting, by the daughter of Martin Drolling, was purchased by the Duchesse de Berry from the 1824 Paris Salon. It is a fitting pendant to the two interiors by her father (plates 184, 185), one of which, the kitchen scene, was also owned by the Duchesse. Again, the influence of Dutch painting of the seventeenth century is apparent, particularly in its portrayal of the subject in the act of some domestic accomplishment. To gain enough light, the draughtswoman has pushed aside the half-curtain. The room is simply decorated and furnished; there is a large bookcase crammed with volumes and a handsome classical bust that contributes to this 'working' room, which must have been austere by choice rather than economic necessity. A very similar painting is in the Musée de Carnavalet, Paris. Also showing an artist at work by the window, it is attributed to a pupil or follower of Martin Drolling, titled 'Young woman in Interior'. The subject is not unusual for the age before gas and electricity, when daylight was the most precious light source and the home was also the workplace, not just for illustrators and engravers but also for many trades.

Louise Adéone Drolling, oil
St Louis Art Museum, Missouri (Miss Lillie B. Randall Fund)

184
Domestic interior with women sewing 1815

Shown as companion piece to *The Dining Room* in the Paris Salon of 1817, this painting by Martin Drolling implies that the kitchen was a room occupied as well as used by womenfolk of the household. The utensils and furniture are of the unchanging provincial French tradition and the room is in Paris, yet the whole effect is deliberately seventeenth-century Dutch. The Dutch schools had been studied by Drolling and had become fashionable in Restoration Paris. This picture belonged to the Duchesse de Berry, one of the great collectors of Dutch interiors.

Martin Drolling, *Interior of a kitchen*
Musée du Louvre, Paris (Réunion des Musées Nationaux)

184

185

185
A dining room in Paris 1816

Although modest, this room bears all the marks of careful,
artistic taste. On the wall are gilt-framed engravings; two
large classical urns flank the doorway leading to the room
beyond, in which the mistress of the house plays the forte-
piano. Over the door is a roundel with a sculpted head of
Medusa. The man is taking breakfast, drinking from a
delicate porcelain cup. The armchairs are of an eighteenth-
century style, upholstered in a green figured material,
perhaps Genoese cut velvet. The chair by the stove is
contemporary with the date of this painting by Martin
Drolling. For all the studied elegance, the tiled floor is
without a rug, and the half-curtain is suspended by wire.
The scene has been identified as a bourgeois Parisian
interior (see *Les Parisien chez eux au 19e siècle*, Hôtel de
Rohan, exhibition catalogue 1977).

Martin Drolling, *Interior of a Dining Room*
Private collection

186
A French fireplace 1820

Pierre Duval-Lecamus (1790–1858) was a pupil of David,
well known for his small full-length portraits of this kind.
By showing the subject thus in his own room, much can be
conveyed about his character and circumstances. Such
paintings provide a convincing semblance of reality for
the information of future generations, and although the
inevitable artfulness of a posed portrait should not be
discounted, there is much in this painting of interest to
the historian. Many such French rooms survive complete
with the simple but boldly architectural fireplace in black
marble. French taste still dictates the chimney ornaments
of clock and candlesticks in ormolu and bronze posed
before a plain overmantel glass reaching to the cove of the
ceiling. In this case the frame with its flat pilasters echoes
that of the door. The decoration of the walls is plain
almost to the point of austerity, but bands of border
ornament at the junction with the bold hollow of the
ceiling moulding and above the heavy chair rail enrich the
scheme to an astonishing degree. The Napoleonic furniture has remained a hallmark of French taste since the
plain but ample and comfortable shapes were first devised. The paintings in their deep plain gold frames are
probably landscapes, typical of the taste of this period.
The needlework rug has the black ground that character-
izes textile designs in the first half of the nineteenth
century, giving a bold prominence to the naturalistic
flowers and leaves of the embroidery.

Portrait of a Man Standing before the Fire
Private collection, London

186

187

187, 188, 189
A country house on the heights of Campden Hill 1817

In the eighteenth century Aubrey House was lived in by the diarist Lady Mary Coke. In the early years of the next century P. N. de Visme took the lease. He died in 1817, but his wife remained in residence for another two years. Their daughter Louisa, who married one John Louis Goldsmid, painted a series of views of both the exterior and interior. The latter is simply furnished with the clear uncluttered lines of the eighteenth century. However, the furnishings have clearly been brought up to date, and attempts made at fashionable decoration, with a frieze (left) imitating the fabric-draped walls popular in France. Chairs dating from the late eighteenth century have been banished to the nursery (below). In what is otherwise a rather austere early-nineteenth century series of rooms, the curtains appear quite startlingly elaborate. Probably influenced by French pattern-books, these treatments were certainly expensive to create.

188

189

These pictures, and the fact that Aubrey House has survived relatively unchanged up until the present day, make the house of compelling interest. A later occupant was to be W.C. Alexander, patron of Whistler, for whom Whistler did the first drafts of various schemes, one of which was to become the infamous 'Peacock' decoration that would adorn Frederic Leyland's dining room at Prince's Gate.

Louisa Goldsmid: *Drawing Room*, *Children's Room* and *Dining Room-Gallery at Aubrey House*, watercolours
Royal Borough of Kensington and Chelsea, London

Drawn by C. F. Porden.   Etched by John Cleghorn.   Engraved by Rob.t Havell & Son, Chapel Str. Fitzroy Squ.

190

190, 191

'A grand and comfortable effect'

1823

Rutter's *Delineations of Fonthill and its Abbey* contains detailed descriptions of the rooms at Fonthill, enumerating the works of art and the furniture as well as the glories of the architecture and decoration. In the section dealing with the King Edward's Gallery (left) he is particularly eloquent on the subject of the great blue and scarlet curtains that flank the windows with their pointed Gothic arched tops, and those on the opposite wall which were to protect the books in their built-in library shelves from the effects of the light pouring in from the west-facing windows. According to Rutter, these windows admitted 'a strong influx of light, which, when the scarlet curtains are drawn, sheds a general and magical tint over every part'. Beckford himself insisted on the 'powers of drapery'. In conversation with Dr Lansdowne towards the end of his life, Beckford states that 'Nothing produces so grand and at the same time so comfortable an effect.' He goes on to boast of the Great Octagon at Fonthill, where there 'were purple curtains fifty feet long'. In the magnificently vaulted St Michael's Gallery (right) were housed 'splendid cabinets of ebony and gold, which contain within them, and bear upon their marble slabs, the most precious specimens of virtu' (p. 52).

After his departure from Fonthill, Beckford transferred his allegiance from the soaring cathedral style of the Gothic interior to an idiosyncratic Italianate manner. On Lansdowne Hill, overlooking Bath, he employed the architect H. E. Goodridge to build him a tower where he installed, in rooms of a comparatively minuscule size, the survivors from his collection of *objets d'art*, antiquities, silver-jewelled Renaissance cups and vases and oriental ceramics. The rooms here are again recorded in considerable detail, in a series of colour plates by the Bath artist Willes Maddox. Although so different in conception and purpose, Lansdowne Tower demonstrates the consistency of Beckford's decorating taste. In colouring and in the general disposition of the furniture he has remained faithful to the principles established at the Abbey. The rooms are now Italianate and yet the drapery remains opulent and bright. Rutter's account of the interior of Fonthill concludes with some 'General Observations' on the Abbey and the fact that its character is very much determined by its vast size. The one conclusion he reaches, as did Repton, was that the 'Abbey Character' of the house involved a great diminution in domestic convenience.

King Edward's Gallery and *St Michael's Gallery* from
J. Rutter, *Delineations of Fonthill and Its Abbey*, 1823

191

193

192, 193
Chinoiserie Royale 1819

In Europe the taste for chinoiserie had a long tradition. From the seventeenth century small lacquer panels had been imported to decorate furniture and the advanced technique and painting of Chinese porcelain made it prized by European collectors. The most conspicuous Chinese artefacts in the European house were hand-painted wallpapers and embroidered silks, their sinewy designs forming the perfect complement to the rococo taste of the mid-eighteenth century. By the 1780s royal and aristocratic estates all over Europe were provided with chinoiserie pavilions, garden buildings and pagodas, while the house itself had *salons* and suites of furniture in the Chinese taste. Pattern books of the eighteenth and early nineteeth centuries included everything from *cottages ornées* to fireplaces in the Chinese taste. The Pavilion at Brighton represents the high point of chinoiserie, but the Prince Regent's studied fantasy of the Celestial Dream left little more to be said and the Chinese taste fell from fashion. The Green Cabinet (left) and the Red Japan Room (above) at Frogmore were oriental fantasies in the vein of the famous Chinese rooms at Orainenbaum outside Leningrad and Drottningholm near Stockholm. These rooms tended to be decorated in the same style as elaborate pieces of chinoiserie furniture. The panels of imitation japanning, and the oriental motifs of birds and branches provided inspiration for imported oriental chinaware.

C. Wild, *The Green Cabinet* and *The Red Japan Room* for W.H. Pyne's *Royal Residences*, 1819, watercolours
Royal Library, Windsor Castle; HM *The Queen*

194

195

194, 195, 196

Schloss Rosenau, Coburg 1861

Queen Victoria made the journey to Coburg in 1845 in order to see for herself the birthplace and childhood home of her husband, Albert. She records in her diary for 20 August:

How happy, how joyful we were, on awakening, to feel ourselves here, at dear Rosenau, my Albert's birthplace, the place he most loves. . . . Before breakfast we went upstairs to where my dearest Albert and [his brother] Ernest used to live. It is quite under the roof, with a tiny little bedroom on each side, in which they both used to sleep with Florschutz their tutor. The view is too beautiful, and the paper still full of holes from their fencing; and the very same table is there on which they were dressed when little.

Ernst I, Duke of Saxe-Coburg Saalfeld, the father of Prince Albert, came into possession of Rosenau in 1806. He began Gothicizing it with the help of his sister, the future Duchess of Kent and mother to Queen Victoria; she herself painted one of the rooms with a leafy arcade. In the bedroom of Duke Ernst the Gothicizing has taken the form of small panelling in the window embrasure and neat trimmings beneath the ceiling moulding. The furniture is of a plain Biedermeier style.

F. Rothbart, watercolours
Royal Library, Windsor Castle; H M The Queen

196

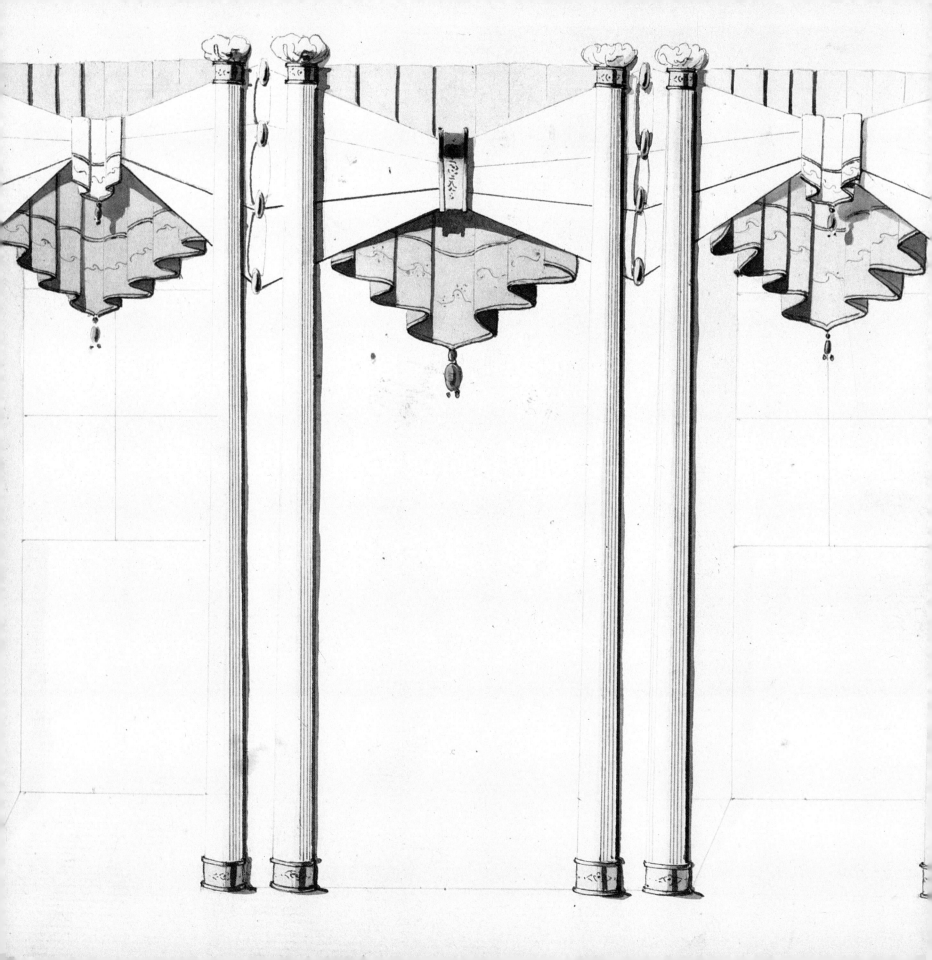

Part Two
1820-1840

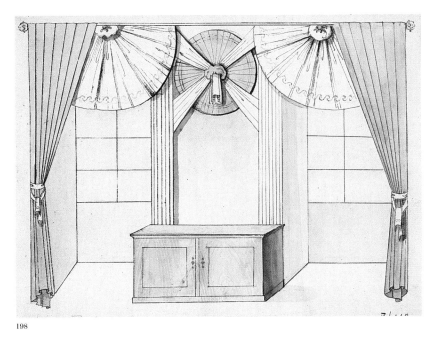

198

197, 198
Biedermeier wall treatments 1820s

The furniture factory founded by Joseph Ulrich Danhauser in 1804 was prodigiously successful. By 1808 no less than 130 workers were employed on the manufacture of all types of furniture, including gilt, silvered and bronze ornaments. The survival of a collection of some 2,500 designs representing every aspect of Danhauser's many-sided production is one of the most valuable records of the Biedermeier period.

From the design archive of the Danhauser firm
Österreichisches Museum für Angewandte Kunst, Vienna

Only with the end of the Napoleonic Wars did something approaching a coherent 'European' language in architecture and decoration re-emerge. In England the lack of communication with the fountainhead of refined taste – that is, Paris – had been a deprivation. No such deprivation existed for America, whose decorative preferences continued to be shaped by French influences throughout the century. With the restoration of the Bourbon line in France, the enduringly popular Louis Quinze and Louis Seize styles returned to favour in England and would remain the hallmark of grandiloquent respectability well into the twentieth century. This manner of interior decoration was well suited to the increasingly opulent terraced developments in London, especially the great stuccoed houses built by Thomas Cubitt in Belgravia and Pimlico. More appropriately, the Louis Quinze style was redeployed in the rebuilding of Paris's medieval centre and its expansion on the Left Bank.

During this period the taste for Gothic and Tudor styles gained ground. The fashion was accelerated by the publication in 1836 of Henry Shaw's *Specimens of Ancient Furniture*, which provided a shopping list of desirable items suitable for a mansion newly decorated in the Elizabethan and Jacobean manner. Some years earlier, in 1826, John Nash and A.C. Pugin's handsomely illustrated *Views of the Royal Pavilion* had revealed the possibilities of Eastern architecture and ornament, principally Indian and Chinese. The Brighton Pavilion had taken these intricate novelties near to extremes, and the bluff philistinism of William IV had a sobering effect on decorators intoxicated by the elegant devices of Prince Albert's seaside fantasy. Lower down the social scale, the influential morality of the Clapham Sect created an ideal of middle-class homeliness which expressed itself in a plain mahogany solidity.

The restored French monarchy inclined, for different reasons, towards restraint. The grandiose extravagance of French decoration did not reassert itself until another Napoleon captured the state. As in England, the past provided the inspiration for fan-vaulted, crocketed and stained-glass arrangements. Largely antiquarian in inspiration, this new interest in the Gothic, as exemplified in the Hôtel de Cluny, served a political cause in re-establishing links with French and Catholic traditions after the dramatic break of the Revolution and Empire.

This period was to see the first publication by A.W.N. Pugin, *Gothic Furniture in the Style of the XVth Century* (1835), and the beginning of work on one of the greatest neo-Gothic edifices, the new Palace of Westminster. This was also the time that the young Viollet-le-Duc converted to the Gothic style. While Gothic was developing in France and Britain, Biedermeier – a severe and restrained neo-classicism – was the dominant style in northern Europe.

199

199
The apartment of the
Comte de Mornay 1833

Having been in Morocco while serving as a diplomat, de Mornay acquired a taste for a North African style of decoration, which he re-created in his room in the Faubourg St-Germain. It is furnished with a cushioned ottoman, covered in the same material as the striped tenting. This 'Moroccan' style of interior is associated with the Bohemian bachelor social life of *juste-milieu* Paris under Louis-Philippe. The *Salle de Conseil* at Malmaison was decorated in the same striped and tented style by Percier and Fontaine in 1800, the time of the French adventures in North Africa.

Eugène Delacroix, oil
Musée du Louvre, Paris (Réunion des Musées Nationaux)

Biedermeier and bourgeois domesticity

The Biedermeier period is defined as spanning the years 1815 to 1848, an age dominated by the repressive policies of Metternich, the Prime Minister of Hapsburg Austria. The resulting political climate in Austria – the centre of Biedermeier culture – bred an introverted attitude that focused on family life and the cultivation of domestic accomplishments and interests. The home became the heart of Austrian life, and it was celebrated in sketches and watercolours both professional and amateur. The numerous interiors depicted during this period represent the pinnacle of achievement in the nineteenth-century art of the interior view. Rooms now began to be equipped with countless items whose function was to divert and amuse the inhabitants. To be able to pick out from among the minutely detailed contents each piece of china, each laboriously embroidered cushion, each family portrait, each flower in each vase, gives these works special documentary importance for the history of interior decoration.

In the forefront of Viennese furniture manufacturers of the period, far surpassing competitors in the scale of his production, stands Joseph Ulrich Danhauser (1780–1829). His distinctive style of furniture design is well recorded in the collection of his drawings at the Österreichisches Museum für Angewandte Kunst, Vienna. Versions of these simple linear forms can be identified in rooms all over northern Europe at this date. Less easy to trace are his idiosyncratic designs for curtains and draperies. These seem to have much in common with the film sets of Hollywood between the wars, or Parisian Art Deco. His patterns for wallpaper and fabrics seem to reach even further forward in time, to the 1950s, perhaps. This 'modernity' of expression extended to the design of silverware and ceramics and achieved, long before the advent of the Arts and Crafts movement, the ideals of

200
A Biedermeier decorative scheme   1820s
Another wall treatment from the Danhauser collection.
Österreichisches Museum für Angewandte Kunst, Vienna

203

204

203
The Tea Room in the 'Altes Palais' 1830s

The room is identified by an inscription on the original mount as being in the 'Altes Palais', presumably the Hesse palace in the Wilhelminenstrasse in Darmstadt (see plate 208). The rooms depicted in the series of pictures are all furnished and decorated in the latest style, reflecting the taste and great interest in this domestic art of the Grand Duchess Wilhelmina.

Franz Barberini, watercolour
Private collection

204
A blue neo-classical salon 1830s

The elegant furniture of the 1820s and '30s was perfectly adapted to domestic comfort and convenience. Without being in any way flimsy or insubstantial, it could very easily be moved about the room in order to create groupings or to make good use of light and heat. This room in a suite of palatial proportions is arranged for family use rather than grand receptions. Hilaire Thiery, the artist of this interior view, was a sculptor. Perhaps the reliefs set into the walls are his own work.

Hilaire Thiery, *A Salon Interior*, watercolour
Eugene Victor Thaw Collection

205

205

A red room in Germany or Russia

c. 1845

This elegantly decorated red sitting room, with its painted blind lowered, awaits an occupant. The height of the room suggests a house of some size; the furniture and decorations are modest, but the voluminous curtains, with their heavy pelmets and full-length lace under-curtains, are of princely grandeur. The ceiling decoration is typical of the private apartments in German princely residences or Russian palaces in the late 1830s and 1840s, particularly the antique-style painting in the rooms of the Winter Palace in St Petersburg, redecorated after the fire of 1837. This may be a room prepared for visitors, the empty shelves and desk ready to receive the innumerable trinkets and toilet articles of the temporary owner.

German school, *Red Interior*, gouache
Eugene Victor Thaw Collection

206

Grand Duchess Cäcilie von Oldenberg's study 1839

Such charming watercolours of the private apartments in northern European aristocratic and princely residences show how modestly they were appointed as a general rule. The furniture is no more remarkable than that of any prosperous household. Many of the accessories were made by members of the family, for example the embroidered firescreen and the sofa cushions. The room is dominated by a portrait of a uniformed officer, probably the Grand Duke himself.

Ernst Christian Anton van Lawtzow, *Arbeitszimmer der Grossherzogin Cäcilie von Oldenberg*, gouache
Eugene Victor Thaw Collection

207

208

207
Dressing room of the Tsarina 1821

Louise of Hesse (1779–1826) married Alexander, heir of Tsar Paul I of Russia, in 1793. On his accession, they took up residence in the Winter Palace. The furniture of this lofty room, with its impressive stucco-work *à l'antique* in the style of the decorations at Pavlovsk by Andrey Voronikhin or Vincenzo Brenna, is of the very plain type fashionable in Russia at this date. A particularly severe form of Biedermeier, it is often executed in birchwood with the very minimum of gilded or ebonized ornament. The incredibly sumptuous curtains and festooned pelmet with lavish fringing make a startling contrast. Both the inlaid wood floor and the vast mirror on the left are characteristic.

T. Brullo, *In the Winter Palace, St. Petersburg*
Schlossmuseum, Darmstadt

208
The Grand Duchess's living room in Darmstadt 1830s

The Grand Duchess Wilhelmina of Baden (1778–1836) was the wife of Ludwig II of Hesse and the Rhine. This view shows one of the rooms in the 'Altes Palais' in Darmstadt, one of six grand-ducal residences in the capital. Although the family owned in all thirty properties, the Grand Duchess indulged her own building and decorating wishes in the romantic Heiligenberg Castle in Hesse. This room is furnished, like others in the palace, in the fashionable neo-classical taste, with plain pieces ornamented with ormolu mounts. The windows are dressed with summer curtains of muslin.

Watercolour
Schlossmuseum, Darmstadt

209

209–214
Rooms new and old in the Munich Residenz 1830s

The dressing room of Ludwig I (overleaf, plate 214) was in the massive new building designed by Schinkel's pupil and follower Leo von Klenze in 1835. It is based on the Palazzo Pitti in Florence. Compared with the charmingly appointed dressing and sitting rooms in the old part of the building, this room has all the severe grandeur of a public or state room. In Murray's 1871 *Handbook* the new

210

apartments are described as '... a style of decoration which is a revival or imitation of the ornaments of the Loggie of the Vatican, and of a still more ancient model, the houses of Pompeii'. In this room the panels are painted with subjects taken from the plays of Aristophanes by Hiltensperger who worked with von Klenze on the New Hermitage in St Petersburg from 1839 to 1852. The dressing room of Queen Thérèse (plate 210) as it was in 1834, and the bedroom (plate 213) and sitting room (plate 209) of Princesse Mathilde painted in the same year, show the character of the private rooms in the older part of the palace. Ludwig himself had a similarly arranged room before the building of the new palace (see Peter Thornton, *Authentic Decor*, 1984, plate 299). In all three rooms the intricately draped curtains and pelmets in the French style first promoted by La Mésanger are the most striking feature; otherwise the furniture, mainly of pale or gilded wood and all upholstered in the same colour to give unity, is quite plain and modest when seen in the context of a royal palace. The 1831 view of the adjoining blue dressing room (plate 212) with its cheval glass or *psyché* prominently in the foreground shows, rather

211

212

unusually, the room in use. When Princesse Mathilde married into the Bavarian royal family in 1826 her trousseau was displayed in an elegant *salon à l'antique* (plate 211) with sculptures in niches and *trompe l'oeil* reliefs in black on panelled walls decorated in grey, white and gold, like the decorations designed for the Yelagin Palace in St Petersburg in 1817 by Carli Rossi.

Watercolours by F.X. Nachtmann:
The Sitting Room of Princesse Mathilde, Munich, 1834 (plate 209); *The Dressing Room of Queen Thérèse of Bavaria*, 1842 (plate 210); *The Trousseau of Princesse Mathilde of Bavaria*, 1826 (plate 211); *The Dressing Room of Princesse Mathilde, Munich*, 1831 (plate 212): *The Bedroom of Princesse Mathilde*, 1834 (plate 213)
Schlossmuseum, Darmstadt
The Dressing Room of King Ludwig I at the Munich Residence, 1836
Eugene Victor Thaw Collection

214

213

215

216

215

A Biedermeier living room in Vienna 1841

The flowery patterns – particularly characteristic of Biedermeier taste is the tiny all-over pattern on the two upholstered bench-seats against the walls – and the muslin curtains, combined with very unpretentious and unornamented furniture, make up a scheme entirely typical of this place and period.

M. Sekim, watercolour
Eugene Victor Thaw Collection

216

Leo von Klenze's Study 1864

The decoration of a ceiling in the Pompeian style became a hallmark of Klenze's schemes. Though he spent his professional life creating effects of elegance and opulence for German princes and Russian autarchs (see plates 209–14), his study displays his own preference for Biedermeier taste with pale, practical furniture and a geometric parquet floor overlayed with needlework rugs.

Angelo Jank, watercolour
Staatliche Graphische Sammlung, Munich (Artothek)

217

217
A neo-classical salon in Naples 1829

This watercolour by L. Iely came from an album as assembled by Comte Paul de Gontaut and his wife, the former Princess Hélène Troubetskoy. It is inscribed on the original mount '*Salon à Naples au Palais Satriano chez Mdme Candide*', and dated. The seventeenth-century Palazzo Satriano was enlarged in the eighteenth century by the Neapolitan architect Ferdinando Sanfelice (1675–1748). The decoration in the neo-classical style was undertaken by Gaetano Genovese (1795–after 1860) who came to Naples from Eboli in 1822. This example of severely plain neo-classical decoration with a whole suite of matching furniture makes a prominent feature of the ceiling.

Eugene Victor Thaw Collection

218
Exporting English taste 1840s

Everything about this room suggests an English occupant except the room itself. On the walls are a number of horse paintings, and a small sculpture of a horse stands on the glass-fronted eighteenth-century English cabinet in the corner. A chair, in simulated bamboo, is typical of the English taste for chinoiserie promoted by the Pavilion at Brighton. By the sofa, in a blue cover and standing against the wall, is an English Regency sofa table. The table in the foreground is laden with English-looking books, and the flowers are arranged in the sort of informal manner more in line with English taste. However, the room itself is entirely continental in character: the windows open inwards like those in continental houses, and through the door can be seen closed external shutters, which are very rare in England. The window looks on to an Italianate palazzo framed by the sprig-patterned voile curtains trimmed with black fringe that feature so frequently in Italian houses in the mid-nineteenth century.

Unknown artist, watercolour
Victoria and Albert Museum, London

218

219

219

A sitting room with blue curtains, possibly German *c.*1850

Much of the decoration and furnishing of this room seems to have been contrived by amateur hands. The curtains, pelmets and matching bookshelf *lambrequins* have an engagingly handmade look. The artless disarray of the cushions and the tabletops suggests a room in constant use and also a degree of sophistication in the unknown artist, who has set out to achieve something more evocative than a mere record of colours and contents. The name Pauline is inscribed on the mount.

Unknown German artist, watercolour
William Drummond, London

220

A green-and-white boudoir *c.*1840

Here is another example of the tall, narrow rooms characteristic of the private living quarters of princely residences in northern Europe. The way in which these rooms are furnished and decorated is very personal with no attempt at grand effects, but the number of pictures and ornaments suggests the greater riches in the public reception rooms. This room is a combined bedroom and boudoir equipped with the materials for sewing and painting and with a writing desk laden with ornaments and family pictures. The curtains that can be closed to screen the bed are drawn back, making, with the *lambrequin* in a Moorish style, a frame for the scene beyond.

Unknown Austrian artist, *Green-and-White Interior*
Eugene Victor Thaw Collection

221

221, 222

Adjoining rooms in
Schloss Fischbach *c.* 1840

In 1822 Prince Wilhelm of Prussia, brother of King Friedrich Wilhelm III, bought the sixteenth-century castle of Fischbach in Silesia as a summer residence. In 1838 he started to rebuild and redecorate the rather old-fashioned castle, using plans and sketches provided by the German architect Karl Friedrich Schinkel. Externally Fischbach was Gothicized and given a Jacobean-style tower; the garden buildings were also in the Gothic taste. The interior is an attractive undogmatic mixture of Gothic and classical, with Jacobean touches and floral carpets. In the 'Red Room' the furniture is a somewhat heavy interpretation of late Renaissance taste, with handsome neo-Gothic chandeliers. The upper panes of the windows have insets of heraldic glass like so many English houses at this date. In the 'Blue Room' the effect is lightened by Schinkel's neo-classical chairs drawn up to the table and the many vases of flowers. The chairs are of the type designed in 1825 for the Schloss Glienicke and also used in the Schloss Charlottenhof in Berlin. In the window a seat in the antique style has been contrived, mimicking an earlier version in marble designed by Schinkel about 1815. In both rooms the windows are dressed for summer with curtains of muslin or voile instead of the heavy draperies that might have been expected to accompany the stiff, neo-Gothic pelmets decorated with large tassels.

Friederich Wilhelm Klose, *The 'Red Room'* and *The 'Blue Room' at Schloss Fischbach*, watercolours
Hildegard Fritz Denneville

222

223

223
The 'Chamois Room' at the Kronprinzenpalais, Berlin *c.* 1840

The room was given this name in 1793 when it was decorated with a striped chamois-coloured damask. This was the year in which the palace was given to King Friederich Wilhelm III of Prussia. He redecorated the palace completely and then lived there until his death in 1840. The magnificent glass chandelier was designed by Karl Friedrich Schinkel in 1809. The lustres hang from a ring at the top decorated with dancing nymphs. The lower ring is of palmettes and lotus blooms. The Chamois Room was used as a gaming room but the furnishings, and the closely hung copies after paintings by Raphael, hardly suggest such a light-hearted purpose. The parrots in their gilded cages were given to the King's relations after his death.

Friederich Wilhelm Klose, *The 'Chamois Room'*, *View towards the Study*, watercolour
Hildegard Fritz Denneville, by courtesy of Marianne Feilchenfeldt, Zurich

224

A bourgeois interior   Mid-19th century

This scheme, while retaining many of the more attractive characteristics of the Biedermeier taste, is beginning to show signs of a heavier-handed manner based on a revived, but reinterpreted, rococo style. The wallpaper is charmingly unpretentious and the ceiling not yet very heavily ornamented, but the flourished and curving lines of the neo-rococo are already more than suggested in the design of the furniture. That these more extravagant pieces have been introduced into an earlier and rather more severe scheme is suggested by the uniform row of very plainly framed prints above the piano, and the unadorned double door frame painted in two tones of grey with its panels of mirror glass. The simple white curtains have been given additional importance by looping heavy tassels from the rail. The furniture is of the type that was to be developed in a more elaborately decorated form in America by the German *émigré* cabinet-maker John Henry Belter. In origin the style is French, but Belter was to load the frames of his distinctive pieces with the most intricate pierced and carved ornament. The wallpaper in this room is also French in inspiration, possibly even French-manufactured. Papers with sprays of naturalistic flowers on a creamy white ground, designed to be finished with a border as seen here, were popular in the 1820s.

Unknown German or Austrian artist, watercolour
Victoria and Albert Museum, London

225

A Biedermeier interior   1830s

In an austerely plain room a heterogenous collection of rather elegant but severe furniture is disposed informally on a geometric-patterned parquet floor. The inevitable mirror is placed between a pair of windows with the light voile curtains that feature in so many interiors of this date and type.

Unknown German or Austrian artist, watercolour
Victoria and Albert Museum, London

224

225

226

A bedroom in a Russian *dacha* 1839

Life in a *dacha* (country cottage) was informal and unpretentious. Among the unmatching oddments of furniture is a chair (on the right in front of the desk) that appears to be an example from the Tula steelworks. Ornamental items in Tula steel were highly prized curiosities. Miss Catherine Wilmot was presented with a pair of candlesticks during her stay in Russia in 1816, and greatly cherished them. Pieces of this distinctive furniture with damascened decoration survive in many of the imperial Russian palaces. A feature of many of these *dachas* was the bare walls, the wooden construction being emphasized rather than concealed with plaster or paperhanging.

Unknown Russian artist, watercolour
Eugene Victor Thaw Collection

227

228

227, 228

Two rooms occupied by an English visitor in the Palazzo Stiozzi Ridolfi, Florence 1833

The Palazzo Stiozzi Ridolfi, now known as the Palazzo Ginori Venturi, is in the via della Scala in Florence, and was built in the famous garden of the Rucellai, which at one time belonged to Bianca Cappello, wife of Francesco de' Medici. At the beginning of the nineteenth century the gardens were remodelled for Giuseppe Stiozzi Ridolfi by Luigi Digny, and in 1832, the year before these interiors were painted, were reproduced in the *Vedute del giardino del Marchese Stiozzi Ridolfi già Orti Oricellari* (1832). The garden, with its colossal figure of Polyphemus by Novelli and other massize sculptures, is one of the sights of

Florence. In these watercolours it is apparent that the fine Renaissance rooms of the Palazzo have been redecorated in the Empire style: the bed is hung with draperies ruched over rails with decorative finials in the form of spearheads. The shape of the bedroom windows, not being appropriate to the magnificent curtains with their crossover festoons in blue and white, has simply been disregarded. Similarly, the great red velvet window hangings in the sitting room rise far above the top of the rather small window. Whereas the curtains and their pelmets are rather too handsome and important for the rooms, the furniture is too modest and too small; but, being in a taste that was currently very popular, the scheme no doubt pleased the inhabitants of the moment.

Unknown artist, watercolours
Private collection

229

229, 230
Refurnishing a palazzo *c.*1850

These two rooms in an Italian palazzo have been furnished, like those in the Florentine Palazzo Ridolfi Stiozzi, with characteristic disregard for their character and proportions. The magnificently decorated coved ceilings and the patterned floors are almost insignificant in schemes with matching walls, curtains, bed hangings and upholstery. Some earlier pieces of furniture have been retained and are interspersed with newly acquired pieces.

Unknown artist, *Two Rooms in an Italian Palazzo*,
watercolour and bodycolour
Victoria and Albert Museum, London

230

231

A palatial French billiard room

1840s

Extensive building, reconstruction and redecoration in Berlin, Leningrad and Munich under K. F. Schinkel and Leo von Klenze produced suites of magnificent apartments decorated in the 'antique' taste which were very influential on the Continent. The inspiration for this billiard room can be traced to the Empire period, its style partly neo-Greek, partly derived from the newly excavated monuments of Roman antiquity, notably Pompeii, and partly influenced by Renaissance decorations in the Vatican carried out under Raphael's direction. (These had been reproduced in a remarkable series of colour plates published by Vasi in the eighteenth century.) The chairs are based on the 'Roman' form fashionable in France in the 1820s and 1830s. However, certain elements, for example the heavy arched fireplace, suggest the next decade.

Decorative scheme by Léger
Musée des Arts Décoratifs, Paris (Sully-Jaulmes)

243

243, 244
Chatsworth and the Bachelor Duke 1822

When the sixth Duke of Devonshire succeeded his father

in 1811 he embarked on a great programme of rebuilding, redecorating and refurbishing the family's various properties. Devonshire House in Piccadilly was redecorated almost throughout. E. Beresford Chancellor wrote of the Saloon of Devonshire House as 'in point of elaborate decoration the most remarkable. We seem here to be entering one of those gorgeous apartments which the wealth and luxury of Venice, at its great period, could alone conceive, and the pencil of Veronese was alone to perpetuate' (*The Private Palaces of London*, 1908, p. 245). This watercolour of 1822 shows the furniture still in a highly formal arrangement. A century later the magnificent house was demolished and the works of art, furniture and some of the curtains went to Chatsworth. The suite of seat furniture in plate 243 is now in the library there. On Chatsworth the sixth Duke lavished some of his most ambitious decorating schemes. The furniture, in figured woods with gold or black trim, was supplied by Crace. Charles Greville, in 1843, admitted of Chatsworth:

[It was] very magnificent, but I looked back with regret to the

house in its unfinished state, when we lived in these spacious cheerful rooms looking to the South, which are now quite useless, being so gorgeously furnished with velvet and silk, and marble tables, but unoccupied, and the windows closed lest the sun should spoil the finery with which the apartments are decorated. The comfort we had then has been ill exchanged for the magnificence which has replaced it, and the Duke has made the house so large that he cannot afford to live in it, and never remains there above two or three months of the year. (Greville, *Memoirs, 1875–87*, vol. v, entry for 16 October 1843.)

William Henry Hunt, *The Saloon at Devonshire House* and *The Morning Room at Chatsworth*, watercolours *Devonshire Collection, Chatsworth, reproduced by permission of the Trustees of the Chatsworth Settlement*

245

246

245, 246
A squire's library   1836–7

I wish you could see my library here. I think it a model for a book-drawing-room; it is but just furnished, and all in the very cheapest way; but everyone who has seen or sat in it are delighted with it. It is rather odd, and would frighten poor Smirke [the architect] by its angles and irregularities; but it is warm and comfortable and holds 3,000 volumes without diminishing the size of the room, and without harming, I think, any of the sombre formality of a library.

So wrote a Berkshire squire to Sir Robert Peel in 1832. J.W. Croker lived at West Moulsey, not so very distant from the Walsh family at Binfield who installed their library-drawing room four years later. The room has one free-standing bookcase of an earlier date and a built-in one which has been given some character by the centre section that stands proud. With the introduction of a more comfortable library *à la* Repton, the newly dis- covered pleasures of fiction could be indulged. The furniture is pattern-book taste of the 1820s; the Grecian- style couch and the bobbin-turned chairs are such as to be found in the Gillows catalogues. The draperies of the windows show the importance attached to imaginative arrangement of hangings to be found in all house- furnisher's manuals.

Edward Hassell, *Two Views of the Library at Binfield*, watercolours

Formerly Hazlitt, Gooden & Fox Limited, London

247

248

247, 248, 249
Three views by Mary Ellen Best
1837–40

Mary Ellen Best's work has been discovered comparatively recently. Like that of many other interior view painters, the bulk of it remained in the possession of her descendants, appropriately as the accumulated watercolours constitute a pictorial diary of the artist's life. Mary Ellen Best was born in York in 1809 into a cultivated, well-to-do family; her father was a doctor and her mother the daughter of a Yorkshire landowner. She was given excellent tuition in drawing and painting at her first boarding school, and when she left school to return to live with her mother and sister in York she set up as a watercolour painter, executing portraits and, for her own instruction and amusement, the highly detailed interior views that are now so prized by collectors. Her life at home in York as well as the family homes supplied her with subject matter, for example her own painting room or a farm kitchen at Clifton, as well as fascinating glimpses of such great country houses as Castle Howard, Howsham Hall, Middleton Hall and Moulton Hall. Her mother's family home, Langton Hall, is frequently depicted; later Continental travels and her marriage to a German schoolmaster, Johann Sarg, have supplied us with a unique record of interiors of guesthouses and hotels succeeded by a series of modest but attractive family rooms furnished with the Sargs' joint belongings – among which can be recognized gifts from members of the family in Yorkshire and other favourite possessions, which survived the moves from one house to another. Mary Ellen Best seems to have given up painting in her forties. Although there may be albums of work still to be discovered, her biographer, Caroline Davidson (*The World of Mary Ellen Best*, 1985), believes that she did not continue painting beyond the mid-century. She lived to a great age, dying in 1891 when she was eighty-one years old. The view of Colonel Norcliffe's study at Langton Hall shows Mary Ellen's uncle Norcliffe after he had retired from the Army. He had inherited Langton Hall on the death of his mother, Mary Ellen's grandmother, in 1835, but the paintings of military subjects must surely reflect his own tastes. In the painting room, Mary Ellen is wearing mourning for her mother. The cabinet in the right-hand alcove came from her grandmother. The dog, Azor, she brought back from Frankfurt. This room and the drawing room are in the Best family house in York. Mary Ellen was married from this house in 1840 and spent the time immediately after her wedding here.

249

Colonel Norcliffe's Study at Langton Hall, 1837–9;
Painting Room in Our House at York, 1838;
Our Drawing Room at York, 1838–40; watercolours
York City Art Gallery

scheme and flower-pattern carpet as was to be found in rooms of Carlo Rastrelli's original Winter Palace. The carpets in these rooms are laid over geometric-inlay wood floors. In the 1850s and '60s a team of artists recorded the Winter Palace's interiors with minute skill, allowing every detail to be identified. Though the works of art and objects on display in the public rooms are important, their settings are stamped with an imperial magnificence appropriate to the showpiece of the capital, and it is only the private rooms that show a personal identity which makes them interesting.

Edward Hau, watercolour
Schlossmuseum, Darmstadt

271

Living with the past 1857

The blue-and-white Cavalier Room in Frederick the Great's summer palace Schloss Sansouci, occupied by Elizabeth, the wife of Friedrich Wilhelm IV (reigned 1840–57), retained its original rococo decoration. She installed up-to-date furniture and her own personal effects. The furniture has been covered in blue-and-white striped satin, nicely complementing the original scheme. The desk is cluttered with the inevitable accumulation of mementoes, which supply an individual and personal character to a room that was otherwise more historical than cosy.

Watercolour, signed and dated 'F. von Arnim '57'
Hildegard Fritz Denneville, by courtesy of Marianne Feilchenfeldt, Zurich

271

272

272
The Cupid Salon in the Winter Palace 1872

This lavishly gilded rococo interior by Luigi Premazzi is a version of the Cupid Salon on the ground floor of the Winter Palace painted by Edward Hau in 1868 (reproduced in *Hermitage Interiors*, 1983, plate 99). Like Hau (see plate 270) Premazzi executed a number of interiors of the Hermitage which are preserved there, as it is now a museum. He was Milanese by birth, but later moved to St Petersburg and set up a drawing school.

Inscribed on the reverse *Mon Salon, Au Palais d'Hiver,* signed and dated, watercolour
Private collection

273
Redecoration in crimson 1855

This is the Rubens Room at Windsor Castle, so-called because all but one of the paintings are by Peter Paul Rubens. Pieces from Carlton House can be recognized among the mainly French furnishings. In the window, for example, stands the blue Chinese vase with gilt-bronze mounts, added by P.-P. Thomire in 1812, which once appeared in the Rose Satin Drawing Room. So, too, did the gilded griffin tripods. The decoration of the room was carried out during the reorganization of the Castle by Wyatville (nephew of English architect James Wyatt), but the crimson wall-hangings and furniture were installed in 1855 for the visit of the Emperor Napoleon III.

Photograph Weidenfeld & Nicolson Archive

A Russian salon 1850s

The nineteenth-century taste for elaboration in furnishing and decorating naturally encompassed upholstery. The deep buttoning evident in the seat furniture of this mid-century Russian drawing room is typical. The Empress Eugénie had introduced chairs upholstered in this way into the reception rooms at the Tuileries and at St-Cloud, where they mingled uneasily with Empire decorations carried out by Napoleon I. Here, the crimson buttoned upholstery fits much more appropriately with the sinuous curves of the Louis XVI desk, commodes and fireplace. The rooms decorated for the Empress Marie at the Winter Palace in St Petersburg mix just such crimson damask upholstery with the same kind of flower-patterned carpet in an eighteenth-century style setting.

Russian school, watercolour
Photograph courtesy of A la Vieille Russie

274

275

276

275, 276

Alexander II's private apartments, Gatchina 1890s

Catherine the Great gave Gatchina to her lover Peter Orlov; after his death she gave it to her heir Paul I. In spite of its connection with Peter Orlov, the murderer of Paul's supposed father, Gatchina was Paul's favourite residence. Situated some distance from St Petersburg, in a setting of parkland and lakes, Gatchina remained a country retreat of the imperial family throughout the nineteenth century. Alexander's rooms were left unchanged after his death. Visitors were surprised to see the almost spartan nature of the imperial living quarters at Gatchina. Alexander II was seemingly indifferent to luxury or modern convenience. After the Revolution, Sir William Martin Conway explored the Tsar's cramped quarters in the Winter Palace in Leningrad:

He seems to have worked in his bedroom, or slept in his study, whichever way you like to put it. The bed was hidden behind a piece of wall round which you could walk to either end of it. . . . There is a washing-stand close to his desk. On the latter is a calendar still showing the date of his last day, his pens, ink-pots, blotting-pad, photographs, and all his little things just as he left them. It is an ugly room and contains nothing in it of value. The blue bedroom of his wife is adjacent. It has no view. Then comes a gold and red reception room from which you can look out, and then a dining room with a top light rather well decorated in plaster work. The suite also contained one or two rooms for secretaries and books; that is all.

What mystified the English baronet most about Nicholas I and Alexander II's private rooms was the contrast between the public and private styles. They were, as Conway puts it, 'the wealthiest family in the world. Whatever they desired they could have. They possessed endless treasures of matchless beauty and rarity.' And yet what 'they actually did was to hunt down out some obscure set of small rooms in some remote corner of the huge building and to furnish them in the simplest, least tasteful, and most bourgeois style of their days. (*Art Treasures of the Soviet Union*, 1925, quoted in Laurence Kelly, *St Petersburg. A traveller's companion*, 1981, pp. 88–9.)

Alexandre Benois, watercolours
Eugene Victor Thaw Collection

277

277

A grand Russian room *c.*1860

The royal taste of mid-eighteenth century France dominated the decorative style of grand reception rooms throughout Europe until the last years of the nineteenth century. These white and gold rooms, the furniture typically upholstered in a delicate, pale version of Aubusson tapestry, with naturalistic flower bouquets on a white ground, imported an air of fragile elegance to rooms planned principally for after-dinner conversation.

Max Sadovnikov, pen and watercolour
Photograph courtesy of A la Vieille Russie

278

278, 279, 280

Before the fire at Capesthorne 1843

Capesthorne Hall, home of the Bromley-Davenports, is now a gabled, pinnacled, turreted, mullioned Tudor-bethan mansion. The transformation of the eighteenth-century Palladian house was undertaken in the first instance by Edward Blore for Edward Davenport (1778–1847), who succeeded his father in 1837. The works took from 1837 to 1839 and included a vast conservatory, allegedly to Paxton's design. In 1861 fire gutted the centre of the house. Edward Davenport's successor, Andrew Henry Davenport, engaged Anthony Salvin to carry out the reconstruction. These watercolours show the rooms as completed by Blore. The Great Hall (above right), however, survives today much as depicted in 1843.

The upper parts of the window are filled with heraldic glass arranged by Thomas Willement. Blore's plaster ceiling survives, but the plain chimneypiece has been replaced by a larger confection that includes two early Flemish figures which had once supported the two-decker pulpit in the chapel. The hall was used as a billiard room as well as a sculpture gallery. The Drawing Room (below) was entirely destroyed in the 1861 fire. Salvin did not attempt to re-create its sky-painted ceiling; instead, he put up the present Jacobean-style one. The West Library (left) was two drawing rooms knocked into one and separated by an ante-room from the new Drawing Room. Beyond this suite of rooms stood the Great Conservatory. The famous Davenport book collection was largely assembled by Edward. He also collected bronzes and the Etruscan votive heads which line the tops of the bookcases. The decoration of these rooms is of the 1780s, possibly by James Wyatt, and was left untouched by Blore. These pictures are by James Johnson of Macclesfield, a joiner employed as part of the 150-strong workforce that remodelled Capesthorne under Blore.

The West Library, Drawing Room and *Hall and Entrance Corridor*, watercolours
Col. H. Bramley Davenport

280

279

282

281, 282
Knebworth House, Hertfordshire

Late 19th century

These photographs show the interiors at Knebworth as they appeared after the alterations undertaken by Mrs Lytton Bulwer, from 1811, and by her son the writer, Edward Bulwer Lytton, from 1843 onwards. No contemporary photographs survive at Knebworth of John Crace's State Drawing Room, one of the finest extant examples of the Victorian Gothic interior. These photo-graphs are interesting because they show rooms now much altered. The Staircase Hall has been tidied up, as has the Banqueting Hall. In the early years of this century, Lutyens worked on alterations at Knebworth – he had married Lady Emily Lytton, the daughter of the house, in 1897. In 1909 he wrote to his wife: 'The Tudor Corridor [is] a puzzle indeed.' The entrance hall screen of archways is appropriate to the predominately Tudor character of the house; it is surprising that such an essay in historicism should have puzzled the architect.

The Hon. David Lytton Cobbold of Knebworth House

287

287, 288, 289
Curiosities for the antiquarian interior Mid-19th century

In the worst excesses of antiquarianism, rooms could become domestic 'Old Curiosity Shops'; indeed, it was from such shops that many of the objects that filled the Tudor Revival country house had originated. Such an assemblage filled the rooms at Horton Hall near Bradford in the mid-century. Cattermole's illustrations to the Dickens novel bring to life contemporary descriptions of brokers' shops. When the Pre-Raphaelite painter R.B. Martineau came to portray the background to *Kit's Writing Lesson*, he added a number of fragments of stained glass of the kind that had been keenly sought by collectors since the mid-century to embellish the new style of Gothic window.

The bedroom window at Horton Hall has been so embellished, the roundels and panes of ancient glass being suspended in front of the plain lights of the window. A great carved oak Tudor bed dominates this room, but otherwise, as elsewhere in the house, the furniture is a random mixture of old and new, like the house itself.

288

289

Indeed, in the drawing room (above and above left) there are Chinese and Japanese curiosities and furniture, low tables with fretted ornament and a painted fan with an African fly-whisk hung over it. The room bears many of the signs of antiquarian fervour, notably the Sinhalese carved black sofas and chairs of which there seems to have been an unending supply for buyers in search of 'medieval' furniture.

Unknown artist, watercolours, mid-19th century
Clarendon Gallery, London

290

291

290, 291

Osborne House 1851

Built as a seaside residence at the Queen's own expense, Osborne was never a palace. It was designed by Prince Albert and Thomas Cubitt, and building lasted from 1845 to 1851. It was in the Italianate style which was popular for country houses and was regarded as Sir Charles Barry's forte. However, here Albert did most of the design himself, leaving the details to Cubitt; a working arrangement that would have been impossible had Barry been the architect employed. After the Prince's death in 1861 the Queen left Osborne largely unaltered as a pious act of memory to its designer and her lost happiness. Today, despite alterations for opening it to the public, the furniture of the dining room is disposed much as it was in the nineteenth century. The furniture was supplied by Holland & Sons. The large family group is a Winterhalter painting of 1846. Over the door is a portrait of the young Duchess of Kent, Albert's aunt and the Queen's mother. The royal dressing rooms at Osborne were hung with works purchased by Albert, who was a knowledgeable collector and patron of contemporary artists, and Queen Victoria. The Queen's tastes had been less intellectually formed and her preferences probably ran parallel with those of her subjects.

James Roberts, *The Dining Room*, watercolour
Jeremy Maas Gallery, London
James Roberts, *The Dressing Room*, watercolour
Royal Library, Windsor Castle; H M The Queen

292

Decoration on scientific principles at Pitfour 1890s

The decorations at Pitfour Castle were, like those at Holyrood, the work of David Ramsay Hay. His subtle but rich effects, with their highlights of gold, provide a background of greater sumptuousness than the rather miscellaneous assemblage of lightweight – even cheap – furniture deserves. Hay's schemes transcended the conventions of the Scottish Baronial or neo-Gothic styles, but their subtleties were to pass over the heads of later generations, who saw the rich dark colours as too sombre and could not – as with a full-blown Gothic extravaganza – regard the rooms as 'amusing'.

Photograph, *c.* 1890
Perth Museum and Art Gallery

293

293, 294

Rance's Folly 1850s

The large red brick house in Cambridge known locally as Rance's Folly was built by a solicitor, Henry Rance, in the 1850s. It contained his office as well as accommodation for a procession of guests whom the open-handed owner encouraged to visit him. In the context of a mid-nineteenth-century university town, the catalogue of its amenities is extraordinary and anachronistic, reminiscent of a Beverly Hills lifestyle of our own day. There were several lifts, a swimming pool, four bathrooms and the vast luxury of central heating; there were even rumours of young guests playing tennis on the roof. The rooms themselves show little flair but for the unique 'mathematical' ceiling. The house was demolished in 1957; these photographs were taken by Rance's son-in-law, Rev. F.C. Lambert.

Dining Room and Library of 62 St Andrew's Street, Cambridge
Cambridgeshire Collection, Cambridge Folk Museum

295

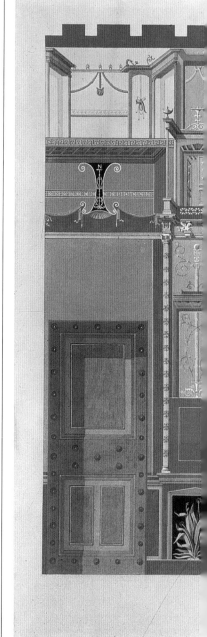

296

295, 296
A Pompeian palace in Paris 1856

The Maison Pompéienne was built for Prince Napoleon (1822–91), brother of Princesse Mathilde, in the avenue Montaigne in 1856. It was sold after only ten years, and in 1891 it was demolished. The Prince was a patron and collector, and numbered many writers and artists among his entourage. This exotic milieu was designed almost in the spirit of a museum to house his collection of works of art and antiquities. The commission for this neo-classical edifice was originally given to the German architect Hittorff, but he was too occupied to complete the work, and in the event the actual construction of the Maison Pompéienne was achieved by Alfred Normand, a young architect recently returned from Italy who was particularly interested in Pompeii and the excavations there. A number of Normand's drawings for the commission survive, including these highly finished schemes for the decoration in the Pompeian style of the Atrium (right) and Vestibule (above). Jacques-Ignace Hittorff is the link between this late polychromatic and highly ornamental neo-classicism of the mid-century, and the spare, pale elegance of the First Empire. He studied architecture under Charles Percier at the Ecole des Beaux-Arts and

drawing under Jean-Baptiste Isabey. In 1821 he was in Germany, where he made contact with Schinkel, and during the next four years he travelled in Italy with Karl Ludwig von Zanth, becoming increasingly absorbed in the study of polychromy in the architecture of ancient Greece. His influential *Architecture polychrome chez les Grecs* (1830) was to be one of the sources drawn upon by Owen Jones for his stunning polychrome schemes for Paxton's Crystal Palace in 1851. When the house was put up for sale in 1866 it was bought by a group including Arsène Houssaye, the man of letters, and Ferdinand de Lesseps, who built the Suez Canal, and it was turned for a while into a museum. Hardly any of the historical and classical revival palaces of mid-century Paris have survived: the Maison Gothique, also in the avenue Montaigne, built in 1848, was demolished before the Maison Pompéienne; M. de Lesseps' Pavillon Mauresque, nearly next door to the Maison Gothique, was also demolished. The much earlier Maison Grecque, built in 1812 in imitation of the Erechtheion in Athens, and occupied in the 1850s by the Comtesse de Montijo, mother of the Empress Eugénie, was demolished in 1860.

Alfred Normand, Two project drawings, watercolours
Musée des Arts Décoratifs, Paris

ATRIUM — FACE COTE DE LA SALLE A MANGER

297

297
A neo-Greek New York house

c. 1845

A 'Greek-revival double parlour' in the John Cox Stevens House was designed by the celebrated American architect Alexander Jackson Davis. It is sparsely furnished, but with pieces of great interest, based on designs by Thomas Hope. The 'Klismos'-style chairs are taken from the Second Vase Room and the side table from the Picture Gallery in the Duchess Street mansion, and were featured among the illustrations to Hope's *Household Furniture and Interior Decoration* (1807), as were the firescreen and the tripod supporting a vase; the tables are the same as the ones Hope had in his boudoir at The Deepdene. The sofa is also based on a design by Hope. Hope might well have deplored the mixing of elements that in his own house were deployed with archaeological exactitude. The effect achieved here is grand and chilly, without the domesticating clutter that humanized the scheme.

Watercolour
By courtesy of The New-York Historical Society

Second Empire Taste 1844

298–304

Schemes by Léger, a successful Parisian decorator, showing the Imperial Taste of the Second Empire as adapted to a private mansion. The rooms include a ballroom (plate 302), with seating in stages for spectators. These tiered *banquettes* were a common nineteenth-century feature found, for instance, in the Red Ballroom at Buckingham Palace in the 1850s. Then there is a more intimate room with a table and upholstered settles in the Renaissance style (plate 304), where the older party-goers would have played whist, as well as the usual private and reception rooms. The colour schemes are conventional: airy blues and whites for boudoir and bedroom (plates 298, 299), rich velvety reds and bright golds for the public reception rooms (plate 301), and green and gold for the dining room (plate 303).

Léger, watercolours
Musée des Arts Décoratifs, Paris (Sully-Jaulmes)

299

298

300

301

302

303

304

305

A Royal Sculptor 1840s

The *salon* of Princesse Marie d'Orleans in the Tuileries shows the influence of the latest 'Cluny' style, here deployed with the assurance of the accomplished artist rather than the stylized confusion of the antiquarian. The Normal Revival style was the most enduring of the many revived styles of nineteenth-century France; its solidity appealed to the newly prosperous bourgeois gentilhomme.

Prosper Lafaye, oil
Musée des Arts Décoratifs, Paris (Sully-Jaulmes)

306, 307

The *juste milieu* at the Tuileries

1842

Eugène Lami's projects for the decoration of the Duc de Nemours' apartments in the Tuileries are in marked contrast to the cool imperial blues of the next decades. The Château d'Eu was depicted with its rich neo-Renaissance decor at this date, also by Lami (see plate 261).

Eugène Lami, watercolour
Musée des Arts Décoratifs, Paris (Sully-Jaulmes)

306

307

308

308, 309
A family gathering around the table 1845/1857

In the eighteenth century, most public rooms of the house contained furniture ranged around the walls and the centre was left almost empty. Nineteenth-century domestic arrangements created 'islands' for different activities and made the table a feature of great importance. Early nineteenth-century interior views, if they show people, depict the family clustered around the table sharing the light of a lamp for their different occupations which would include reading and sewing, letter-writing or drawing.

Charles Augustus Carter and his wife are shown in circumstances not dissimilar to those of the family below, but the treatment of both sitters and their setting is less informal. The suggestion of a more indulgent regime is subtly conveyed in Kyhn's household, where as the Carters pose stiffly for posterity in their well-appointed room.

Nicholas Biddle Kittell, *Mr and Mrs Charles Augustus Carter*, 1845
Museum of the City of New York
Wilhelm Kyhn, *Interior with Artist's Family*, etching, 1857
Statens Museum for Kunst, Copenhagen

310

310
A book-lined study *c.* 1850

Books dominate the room to the exclusion of all conscious decoration. Even the chimneypiece has been annexed to provide three more shelves. The artist of this picture was R. Parminter Cuff, an architect who also made engravings after Ruskin's drawings for the illustrations to *The Stones of Venice* (1851).

R. Parminter Cuff, *Lady Writing in a Study*
William Drummond, London

311

312

311, 312
Pre-Raphaelite precision 1849–50

These two Pre-Raphaelite works are uncharacteristically devoid of narrative or symbolism, but the minutely observed detail employed by the artist at this date has left us with an unusually faithful record of the type and disposition of this family's possessions. James Wyatt was a collector and art-dealer in Oxford. He carried on his business at 115 High Street, where he also lived. The setting for Wyatt himself gives a clue to his tastes; in contrast to that of his daughter, he is shown with the furniture and china (in the glass-fronted cupboard behind him) of an earlier date. This window embrasure must have been his preferred sitting place, as the damask-covered wing chair is furnished with a footrest and a convenient table, circular and possibly of eighteenth-century date, supported on a delicate turned pedestal. Eliza Wyatt, shown with her younger daughter, is depicted in a setting with newer, heavier furnishings, a work table of much more massive construction than Mr Wyatt's table and a large sofa. Above the sofa are hung prints after Raphael – two circular compositions of Madonnas that both echo and contrast with the studied realism of the portrait's subjects – and Leonardo da Vinci's *Last Supper*, a taste entirely consistent with the ambience of a cultivated collector.

John Everett Millais, *Mrs Wyatt Jr. and Her Daughter*, 1850
Private collection
John Everett Millais, *James Wyatt and His Granddaughter*, 1849
Tate Gallery, London

313
An autocrat in his drawing room
1852–3

This painting shows Henry Cole and his family in the drawing room of his house, 1 The Terrace, Kensington High Street, London. The house dates from 1740, and shows the eminently adaptable nature of the Georgian town house. A simple room, the main effect relying on the architecture's proportions, it tallies with Cole's known preferences in interior design. The walls are painted in a pale stone colour in keeping with the architectonic early nineteenth-century fireplace surround; pictures are symmetrically arranged. Unusually for the date, some are framed with plain gilt square-section mouldings and wide mounts. The chintz curtains are held back with ties, permitting a glimpse of the panelled shutter cases. The sash windows have retained the original twelve-pane models, and hence there would have been no need for blinds or lace curtains, which became necessary with the

313

introduction of glaring plate glass. The furnishings, solidly made and unpretentious, include a country chair similar to those advertised by Edwin Skull of West Wycombe (see plate 137). To the left of the fireplace hangs a large print of the Crystal Palace's interior – not a detail peculiar to this house, since the Great Exhibition represented a national triumph as well as a purely personal one for its foremost organizer, Henry Cole. The statuettes on the brackets between the windows are Parian ware figures, products of Cole's own enterprise, Felix Summerly's Art-Manufactures, which had been operating for six years selling ornaments and small items of furniture designed by Cole's friends and associates. In spite of considerable publicity, this venture did not make money, but it established Cole's interest in design appropriate to machine-made manufacture. Small white statuary ornaments were a familiar feature of mid-century homes; these would soon be rivalled by bronzes issued specifically for domestic display by the Art Union. Cole occupied this house until 1854; in 1860 he built himself a country house at Witley, Surrey. The interior was ornamental and reflected the taste that was developing under Cole's auspices in the buildings of the new South Kensington museums. Elizabeth Bonython concludes from the evidence of his diaries that, in spite of their very different character, both Witley and The Terrace were decorated in line with Cole's own taste. (See 'Art applied to the home: the household taste of Henry Cole and his circle', *Victoria and Albert Museum Album*, No. 3.)

George Smith, *Evenings at Home*
Private collection

Part Four
1860-1880

324

323, 324
Contrasting Morris & Co. designs

The wallpaper, left, first issued by Morris & Co. in 1864, and later accompanied by matching tiles, originated from embroidered hangings of the same pattern designed by Morris for the walls of the principal bedroom of his Red House. Their design was in turn based on that of hangings depicted in miniatures in a fifteenth-century manuscript of Froissart. 'Daisy' was one of the most perennially popular of Morris papers. For carpets Eastlake deplored current tastes in naturalistic floral patterns. His advice to those of moderate means was to 'choose, then, the humblest type of Turkey carpet or the cheapest hearthrug from Schinde, and be sure that they will afford you more lasting eye-pleasure than any English imitation' (*Hints on Household Taste*, 1868). Although 'Bullerswood' (1889), above, has an eastern inspiration it is symmetrical along a single axis.

From the Morris & Co. catalogue

Just when it seemed that the exhibition-promoted extravaganza was set to hold its sway over decoration indefinitely, the tide began to turn and a respect for the achievements of craftsmen captured the imaginations of architects and designers. Barely ten years after the eulogies that accompanied the flamboyant exhibits of the Great Exhibition of 1851, a counter-movement was formed with the inauguration of the firm of Morris & Co., unveiled to the public at the 1862 London Exhibition. During the following two decades the gilded, ornate and over-elaborate manufactures that had been so praised in 1851 were challenged by the Arts and Crafts movement and the allied Queen Anne revival and Aesthetic movement.

In 1868 Charles Eastlake brought out his influential book, *Hints on Household Taste in Furniture, Upholstery and other Details*. In America the book's impact was immediate and long-lasting, ousting the French influences that had dominated the United States since the late eighteenth century. Honest materials and construction, and simple geometric and solid shapes were the basic message, and Eastlake's illustrations of furniture were copied and bought by anyone with artistic *savoir-vivre*.

The 1870s saw the beginnings of the deluge of publications on the subject of decoration. They offered sound advice on all facets of the decoration of the middle-class home. The Victorian woman had begun to play a greater part in the organization of the house, and many of the books on decoration were aimed at women; most of Eastlake's *Hints on Household Taste* had been recast from articles that originally appeared in *The Queen*, a magazine targeted at middle-class women.

The rich were not easily weaned away from a taste for French historical styles, including the 'Fontainebleau' manner and the perennially popular 'Louis Quinze' which covered most of Louis XVI's reign as well. The Queen Anne revival gave little scope for conspicuous consumption, while the Arts and Crafts interior can be said to have totally repudiated the wanton luxury that so attracts the rich. It is perhaps significant that Leighton, Alma-Tadema and Millais, all of whom were successful and prosperous, were not tempted by the 'artistic' style: that is, the revived Queen Anne. They chose, respectively, German classicism with exotic Arab additions (originated by George Aitchison); neo-Roman or Pompeian marble palazzo style (designed by Alma-Tadema himself); and a severe Renaissance palace style (influenced by Philip Hardwick). William Burges created his own private Gothic fantasy in the Tower House; Whistler employed E. W. Godwin, but the typical artist's house was to be a red-brick Queen Anne building by Richard Norman Shaw.

Morris was discovering that only the rich could afford a thorough-going Morris & Co. interior; the short-term commercial side of Morris & Co. is an ambiguous triumph given Morris and Philip Webb's socialist beliefs. Morris, in his own words, spent his life in 'ministering to the swinish luxury of the rich' (quoted in Lethaby, *Philip Webb and His Work*, 1935). However, through his designs and his writings Morris's influence on all sectors of society was immense.

From this intense preoccupation of the period with design and an 'aesthetic' approach to all aspects of life, new criteria of beauty and design evolved which found their conclusion in the directness of the Arts and Crafts interior and adaptation of vernacular forms which embodied both beauty and a simplified way of life without the cruel clutter of mid-Victorian existence.

This suffocation was spiritual as well as the result of hybrid design. Walter Crane recalls the frustration of the young who had to live with what passed for art and decoration in drawing rooms of the 1850s:

. . . big looking glasses, and machine-lace curtains, and where the furniture is afflicted with curvature of the spine, and dreary lumps of bronze and ormolu repose on marble slabs at every opportunity, where monstrosities of every kind are encouraged under glass shades, while every species of design-debauchery is indulged in upon carpets, curtains, chintzes and wall papers, and where the antimacassar is made to cover a multitude of sins. When such ideas of decoration prevailed, having their origin or prototypes, in the vapid splendours of imperial saloons, and had to be reduced to the scale of an ordinary citizen's house and pocket, the thing became absurd as well as hideous.
('The English revival in decorative art' in *William Morris to Whistler*, 1911.)

William Morris

Morris was a man of gargantuan stature and violently held – and expressed – opinions. As a result, his activities in the field of decoration and design have eclipsed those of many of his contemporaries, many no less talented, some much more radically innovatory in their interpretation of current trends. Morris was a romantic medievalist, and it is in this aspect of the Aesthetic movement that his influence was most powerfully at work. The contemporary fascination with alien cultures – for example, Japanese or Moorish – had little effect on his development. He came to decorating through the need to decorate his own house, and his company remained an expression of his own preferences and prejudices. The most notable features of Morris's first real home. Red House at Bexleyheath in Kent, were the patterned and painted walls, ceilings and furniture and the appliquéd and embroidered hangings and curtains. To William Bell Scott the interior seemed extraordinarily primitive. Visiting the house soon after its completion in the early 1860s, he wrote:

The only thing you saw from a distance was an immense

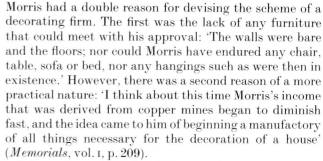

red-tiled steep and high roof; and the only room I remember was the dining-room or hall, which seemed to occupy the whole area of the mansion. It had a fixed settle all round the walls, a curious music-gallery entered by a stair outside the room, breaking out high upon the gable, and no furniture but a long table of oak reaching nearly from end to end. This vast empty hall was painted coarsely in bands of wild foliage over both wall and ceiling, which was open timber and lofty. The adornment had a novel, not to say startling character, but if one had been told it was the South Sea Island style of thing one could have easily believed such to be the case, so bizarre was the execution. This eccentricity was very easily understood after a little consideration. Genius always rushes to extremes at first; on leaving the beaten track of everyday no medium is to be preserved.
(*Autobiography*, ed. William Minto, 1892, p. 61.)

Morris's friends were all expected to involve themselves with this important decorating project. Rossetti was inspanned for the painting of furniture, as was Edward Burne-Jones, who remembered their enthusiastic plans to beautify the house:

As we talked of decorating its plans grew apace. We fixed upon a romance for the drawing-room, a great favourite of ours called Sir Degrevaunt. I designed seven pictures from that poem, of which I painted three that summer and autumn in tempera. We schemed also subjects from Troy for the hall, and a great ship carrying Greek heroes for a larger space in the hall, but these remained only schemes, none were designed except for the ship. The great settle from Red Lion Square, with the three painted shutters above the seat, was put up at the end of the drawing-room, and there was a ladder to its top and a parapet around it, and a little door above, in the wall behind it that led into the roof. There at Christmas time it was intended that minstrels should play and sing.
(Georgiana Burne-Jones, *Memorials*, 1906, vol.I, p. 209.)

Burne-Jones's own rooms were decorated in this highly personal manner, with painted furniture and embroidered hangings and solid, plain oaken furniture designed by Philip Webb, who was to join the group in the founding of Morris's decorating company. Burne-Jones believed that

325
Morris & Co. chairs 1860s

'Lost in the contemplation of palaces we have forgotten to look about us for a chair', wrote Charles Eastlake. This was very close to the Morris & Co. manifesto for a simple elegance applied to household artefacts. Although the firm produced articles of everyday use, the members always insisted on their status as artists. In spite of this, it survived as a commercial venture, though similar firms were short-lived.

From the Morris & Co. catalogue

Morris had a double reason for devising the scheme of a decorating firm. The first was the lack of any furniture that could meet with his approval: 'The walls were bare and the floors; nor could Morris have endured any chair, table, sofa or bed, nor any hangings such as were then in existence.' However, there was a second reason of a more practical nature: 'I think about this time Morris's income that was derived from copper mines began to diminish fast, and the idea came to him of beginning a manufactory of all things necessary for the decoration of a house' (*Memorials*, vol. I, p. 209).

It is a measure of William Morris's achievement that his name, linked with the well known products of his firm, has never been forgotten, unlike those of so many of his contemporaries. However, technically much of the early furniture was of very uneven quality; ignorance of the basic principles of construction led the craftsmen to make mistakes which had to be corrected laboriously by a process of trial and error. Surviving examples of the trestle dining table designed by Philip Webb for Red House in 1859 bear traces of the modifications and alterations needed to strengthen the structure and achieve stability. In addition to problems in the production of the furniture, Morris was hopelessly undercapitalized and he could never afford machines to bypass the lengthy hand work involved in the manufacture of the firm's wares, which inevitably meant that 'Morrisian' style was expensive. For instance, the handwoven Hammersmith carpets cost as much as four guineas per square yard, which was a huge sum at the end of the nineteenth century, far beyond the resources of the average middle-class household. However, the firm's textiles have survived in remarkable condition owing to the quality of the materials and the meticulous hand work, J.W. Mackail, in his illuminating *Life and Letters of William Morris* (1899), records the fact that the very high cost of the decorations carried out by the firm in the Green Dining Room at the South Kensington Museum (now the Victoria and Albert Museum) in 1867 came to be seen as a good investment, as in the space of thirty years no repairs or maintenance had been necessary beyond the repainting of the ceiling. Newly cleaned and restored, the room can again be seen in all the richness of the original gilding and painting, an example of the splendour of the 'Morrisian method'.

Contemporary opinion inclined to the view that Morris was more used to splendour than simplicity. *The Cabinet Maker and Art Furnisher*, discussing the 1887 Manchester Exhibition, included the following comment: 'That Messrs Morris & Co. should seek business and reputation in the wealthy city of Manchester is most natural, for it requires a long purse to live up to the higher phases of Morrisean taste.'

Finally it was the innumerable 'artistic' interiors, decorated with Morris paper, hung with Morris chintz and furnished with a Sussex chair or two – which, at a few

shillings each, must have been seen as cheap by any standards – that were to be the visible monuments to Morris's idealism and a practical realization of his socialist theorizing.

The firm of Morris, Marshall, Faulkner & Co. was founded in 1861, and set up business premises at 8 Red Lion Square, near to the studio which Morris once shared with Burne-Jones. The notion of being an old-fashioned tradesman obviously appealed to Morris. In later years, when the firm was carrying out work on a house, a board would be put up outside advertising the activities of 'Morris and Company – upholders', an archaism for 'upholsterers' which even a century ago must long have fallen into disuse. The members of Morris & Co. always referred to it as 'the firm'.

In the early years of the firm almost all the furniture was designed by Philip Webb. Later, a new style was introduced by Webb's assistant, George Jack. Although this was superficially conventional in proportion and ornamentation, Jack had taken eighteenth-century forms and remade them in a way that is reminiscent of A. H. Mackmurdo. The debt to Webb is apparent in the arrangement of the panelling, but the cabinet work is of the finest quality, owing no doubt to the fact that in 1887 Morris & Co. had acquired one of the workshops in Pimlico owned by the cabinet-making firm, Holland & Sons. The firm's retail premises survived in London until 1942. The closure took place when Morris designs were no longer admired, and the remaining stock as well as all the records were consigned to oblivion in the dustbin. Now the wheel has turned full circle, and Morris designs are familiar products in households throughout the world.

Morris had been appalled by the Great Exhibition; in fact the shock gave him the impetus for his decorating career. However, the collections in the South Kensington Museum, which was established with the exhibition's profits, were a source of inspiration to him. This museum was set up to promote good design: Prince Albert and Henry Cole conceived the idea of a repository of the design works of past and present to provide inspiration for designers and manufacturers and to influence the taste of the general public. Moncure Conway, writing in 1882,

326
Tiles for an 'artistic' house 1880s

These anonymous watercolour designs are in the same style as surviving examples from the firms of Simpson and Jeffrey & Co., who specialised in tiles and wallpapers respectively. They have the fashionable Anglo-Japanese touch. The corner piece may have been intended as part of a ceiling decoration. Ceiling papers were a cheap and quickly installed substitute for the hand stencilling used in the more costly schemes.

Michael Whiteway, London

327

327
The bed at Kelmscott Manor 1880s

Michael Whiteway, London

described how he had met an artist compatriot at work in the South Kensington schools and discussed with her the relative merits of art teaching in her native Philadelphia and in London. She concluded that the association between an art school and a collection of decorative art was very advantageous.

This lady's experience has been several times confirmed by American artists with whom I have walked through the South Kensington Museum. One of the most eminent of them said: 'What a revolution it would cause in American art to have such a museum as this in each large city! It would in each case draw around it an art community and send out widening waves of taste and love of beauty through the country.'
(*Travels in South Kensington*, p. 114.)

The museum was founded in 1852 as the Museum of Ornamental Art, and was first housed at Marlborough House. In 1856 it moved to South Kensington, occupying a complex of rather miscellaneous buildings and temporary shelters on the site of the present building. In 1899 it became the Victoria and Albert Museum. In the meantime, however, the visible improvement in design and manufactures in Britain had inspired the setting up of similar institutions abroad; their collections and those in the Victoria and Albert Museum can therefore provide evidence of both sides of the coin of taste – the source of ideas and the results of the application of those same ideas.

One aspect of this cross-fertilization of talent through the museum's collection has been investigated in considerable detail: the extent of William Morris's dependence on the collection of historic textiles for inspiration in his own pattern designs for Morris & Co. is a subject of crucial importance to the history of interior decorating in the nineteenth century. In her recent book, *Inspiration for Design. The influence of the Victoria and Albert Museum* (1986), Barbara Morris has gathered the myriad strands of information together to demonstrate the way in which Morris derived his pattern designs from the important textile collections at South Kensington. It is, of course, the subtle transformation of his source material that makes Morris such an interesting figure. He forged a style appropriate to the antiquarian tastes of the era, but transcended antiquarianism with its dependence on ancient artefacts supported by straightforward copying of surviving material.

The Morris & Co. decorating commissions, of which a number survive in country houses of the later Victorian period – and, indeed, in Normandy – have an ageless quality which has stood the test of time better than the more flamboyant 'antiquarian' taste of the earlier period. Although two of the most fully realized of Morris's decorating schemes were in town houses – for George Howard (later Lord Carlisle) and Alexander Ionides – the vernal character of his work makes it appropriate to the environment of the countryside. This is hardly surprising given Morris's views on town life; and the two houses that he himself occupied in the country, Red House and Kelmscott Manor, should probably be regarded as the most perfect expression of his romantic medievalist taste. Moncure Conway understood Morris's achievement well; he wrote the following before describing in detail the Ionides house in his *Travels in South Kensington*:

Although the hangings of Morris & Co. do not imply a lavish, but only a liberal, expenditure, they do not readily adapt themselves to a commonplace house inhabited by commonplace people. There must be thousands of these square-block houses with square boxes for rooms which would only be shamed by the individualities of their work ... (p. 202.)

Morris was aware of his failure to solve the economic realities of 'art for all'; he cannot have been reassured by reading these words.

Godwin and Dresser: Aestheticism and the Japanese mania

Max Beerbohm described Godwin as the 'greatest aesthete of them all'. Aesthetes derived their inspiration mainly from the cult of Japan and the Queen Anne revival. Edward William Godwin (1833–86) was in the forefront of a design reform movement which wanted to supply the public with 'art' furniture, 'art' embroidery, 'art' pottery, 'art' wallpapers; in fact all materials for an 'Aesthetic' interior. This insistence on 'art' made the Aesthetic movement an easy target for 'philistines', 'barbarians' and satirists.

The Queen Anne revival was an important element in the 'artistic' style of architecture and decoration. It was a reaction against the fussy opulence of mid-nineteenth century taste. Its style as far as decoration and furniture were concerned was something of a hotch-potch, with a large admixture of Georgian style and a nostalgic interpretation of medieval and Gothic detail. The possession of a Queen Anne house was a statement of rebellion against the crasser materialism of the industrial and commercial élites of Victorian England; the decoration and furniture followed this lead.

The story of the opening up of Japan after centuries of isolation has been told in detail elsewhere. The legend that the fame of Japanese art spread via the discovery of some old prints being used as wrapping paper has proved to be apocryphal. Godwin was an early and eager admirer of Japanese prints, which he purchased, as did Rossetti and Whistler, from Farmer & Rogers's Oriental Department, where Arthur Lasenby Liberty had his first job.

Godwin's professional career and his involvement with things Japanese began in Bristol. He was creating his first home at much the same time as Morris was furnishing his own 'palace of art'. Reputedly, Godwin's house was the first to be decorated in accordance with Japanese principles, with plain coloured walls ornamented only with Japanese prints. The attractive simplicity of this style of room, perfected by Godwin and Whistler, which deployed choice specimens of blue-and-white porcelain as the sole decorative feature, caught on rapidly. Newly opened trading channels supplied a barely sufficient supply of Japanese art objects to satisfy increasing demand. Information on Japanese architecture, design, interiors, customs and methods of manufacture began to be available through travellers' reports and books.

Christopher Dresser, like Godwin and Whistler, had been influenced by the Japanese stands at the 1862 International Exhibition in London, and he travelled to Japan on what today would probably be called a 'fact-finding mission' from 1876 to 1877 – the result was his book *Japan, its Architecture, Art and Art Manufactures* (1882). France, Canada and the United States also absorbed the Japanese influence. John La Farge, an

American, wrote about his epic journey to Japan in *An Artist's Letters from Japan* (1886), a trip that was to inspire his art for the rest of his life. He writes about the interior of the Japanese house with all the fervour of a convert:

Within, the Japanese house is simplicity itself; all is framework, and moving screens instead of wall. No accumulations, no bric-à-brac; any lady's drawing-room with us will contain more odds and ends than all I have seen in Japan. The reserved place of honour, a sort of niche in the wall, the supposed seat of an ideal guest, has upon its bench, some choice image on a stand or a vase with elegant disposal of flowers or plants, and above it the hanging roll with drawing or inscription. Perhaps some other inscription or verse, or a few words on a tablet or some cross-beam, and perhaps a small folding screen. . . . The woodwork is as simple as can be – occasionally, some beautiful joinery; and above all exquisite cleanliness. For there are no beds – only wadded coverlets and the little wooden pillow, which does not disturb the complicated feminine coiffure in the languors of the night. No tables; food is laid cleanly on mats, in many trays and dishes. No chairs; the same mats that serve for bedstead and table serve for seats with, perhaps a cushion added. . . . It is possible that when I return I shall feel still more distaste for the barbarous accumulations in our houses, and recall the far more civilized emptiness persisted in by a more esthetic race.

Dresser's *Japan* also compares the plain Japanese interior with its Western counterpart and finds his native land wanting; he considered that:

. . . we in England overestimate the decorative value of pictures. Many who cover their walls with costly paintings have scarcely an object in their houses beside these which has any art merit. The vases on the chimney piece, the épergne on the table, the nick-nacks in the cabinets, and the service for the afternoon tea drinking are all alike incongruous and meretricious. Surely persons whose houses are thus furnished have but little real love of beauty . . . ?

In the West, the Japanese style of interior could consist of anything from a display of blue-and-white china to a full-scale extravaganza of authentic silk-panelled walls, masks, samurai weaponry, screens, embroidery and the like. Much of what was termed 'Japanese' was simply a radical paring-down of relatively traditional forms. The actor Forbes Robertson describes Godwin's London house which can hardly be said to be purist:

The floor was covered with straw-coloured matting, and there was a dado of the same material. Above the dado were white walls and the hangings were of a cretonne with a fine Japanese pattern in delicate grey blue. The chairs were of wicker with cushion like hangings, and in the centre of the room was a full size cast of the Venus de Milo.
(*A Player under Three Reigns*, 1925.)

At the other end of the scale was the house commissioned in the 1890s by Mortimer Menpes fitted out with carved panels and slatted wooden screens all made in Japan.

What Godwin sought in the Japanese taste was an austerity of design and execution that was rare in contemporary art and manufacture. Cost, too, was a reason for his search for simpler forms of furniture and décor. Japanese models supplied the shapely elegance which was hard to achieve on a low budget in the Gothic style.

The Japanese prints that hung in his Bristol house were said to have been purchased from material that was intended for the 1862 exhibition, but arrived too late for inclusion. The same source, it is thought, supplied Rossetti with Japanese porcelain and William Burges with examples of leather paper. Burges had been impressed by the Japanese exhibit, admiring its asymmetry. He advised: '[for] any student of our reviving arts of the thirteenth century an hour or even a day or two spent in the Japanese Department will by no means be lost time for these hitherto unknown barbarians appear not only to know all the middle ages knew but, in some respects, are beyond them and us as well.'

Burges took every influence, including that of Japan, and engulfed it in his own version of thirteenth-century Gothic. Godwin achieved a personal synthesis of Gothic, Japanese, antique and classical forms in a search for an ideal of simplicity and purity. An idea, rather than a style, lies behind his furniture and decorative schemes.

As an example of his dedication to his art, one of his notebooks records the 'colours of a partly faded pineapple': 'yellow ochre, white & lower green/vermil[ion] Pruss[ian] blue & upper yellow/Pruss[ian] blue vermil[ion]/gamboge white . . .' (Notebook E223–1963, Victoria and Albert Museum, London). This elaborate notation went on to form the basis of the decoration of a room in the house at Harpenden, which he shared with Ellen Terry. It had woodwork 'painted the pale green sometimes seen at the stem of a pineapple leaf when the other end has faded'. Not surprisingly, this degree of perfectionism was the subject both of incomprehension and of the satirist.

Godwin cannot be blamed for his imitators. Significantly, he spent the last years of his life producing both theatre designs and a radical couture, Greek in origin and simplicity. The 1880s witnessed the 'extravagances of the pseudo-aesthetic school', as H. J. Jennings put it in *Our Homes and How to Beautify Them* (1902). Such 'pseudo-aesthetic' devotees are best known through du Maurier's cartoon family, the Cimabue Browns. Jenkins categorized them as 'effeminate, invertebrate, sensuous, and mawkish. . . .' However, he concluded his scathing résumé of their excesses: 'But it must in fairness be admitted that the aesthetic movement, of which this craze was but the rank growth, sowed precious seed. People began to realize that it was possible to make their homes more beautiful.'

Richard Norman Shaw
and the Old English style

The idea of an 'artistic' and 'intellectual' house crystallized in the 1860s and 1870s with the designs of Richard Norman Shaw and his 'artistic clients'. Beginning in the Surrey and Kent countryside, the Old English style soon colonized Hampstead, Chelsea and Kensington. The western reaches of Kensington at that date were something of an artists' quarter: from Melbury Road, where Burges had built his Tower House, to Burne-Jones's house in the North End Road, and almost to William Morris's Kelmscott in Hammersmith. Here was the start of a new wave of expansion. Luke Fildes and Marcus Stone commissioned studio houses designed by Shaw. Both the fashionable status of the artists and the lightness and freedom of Shaw's design gave the 'Queen Anne' style a wide popularity.

These houses exploit the vernacular vein as in Queen Anne and Old English styles. They are built of brick, with pitched tile-hung roofs, picturesque chimneys, and frequently, half-timbered gables. Where the site permitted, the house could be rambling without a central entrance or any symmetry of fenestration. The eccentric arrangement of the windows began as a practical necessity to allow the correct light for an artist to work. Its effect was to add to a streetscape the excitement that had been so often lacking in the terraces of early Victorian stucco or Georgian brick town houses.

Shaw's own house in Ellerdale Road in Hampstead was well supplied with quaint corners, inglenooks, and changing floor levels even within the same room. This informality reflected a conscious attempt to re-create an old house that had been added to and altered over generations, and was also a sign that artistic families no longer obeyed the rigid social customs of the previous generation. Later on in Shaw's successful career, his houses return to a tighter and more classical arrangement. In Queen's Gate, where his commissions of the 1880s were for the wealthy and professional classes, the informality has been reduced and the decoration of their lofty rooms serves as the setting for antique furniture and gold-framed paintings.

Shaw, like William Morris, favoured tapestries as adornments for walls. Like Morris, he was chary of paintings in a picturesque setting, regarding the pictures as rivals in a scheme that should be controlled by the architectural elements. In other respects Shaw and Morris were less compatible. Morris's bold patterning does not suit Shaw's interiors: the effect of so many different patterns in Morris's scheme in the drawing room of Shaw's Old Swan House of 1875 in Chelsea is to promote Morris's contribution at the expense of Shaw.

The 'resident' architect of Morris & Co. was an inappropriate label for Philip Webb. Webb worked for Morris – his designs for animals feature in many of the tapestries the firm produced – yet he also had his own office and architectural practice. In some projects, such as Clouds or Palace Green, Webb wore both hats as architect and as a Morris & Co. designer. Webb never had the commercial success of Shaw, though he was equally influential. Palace Green, built for the Howards in 1868, and the Glebe Place house, built for the watercolourist G. B. Boyce in the same year, contained all the ingredients of the future artistic house.

Webb's output was restricted by the fact that he had a small staff and insisted on supervising every detail of the work himself, right down to selecting the bricks, specifying as many 'seconds' and 'dark headers' for the patterning of his buildings as possible. His perfectionist temperament expressed itself in an autocratic insistence on doing everything conscientiously *his* way. In 1888 F. A. White, who had been impressed with the Glebe Place house, wanted to employ Webb to build his house in Queen's Gate and 'sought an interview to feel his pulse about accepting me as his client'. White recounts the ensuing colloquy:

I told him the sort of house I had in mind, and listened to him as he expounded at length as to the relations between architect and client and the supreme importance of quality in work. Though he must have seen how I appreciated his genius and my own ignorance, I suppose I managed to excite his suspicion that as I was to live in the house, I, too, might have a view or two now and then, and might here and there want a voice which might be dissonant from his own, for he bid me reflect that he was very despotic, and that he would never make a concession he might think unwise to economy, nor please his client at the expense of his conscience. Had I better not think twice before committing myself to one who might become my taskmaster?
(Quoted in Lethaby, *Philip Webb and His Work*, 1935.)

Mr White thought twice, settled for second best and employed Norman Shaw.

Ernest George and Harold Peto made as much of a mark as Shaw on the development of brick houses of the 1870s and '80s. Their Harrington and Collingham Gardens work possesses dramatic façades and more striking outlines than Shaw's Melbury Road houses. The interiors, however, are conventional in plan even if this fact is concealed beneath a wealth of ornamental detail. The recurring feature of a George and Peto interior is the dominant fireplace, often towering over the room and covered in neo-Renaissance ornament. At Grims Dyke, a house built by Shaw for the artist Frederick Goodall, George and Peto were called in by its subsequent owner, W. S. Gilbert, to install a particularly large and ornate chimneypiece. Gilbert had been one of the first owners of a George and Peto house in Harrington Gardens, and at Grims Dyke he had presumably wanted similar bravura to stamp his mark on Shaw's refinement. Goodall had been forced to sell Grims Dyke when his ambitions outran his purse, and one can guess that Gilbert needed to assert his own taste over his predecessor's.

Many of the interiors of Harrington Gardens were photographed by the rising architectural photographer H. Bedford Lemere (d. 1944). These were the houses of art-lovers; their interiors are loaded with bric-à-brac and collected treasures which compete against the wall hangings of stamped and gilded leather, decorated plasterwork ceilings, many-paned windows with some lights of stained glass casting a rainbow light on the dark polished wood, and oriental carpets on the floors. Many hands had been at work to complete this final result: De Morgan tiles in one, Walter Crane wallpaper in another; a Jeckyll fireplace, a chair by Godwin, a Morris table and a Burne-Jones window all added their voice to the effect.

Just before the turn of the century, Bedford Lemere assembled a collection of his photographs into two portfolios entitled *Intérieurs anglais*. Numbering eighty-six in all, they were intended for the Continental market, and the selection is a helpful guide to the best of the Old English style, which is represented in the majority of these pictures. Some are of genuinely old houses of the Tudor period, such as Wollaton and Audley End. George and Peto's work is well covered as is, of course, Norman Shaw's. Curiously, there is little overlap with the examples selected by Hermann Muthesius for his important study *Das englische Haus* (1904). Shaw's Cragside and Dawpool are the only two that feature in both selections. Bedford Lemere includes only two Morris schemes, the grandiose staircase at Stanmore and Old Swan House, Chelsea. The relative absence of Arts and Crafts in Bedford Lemere is surprising – Sidney Mitchell's own house, The Pleasance in Gullane being the only other example – given that Muthesius draws on it so heavily only a decade later.

Of course, Bedford Lemere's published portfolios were spin-offs from photographs commissioned by architects, decorators or houseproud owners, and the implication is that Arts and Crafts architects did not like publicity photography – or could not afford Lemere's services in the 1890s. Secondly, the Arts and Crafts style had a wider currency in Germany than it ever did in Beaux-Arts dominated France. One assumes that Bedford Lemere knew his market, and he judged that Old English would be of interest to French and Belgian markets; indeed there is some reason to suspect the choice of pictures was made by someone unfamiliar with English.

The 1890s saw a rekindling of an interest in Renaissance styles, inspired by the increasing nationalistic feelings of the years which led up to the Great War. The trend particularly affected town halls and other public buildings.

Shopping for the aesthetic interior

Farmer & Rogers were amongst the first to supply enthusiasts with Japanese prints and porcelain. After the 1862 International Exhibition closed, they took on the disposal of the exhibits from the Japanese display. In the following year, Arthur Lasenby Liberty took over Farmer & Roger's Oriental Department, where he remained for twelve years. In 1875 he opened his own small shop in Regent Street and many of his customers followed.

In these early years the trade in Japanese objects was an important contribution to taste in interior decoration; at the turn of the century, Liberty had a greater influence on a new development, the Art Nouveau style, whose roots were to be found in the cult of Japan and to some extent in the revived Queen Anne style.

A major rival to Liberty in London was the dealer Murray Marks. Marks was an important source of blue-and-white china for collectors. He was an admirer, patron and friend of Rossetti, who used him shamelessly as a general dogsbody. The great painter used the great shopkeeper to run small errands, like finding matting for the studio floor, acquiring a marquee for the garden to house his small menagerie, and scouting out a table for Rossetti's room at Kelmscott Manor. 'It should be of the Pembroke kind,' ordered the painter. 'More or less firm, very moderate in size, with a flap or flaps (*one* I should think best) . . . and going on castors.' On another occasion Marks was asked to find 'two square tables, one mahogany and one satin wood'. These little tasks were performed by the good-natured Marks in between supplying an important clientèle which included Frederic Leyland, Whistler's patron; and Wickham Flower, a patron of Webb and collector of Italian Old Masters.

The origins of the Japanese influence in Europe are to be found equally in France and in England, and the exact chronology of its discovery by European artists and designers has been the subject of detailed discussion. Suffice it to say that in both France and England there was a considerable awareness of the Japanese 'aesthetic', and its influence was increasingly widespread. For instance, a recent study of Impressionism emphasizes Claude Monet's involvement with Japanese art; the painter collected Japanese prints and his house at Giverny was decorated with Japanese colour combinations in mind (see Théodore Duret, *Les Peintres impressionistes*, 1878). Monet's schemes have been re-created, and stand as evidence of this particular strand of nineteenth-century artistic taste.

The difference between the cult of Japan in England and in France is largely one of diffusion. French books on Japanese art tend to be analytical and scholarly; the English lean to the travelogue. In France, Japan remained a taste of the practising artist; in Britain the

328

328
The drawing room at Old Swan House, Chelsea 1890s

'Hammersmith' carpets, Morris & Co. furniture and green-painted woodwork furnish the drawing room at Old Swan House, its walls hung with St James's silk.

From the Morris & Co. catalogue

manifestations of Japanese influence were more far-flung, often embracing crude vulgarization that retained a mere whisper of anything authentically Japanese.

In Paris of the 1860s *cognoscenti* shopped for Japanese prints, ceramics and bronzes at the Porte Chinoise, and visited expositions sponsored by the Union Centrale des Arts Décoratifs. In the 1870s, the Parisian scene was enlivened by the entrepreneurial genius of Siegfried Bing, later the proprietor of the famous furniture and decorating business, L'Art Nouveau. Bing is a visible link between *le Japonisme* and Art Nouveau and was an instigator of fashions, whereas his closest London equivalent, Arthur Lasenby Liberty, was a commercial imitator. However, Liberty obtained his slice of immortality by giving his name to *lo stile Liberty*, which was the Italian term for the Art Nouveau style.

American Gothic

The obvious drawbacks of Gothic as a domestic style did not deter nineteenth-century patrons from demanding it for their country houses. In America the origins of neo-Gothic can be traced to the final years of the eighteenth century, when the fame of Horace Walpole's Strawberry Hill had begun to spread beyond British shores. In 1799 the architect Benjamin Henry Latrobe designed the Gothic Revival house, Sedgeley, for William Crammond of Philadelphia. It is now demolished, but it was illustrated in 1808 in William Birch's *The Country Seats of the United States of North America*. Of course it was no Fonthill, simply a foursquare, modestly sized house with neo-Gothic features; but Latrobe was a sufficiently highly regarded architect to establish the style in public esteem, and many more Gothic-style houses were to follow.

In the 1840s Andrew Jackson Downing, an admirer of J. C. Loudon, promoted the Gothic style in his writings on architecture. His own house, a handsome Gothic mansion of stone, now demolished, was illustrated in his *Treatise on the Theory and Practice of Landscape Gardening* (1841). Downing admired Alexander Jackson Davis, the most successful architect of the period, and promoted him enthusiastically. One Gothic-style house designed by Davis, dating from 1844, survives: Lyndhurst at Tarytown on the Hudson River. Lyndhurst has a magnificence of scale unusual in American domestic architecture at this date. The house eventually came into the possession of the railroad millionaire Jay Gould. It was lived in after his death by his daughter, and she gave it to the American National Trust. The interior recalls English examples dating from the mid-nineteenth century in the splendour and elaboration of its decoration.

Other similarly monumental houses followed Lyndhurst, some in the pointed, fanciful Gothic which is closest to the eighteenth-century taste, others square and formidable, typical of the mid-century respect for durability. But the most charming and individual contribution made by American builders to the history of the Gothic Revival is the wooden villa, elaborately ornamented under high-pointed gables and along the verandas and porches with lace-like Gothic motifs. This so-called 'Carpenter's Gothic' found its most appropriate and highly evolved expression in the houses of the summer colony at Martha's Vineyard, Massachusetts.

Of course these houses had to be equipped with consistent furniture. Some of the designs may have come from *The Gothic Album for Cabinet Makers* issued by C. Baird of Philadelphia, 'Industrial Publisher', in 1868. Later a dependence on the advice offered by Charles Eastlake in his *Hints on Household Taste* (1868; first American edition 1872) is very apparent. In 1876 Charles Wyllys Elliott, a Boston decorator, published in book form a series of articles on contemporary American interior decoration. It is apparent from the drawings of the chosen rooms illustrated in *The Book of American Interiors* that the firms of Cottier & Co. and Kimbel & Cabus must have supplied some of the furniture. Pieces shown come very close to examples advertised and exhibited by these firms. There must have been many others, too, but Elliott mentions only one by name, and this somewhat disingenuously: it is his own firm, the Household Art Company of Boston. Whatever Elliott's motives in putting together this collection of interior views may have been, the result is an interesting and informative collection of material.

330

329

The two Kelmscotts Early and late 1870s

Morris rented Kelmscott Manor in Oxfordshire in 1871. Seven years later he discovered a house in London that appealed to him. The Retreat in the Upper Mall, Hammersmith had belonged to Dr George Macdonald, best known as the author of children's books. William De Morgan records Morris's changes:

... the decoration of the principal rooms consisted of red flock wall paper covered by long book-cases painted black, and a ceiling of azure blue, dotted with gilt stars, considerably tarnished. Needless to say, Morris soon changed its appearance; and he altered the name, which he said reminded him of a private asylum, he altered it to Kelmscott House, after his other home on the banks the river [Thames].
(A.M.W. Stirling, *William De Morgan and his Wife*, 1922, p. 119.)

Morris kept up Kelmscott Manor and spent most of the latter part of his life there. It was an unspoilt example of Cotswold stone-building dating from the late sixteenth century. While he was its tenant, Morris did very little to the house. He loved it as he had found it, and wrote eloquently of his feelings for the house and its setting in 'Gossip about an old house on the upper Thames' (*The Quest*, November 1895):

The walls of it are hung with tapestry of about 1600, representing the story of Samson; they were never great works of art, and now when all the bright colours are faded out, and nothing is left but the indigo blues, the greys and warm yellowy browns, they look better, I think, than they were meant to look: at any rate they make the walls a very pleasant background for the living people who haunt the room; (it is our best sitting room now, though it was once the best bedroom) and, in spite of the designer, they give an air of romance which nothing else would quite do.

Morris was responsible in large part for the great revival of interest in textile hangings as decoration. He himself was not much interested in paintings and owned but few, much preferring tapestries and embroidered hangings, as the Tapestry Room at Kelmscott Manor shows. His own houses were plainly decorated, relying on hangings for effect. Other people's houses decorated by Morris & Co. tend to have a claustrophobic effect, partly due to the miscellaneous accumulations that his patrons seemed always to have amassed. The bedroom of Kelmscott Manor (plate 327) is dominated by the Morrises' four-poster bed. The wallpaper is 'Daisy'. The bed hangings were embroidered by May Morris, assisted by Lily Yeats. The long dining room at Kelmscott in Hammersmith is hung with 'Bird', a woollen double cloth designed in 1878.

Royal Borough of Kensington and Chelsea, London

330
The drawing room, Rounton Grange, Northallerton Late 1870s

This was a relatively early Morris & Co. commission. The decorations were carried out soon after the completion of the building works in 1876. Although several patterns are used – the large carpet, which is an early example using a meandering design of acanthus and willow leaves; the two patterns used for the frieze and wall above the dado; and the upholstery of Compton printed cotton – the whole effect is unassuming.

University of Newcastle upon Tyne

331
An 'artistic' bedroom 1892

The Morris & Co. 'Daffodil' printed cotton stands out strongly against the many competing patterns in this voguish bedroom with its fitted cupboards and over-mantel in white, china on display, cane chairs and rush-bottomed chairs which would have been familiar in any 'artistic' scheme.

Bedroom at 37 Augustus Road, Edgbaston, Birmingham
National Monuments Record, London

332, 333

Two rooms in Richard Norman Shaw's Old Swan House 1880s

The long drawing room (below) ran the breadth of the house on the first floor, lit by three great windows of the oriel type, called 'Sparrowe's House' windows from their resemblance to the windows of the Tudor house of that name in Ipswich. The restless patterning of the scheme, with contrasting Morris papers on the walls and the ceiling, and painted decoration in the deep window reveals, the gesso-ornamented grand piano from Morris & Co. and the boldly oriental-style rugs would have given Shaw little satisfaction. He became less and less sympathetic to Morris's ideas. Later he was to write:

333

It is disconcerting, you will admit, when you find that your host and hostess are less noticeable than their wall-papers and their furniture ... present-day belief that good design consists of pattern – pattern repeated ad nauseam *– is an outrage on good taste. A wall-paper should be a* background pure and simple *that and nothing more. If there is any pattern at all ... it ought to be of the simplest kind, quite unobtrusive ...*
('The home and its dwelling rooms' in *The British Home of Today*, ed. Walter Shaw Sparrow, 1904.)

Norman Shaw's much quoted remark, 'William Morris was a great man who somehow delighted in glaring wallpapers', gives an unequivocal flavour of the unbridgeable gap between them. Wickham Flower, Shaw's client for Old Swan House, was a collector and connoisseur of Japanese porcelain. He was a patron of Rossetti, a friend of Leighton and an admirer of Morris and his circle. The sofa in the smaller room illustrated above came from Rossetti's house. The table in the right foreground was designed by Philip Webb for Morris & Co. The fireplace tiles are by William De Morgan. Some of the blue-and-white porcelain may once have belonged to Whistler, Wickham Flower having been one of the buyers when the contents of the White House were sold in 1879. Shaw's words of criticism fit this scheme too well for us to suppose that he liked it, but at this distance of time house and interior have merged into a satisfying entity.

Photographs by H. Bedford Lemere
National Monuments Record, London
Private collection

334
Panelling as pattern 1904

The soaring two-storey hall at Clouds, the Wyndham house in Wiltshire completed in 1885, bears many of the marks of Philip Webb's best style, particularly in the varied geometry of the panelling. The vast space is simply furnished, mainly with eighteenth-century pieces, and hardly ornamented, thus giving emphasis to the Morris & Co. 'Hammersmith' carpet and to the 'Greenway' tapestry, also by Morris. The arrangement of the room reflects Mrs Wyndham's own ideas and is remarkably restrained by the normal standards of a great Victorian country house.

Country Life

335, 336
'An epoch-making house' 1898

These photographs shows the Antiquities Room and Study of the Ionides house at 1 Holland Park Avenue. In an article of 1889 in *The Studio*, titled 'An epoch-making house', Gleeson White remarked:

The real charm of the house is that it is a consistent example of the use of fabrics and patterns designed chiefly by Mr Morris, and it represents the first flower of the 'movement' in aesthetic furnishing which has now developed. . . .

One assumes that Gleeson White wrote about the room's 'aesthetic furnishing' before the introduction of the owner's less than aesthetic taste in camels and *objets d'art*, which return the room to a Victorian clutter. The tapestries suffer from being crowded in an already restricted space. The 'Forest' tapestry was designed by Morris in 1887, with animals designed by Philip Webb (decorative animals were his speciality). The decoration of the Ionides house was completed in 1888, the total cost being £2,361 2s 10d (see Linda Parry, *William Morris Textiles*, 1983).

Photographs Weidenfeld & Nicolson Archive

335
336

338

337

337

Interior with a painted cabinet 1875

The room's main decorative item is a very plainly constructed cabinet with painted decoration in the manner of Morris and Burne-Jones. This kind of furniture was a taste peculiar to a circle close to Morris and Burges, who used very basic forms in order to ensure that the painting was the main interest. The folk tradition of painted furniture had the decoration as subordinate to structure, and it was this aspect that appealed to designers of the craft movement in northern Europe. In England the painting of furniture, often with witty conceits, was a way to make a standard household necessity personal and exciting.

George Pinwell, signed and dated
Private collection

338

The dining room at The Grange, Fulham 1898

For more than twenty-five years Thomas Matthews Rooke worked as assistant to Edward Burne-Jones. This picture which he painted of the dining room is a kind of valedictory to the house and his employer. Angela

Thirkell, Burne-Jones's granddaughter, wrote a poetical account of her childhood visits to this house. The dining room of The Grange, like Rossetti's drawing room, was the creation of a single mind imposing its own order on a collection of personal treasures. In the early days when these hangings and cupboards were installed, Morris and his friends were only playing at being house decorators; the finish and technique lack polish. Like many of his fellow artists, Burne-Jones received guests in his studio on Sunday. Unlike many of them, who filled their studios with the 'props' of the arty *demi-monde*, Burne-Jones maintained his studio as a practical workroom. Visitors had to thread their way through a maze of work in progress. No oriental silks and Persian rugs softened the lofty space. In the rest of the house, for all the painted ornamentation and hangings, the accent was severely practical. The Morris & Co. chairs, designed by Madox Brown, complement the Philip Webb table. Through the opening can be glimpsed stained-glass windows designed by Burne-Jones himself.

Private collection

339
The Morris style in Italy   1871

Painted during an extended honeymoon in Rome, while living in via San Niccolò Tolentino, this picture by Walter Crane foreshadows his frontispiece for Clarence Cook's *The House Beautiful* (1881). The painting's background shows the influences of Morris: a tiled fireplace and embroidered hangings, but all within a classical framework. In the 1890s Walburga, Lady Paget wrote of the Stanhopes' house in Florence as being decorated 'in the Walter Crane style'; a manner that does not move that far away from his illustration work. Indeed, his style was first developed in the form of book illustration, where Crane had 'the habit of putting in all sorts of subsidiary detail that interested me and often made them the vehicle for my ideas in furniture and decoration' (*Reminiscences*, 1907). And it was through these book illustrations that he attracted the attention of architects who commissioned him to do friezes and other works. Crane's *Reminiscences* include a brief note on the circumstances of the painting of this picture. Mrs Crane, née Mary Andrews, even in Rome found herself amid a circle of English art-embroidery enthusiasts and they worked with Roman coloured cottons on linen; these works appear in the background of the picture. This 'fanciful decorative addition' bears another message: in the scene Mary Crane is depicted as Diana the huntress and, accompanied by Cupid, she pursues a crane!

Walter Crane, *At Home. A portrait*, 1871
Leeds City Art Galleries

339

I don't know whether father would approve of our knocking about the house under ordinary circumstances, but he'll forgive anything that's done for her. And then we'll have the painters ... and they shall paint the walls of her room in beautiful colours – or we'll hang them with Morris chintz, or leather paper, or some art stuff; we'll take out the old furniture and put new in. She'll have the easiest sofa at the window and the softest armchair by the fire, and Eastern carpets – the best money can buy –

The Mortlock Library, State Library of South Australia, Adelaide
Photograph Weidenfeld & Nicolson Archive

341

A flamboyant example of the 'Morrisian method' 1891

Stanmore Hall, Middlesex, was built in 1847; in 1888 Brightwell Binyon made additions and alterations for William Knox D'Arcy, who commissioned Morris to decorate the interior. The result is a flamboyant overkill achieved by applying traditional Victorian notions of luxury to the works of the Morris firm. The traditional lumpish furniture sits ill with Morris's patterns which have been applied to all available surfaces and upholstery, creating a restlessness which makes the room far less than the sum of its parts. It was for the dining room at Stanmore that Burne-Jones and Morris designed the series of tapestries *The Quest for the Holy Grail* (see Susan Moore, 'The Marxist and the oilman: Morris & Co. at Stanmore Hall', *Country Life*, 14 September 1985). The *Grail*'s first panel showing the Knights of the Round Table included a number of fanciful chairs that were to influence the Glasgow architect Charles Rennie Mackintosh, and through him many Continental designers in the early days of the Modern Movement. The Grail is the firm's only complete set of Arras tapestries designed for a single room. The scheme was largely the work of Morris's young associate W.H. Dearle, since Morris could feel no sympathy with the client or the house: 'Such a wretched uncomfortable place! A sham Gothic house of fifty years ago now being added to by a young architect of the commercial type.' And yet the tapestries must be regarded as the pinnacle of Morris & Co.'s textile work; and Stanmore's interiors are impressive for all their crammed over-richness. This picture is of the drawing room.

Photograph by H. Bedford Lemere
National Monuments Record, London

340

Morris in Australia 1890s

Auchendarroch was a hill station or summer residence about thirty miles outside Adelaide; it belonged to the Barr Smith family. Robert Barr Smith emigrated to Australia in 1854; his wife Joanna had been a friend of May Morris. Both Auchendarroch and their Adelaide town house contained Morris & Co. furnishings and textiles. The materials were ordered from London and the decorating work carried out by local craftsmen. Some Morris & Co. designs must have been available in Australia, though they would have been relatively dear. Ada Cambridge's novel *A Marked Man* (1891) describes a young woman wishing to make an impression by decorating the house to receive her father's new wife:

341

342

Charles Reade in his study   1870s

Charles Reade is shown seated at a small and probably flimsy ornamental occasional table. It is ironic that a professional – and celebrated – writer should be so ill equipped for the pursuit of his profession when exceptionally well furnished writing rooms were a feature of most nineteenth-century homes. In his biography of Reade, Coleman describes the room shown in this painting:

This pleasant home of delightful memories, though cosy and comfortable, was not spacious; but its owner was fertile in expedients, and he made a new lion's den, big enough for a menagerie, by throwing the passage into the drawing-room, annexing four and twenty square feet of garden at the back, forming one large room with French windows opening to the ground. This palatial apartment served a quintuple purpose. Breakfast in the morning at nine, with the blessed sunshine illumining every nook and cranny; after breakfast, hey presto! 'twas changed to a work-shop; at one he or we, had to

352

wall at the left of the fireplace in Mr Gow's room (below left). Whereas the Christchurch rooms are like those devised for artistic households of that date, the Cambridge rooms are much more like suburban dens or smoking rooms where a little tasteful female intervention has been permitted. In George du Maurier's *Punch* drawings, desperate husbands flee into just such rooms to escape the relentless social demands of their wives. The heavily draped and pelmeted fireplace (above) is a survival from an earlier period; the sporting Mr Custer seems less concerned with the niceties of fashion in decoration, but the dado of woven Japanese straw matting, as recommended by William Morris, and the Japanese fans in Mr Gow's room, suggest a striving after Aestheticism.

Cambridgeshire Collection

353

354

353, 354
At home in the thirteenth century 1870s

In his house in Melbury Road, Burges was able to indulge in the sort of romantic fantasy that he was building for Lord Bute in Wales. In scale, of course, the drawing room of the Tower House bears no comparison to Cardiff Castle, yet for the house of a professional man it is surely exotic. The theme is 'Love, its fortunes and crosses': the frieze by Frederick Weekes depicts legendary lovers, the chimney-piece illustrates Chaucer's *Romaunt of the Rose*, on the ceiling is a Cupid. In his bedroom, Burges chose an underwater theme, with a mermaid fireplace and hooded chimney. The ceiling is studded with tiny mirrors inset into lead stars. The guest bedroom, according to Mrs Haweis's account, 'is made of fire and flowers ... The windows glow with colours of the Alhambra.... The whole room is the shrine of a reliquary' (*Beautiful Houses*, 1881). W.R. Lethaby saw it in 1882–3, 'when it was exactly as he had made and furnished it – massive, learned, glittering, amazing. When the house was finished the hearse was at the door.' And Lethaby's thumbnail description of Burges the man 'as a medievalist indeed, in a peculiarly personal and semi-jocular way, delighting to play the part', also sums up the Tower House. (*Philip Webb and His Work*, 1935.)

Private collection

355
The Central Hall at Wallington, Northumberland 1854–1905

The house dates back to the late seventeenth century, and was altered in the eighteenth century. The Central Hall was part of John Dobson's remodelling of 1853–4 for Lord and Lady Trevelyan, who had decided to make Wallington their home. This hall was devised as a combined sitting room and general meeting place where tea was taken in the afternoons and musical soirées were held. The scheme is Italianate in style; the balustrade at the first level is adapted from a plate in *The Stones of Venice*. The hall was painted by William Bell Scott, an associate of the Pre-Raphaelites, with scenes from Northumbrian history. The piers of the arches were decorated, rather discordantly, with plants and flowers by Lady Trevelyan and friends, Ruskin himself pitching in with the finishing touches. This sort of painted decoration had been popularized by Prince Albert in the 1840s, but it is rare to find it surviving today. The hall painting sessions, which look forward to Bloomsbury 'do-it-yourself' at Charleston, must have resembled Rachel Verinder and Franklin B. Stoke's efforts to paint a door in Wilkie Collins's *The*

355

Moonstone (1868), where 'Mr Franklin's universal genius, dabbling in everything, dabbled in what he called "decorative painting".' Of course some of the 'slow' and 'dirty' work of painting – in this case a door – was enhanced by the charms of the opposite sex:

Miss Rachel being wild to try her hand at the new process, Mr Franklin sent to London for the materials; mixed them up.... put an apron and bib over Miss Rachel's gown, and set her to work decorating her own little sitting room – called

for want of an English name for it, her 'boudoir'. They began with the inside of the door. Mr Franklin scraped off all the nice varnish with a pumice-stone, and made what he described as a surface to work on. Miss Rachel then covered the surface, under his directions and with his help, with patterns and devices – griffins, birds, flowers, cupids, and such like....

Early 20th-century photograph
Private collection

356

356
A neo-Renaissance room in Antwerp 1880

Not a single inappropriate piece of furniture, wall-hanging, table cover, cushion or curtain mars this very completely realized neo-Renaissance scheme in an Antwerp house. Artists in Belgium were fascinated with the Renaissance, and historical subject matter was much appreciated in the work of successful painters like Baron Wappers and Baron Leys. Although C.A.M. Cap belongs to this school of painting, in this highly detailed work he has painted a contemporary subject in a contemporary setting. Yet the copybook Northern Renaissance interior is so perfect as to suggest a stage set. Although the cabinet, with its set of blue-and-white vases, the fireplace tiles and the tapestries all look like antiques, they might equally be modern copies which were available from enterprising manufacturers of the day.

Constant Aimé Marie Cap, *Memory of National Commemoration Day, 1830*, oil
Koninklijk Museum voor Schone Kunsten, Antwerp

357

A Parisian window design 1890s

The Parisian furnishing and decorating firm Schmitt & Co. was started in 1820. They supplied furniture in every fashionable style, and are still in business today. This suggested window treatment has a Renaissance flavour with its heavily embroidered curtains and quaint many-paned leaded windows with painted insets, but the high arched panels with tile pictures strike a modern note.

From the design archive of Schmitt & Co.
Photograph Sims & Reed, London

358

357

358

A Belgian artist's dining room 1869

The dining room in rue de Serment, Antwerp, of the academic painter Baron Leys (1815–69) is, appropriately, in the Northern Renaissance manner. The panelling reaches the frieze, which was painted by Leys himself. The subject matter was taken from the Baron's particular speciality: everyday life in the time of Dürer and Cranach. Minute attention to detail and a skilful technique of realist representation were also hallmarks of the Baron's style, and these professional traits were passed on to his pupil, J.J. Tissot.

Henri de Braekeleer, *Interior at rue de Serment, Antwerp*, oil
Koninklijk Museum voor Schone Kunsten, Antwerp (copyright A.C.L. Bruxelles)

359, 360, 361
Aspects of Aestheticism 1890s

The curious studio below, containing a billiard table, has one wall decorated with a Japanese scheme. During the latter half of the nineteenth century, artists' studios increasingly became haunts of the fashionable set. In his novel of the 1840s, *Cousine Bette*, Balzac had called artists the 'princes of our century'. With social recognition came great financial rewards and public interest in their habitat. The studio of the aspiring or successful artist was

360

expected to have a *demi-monde* feel to it which owed much to deliberate artifice.

Tom Roberts (1856–1931) was a Whistlerian; he had been in London in the early 1880s and had seen Whistler's *Nocturnes* and *Harmonies*. The relationship between the figure and setting in this portrait of Mrs Abrahams (above) owes an obvious debt to Whistler's portraits of the 1870s. The contrast between the painter's 'aesthetic' inspiration and the fashionable 'Old English' taste of the Australian house decorator is more marked than in Britain where the artistic 'style' was more pervasive.

The exotic boudoir, right, could have been achieved without expensive alterations to the structure of the room. *The Lady* and other magazines aimed at women of the 1880s were advising very similar 'oriental' schemes and effects. The accessories used here create their effect by deliberate 'culture shock': No masks, Japanese prints and paintings, ceramics, Samurai weapons and an open parasol provide a theatrical backdrop to the lacquer cabinet with its red interior. The voluptuous silk cushions, the embroidered spread and leopard skin supply an air of luxuriant ease as the model delves into the latest novel.

Unknown artist, *Studio with billiard table*
Private collection
Tom Roberts, *Portrait of Mrs Abrahams*
National Gallery of Victoria, Melbourne
A. Grogaert, *La Liseuse*
Roy Miles Fine Paintings (Bridgeman Art Library)

359

362

362

An English Aesthetic scheme 1880s

Aesthetic schemes, though apparently eclectic, always seem to follow a set of unwritten but inviolable rules that span cultures. The similarity between this room in a Liverpool house and the American Aesthetic scheme (plate 366) is striking. The wallpaper and frieze if not by Bruce Talbert himself are very much in his style. The tile-inset fireplace surround is a slightly unusual version of a standard pattern that was to become popular in houses without any 'artistic' Japanese pretensions. This kind of Japonisme, as opposed to the full-blown re-creation of a 'Japanese' room was a more subtle and long-lived expression of this widespread influence.

Liverpool Museum, National Museums and Galleries on Merseyside

A DRAWING ROOM MANTEL MADE FOR A COUNTRY HOUSE

363

363

'Furniture in the Anglo-Japanese Taste' 1885

This design by E. W. Godwin for William Watt, drawn by Maurice B. Adams, appeared in the *Building News*, 1 May 1885.

364

The fashion for embroidery 1885

Contemporary commentators emphasized the important contribution to an interior made by embroidery, in which there was a revived interest. Walter Crane credits Mrs Morris and Lady Burne-Jones as the pioneers of this revival; certainly the women members of the Morris firm spent long hours pursuing this occupation, and it is hardly surprising, as with Gertrude Jekyll, that their eyesight suffered. The inspiration for Morris & Co.'s tapestries was European; but here the woman is embroidering on silk in the later Japanese fashion, which may simply be a conceit in tune with the Japanese painted screen.

James Cadenhead, *The Artist's Mother*, oil
City of Edinburgh Art Collection

364

365

365

A Contrast in Taste 1880s

The polarities of taste in the 1880s are exemplified by the Aesthetic japonaiseries of the scheme illustrated right and the solidly traditional 'Jacobethan' design by William Frederick Randall above. This 'Design for a drawing room and organ chamber for Warnham Court, Horsham, Sussex' was exhibited at the Royal Academy in 1888. It is in a style that is typical of the English taste in decoration at this period. It straddled the comfortable line between historical allusion and practical requirement; the appropriate furniture for such schemes was made in commerical quantities which helped keep costs low. Jacobethan-style pieces survive in numbers, and today they are the unacceptable face of Victorian taste. Their very popularity and ubiquity in the late nineteenth century made them an obvious and easy target when the revolt against the Victorian age began in earnest.

Courtesy of the Fine Art Society, London

366

366

The Aesthetic movement in the United States 1880s

North American designers quickly annexed and naturalized aesthetic ideas. The various influences – of Godwin in the side cabinets, Morris in the fireplace tiles, Walter Crane in the wallpaper filling and frieze – have been neatly synthesized to produce a scheme with a strong Anglo-Japanese character. The author of this scheme is unknown, but the provenance suggests it to be American. The graining of the woodwork is unexpected; in a similar Godwin scheme, the woodwork would, more than likely, have been ebonized. In a standard English room of this style the blue-and-white porcelain would have been expected to dominate. The scheme shows the typical division of dado, filling and frieze. The dado would probably have been decorated in gold-painted Lincrusta or leather-paper in a geometric Japanese motif. The filling is of a conventional floral pattern, and the frieze might almost be an adaptation of Walter Crane's dado design of pots and lilies which was exhibited at the influential 1876 Philadelphia Centennial Exposition.

Anon., American school, watercolour
Michael Whiteway, London

367

368

367
The library of John A. Burnham, Boston, Massachusetts 1876

The handsome room depicted here was in a house on Commonwealth Avenue, an area of Boston being developed in the grand manner at this date. The furniture, ornamented with decorative brass hinges and incised and carved work, is of the Eastlake type, but the author stigmatized this as 'a most vague and badly used term', preferring 'domestic Gothic' instead. All the furniture was given a dark finish; in the library black walnut, in the dining room dark-stained American ash. All the colours in the room were sombre, dark red and dull green with a brown pattern. The effect can only have been oppressive, but this sort of scheme was common all over the western world in the mid-century.

From C.W. Elliott, *American Interiors*

368
American Eastlake style 1876

Certain elements are common to the British 'Jacobethan' and the Continental Renaissance styles; but Continental taste inclined towards a more tightly conventional historicism, whereas the clients for Old English or Queen Anne in England were of a kind to edge the style towards a greater freedom of interpretation. In the descriptive text accompanying the drawing of the dining room of Dr Chadwick of Clarendon Street in Boston, included by Elliott in *American Interiors*, there is a clue to the underlying rationale of the English taste. Elliott writes of this seemingly straightforward Eastlakian room: 'Its style may be term[ed] "Old English" mainly because in the days of good sense and good taste this kind of timberwork was well done in England' (p. 73).

From C.W. Elliott, *American Interiors*

369
Wightwick Manor, the Great Hall 1890s

The matching wallpaper and sofa upholstery in Morris patterns complement perfectly the Moorish embroidered table cover and the Old English setting, with its heavy exposed woodwork.

Private collection

369

370

371

370
Scheme for a Louis Seize-style salon 1890s

This is from the design books of Mewés & Davis.

Victoria and Albert Museum, London

371
Decorative scheme for 15 Berkeley Square, London 1872–75

Moncure Conway considered 15 Berkeley Square to be George Aitchison's finest decorative achievement. The decoration was conceived around Frederick Lehmann's collection of antiquities, *objets d'art* and paintings. The colours are limpid and cool, set off by gold overlaid with delicate foliate decoration. A frieze of peacocks in the drawing room was painted by Albert Moore. The scheme illustrated here was for the dressing room *en suite* with the master bedroom. The overdoor panels of birds were painted by Frederick Smallfield, an artist who frequently collaborated with Burges. The whole decoration was carried out by hand; no wallpaper was used. The only dark room in the house was the dining room where, mistakenly, in Conway's view, an earlier ceiling and panelling had been retained.

The British Architectural Library, RIBA, London

372, 373, 374
Decorator's historicism 1870s

These three chaste 'Renaissance' schemes are by the Parisian decorator Alexander-Eugène Prignot (b. 1822). There is no 'antiquarian' clutter in this style: the neatly disposed trophies of arms are a common classical and Renaissance motif and have no significance beyond the ornamental. This brand of decoration was very much an urban taste for the urbane Parisian.

Niall Hobhouse, London

372

373

374

375

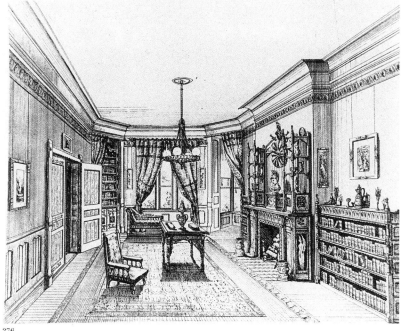

376

377

A·Dining-room·Corner·
Terry & Oakden · Architects·

378

375, 376, 377

Reformed Gothic in England and America 1876

As we can see from the illustrations in Charles Wyllys Elliott's *American Interiors* (1876), the library and dining room of Dr Breck of Springfield in Massachussetts are furnished in the style popularized by Charles Eastlake's *Hints on Household Taste*. In his description, Elliott approves of the form adopted for the furniture in the library:

The style of furniture designed specially for the room may be classed as simple Gothic, adapted to the wants of today, but is not an imitation of anything existing in Henry VII's or any other time. The attempt has been successful, in greater or lesser degree to construct furniture upon true principles, that the grain of the wood should not be twisted or weakened and that the frame which supports the cushions should be distinct and decorative.

Taste in America, as well as deriving from Eastlake, depended greatly on Bruce Talbert's *Gothic Forms applied to Furniture, Metal Work and Decoration For Domestic Purposes* published in the same year.

From C.W. Elliott, *American Interiors* (plates 375, 376)
B.J. Talbert, *Interior in the Gothic Style* (plate 377)

378

A flamboyant example of English Renaissance in Australia 1885

Terry & Oakden architects
La Trobe Collection, State Library of Victoria, Melbourne

379

379
A neo-Gothic steamboat 1861

In the United States infatuation with the Gothic extended even to the decoration of Mississippi steamboats.
Disappointingly, the furnishings of this otherwise carefully Gothicized interior are the kind that would have
formed part of the equipment of any prosperous middle-
class house. A traveller on one of these exotic vessels
commented on the 'gilded saloon', which was 'as clean and
dainty as a drawing room' (quoted by Roy Tyler, *Visions
of America, Pioneer Artists in a New Land*, 1983).

Marie Adrien Persac, *Interior of the Steamboat Princess
Anglo-American Art Museum, Louisiana State
University, Baton Rouge (Gift of Mrs Maimie Persac
Lust)*

380, 381

Americans at home *c.* 1870

The Reverend John Atwood and his family have a predictably austere living room, the pictures few and religious in subject matter, the chairs upright and without cushions or upholstery. However, the curtains are silk, and the table has a handsome green plush cover. The fireplace has been filled with a board covered in the same paper as the walls for the summer months. The lamp with its prismatic drops is, like the furniture and accessories of the room, of good quality, not ostentatious but clearly of the most recent manufacture. The difference in treatment of these two group portraits emphasizes the austerity of the one and the opulence of the other. The Vanderbilt family are gathered in a room with warm yellow walls, crimson plush upholstery and gilt-framed paintings.

Henry F. Darby, oil
Museum of Fine Arts, Boston (Gift of Maxim Karolik to

380

the M. and M. Karolik Collection of American Paintings)
Seymour J. Guy, oil
Biltmore Estate Collection, Asheville, North Carolina

381

382

The dining room of George James, Nahant, Massachusetts 1876

In this room, as in the one from the house in Common-wealth Avenue (plate 367), the style is described as 'domestic Gothic'; but here the furniture is very like examples advertised by the New York firm of Kimbel & Cabus. This furnishing and decorating firm had a stand at the Philadelphia Centennial Exposition in 1876, the year in which *American Interiors* was published. At the level of modest domestic house furnishing they were supremely successful and popular, interpreting in a way that perfect-ly caught the public fancy the Gothic Revival style first promoted by Eastlake. This house on the coast was still unfinished when the book was published. The description suggests that the final result would employ a more delicate range of colours than the town houses. Elliott himself described the room with its light ash furniture and brownish-grey walls as 'light and cheerful'.

From C.W. Elliott, *American Interiors*

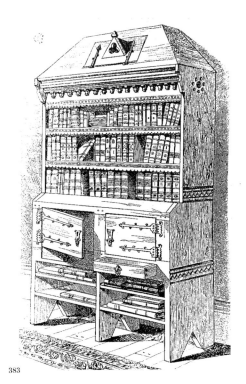

383

KIMBEL & CABUS,

7 & 9 East 20th St.　　New York.

Cabinet Manufacturers and Decorators.

385

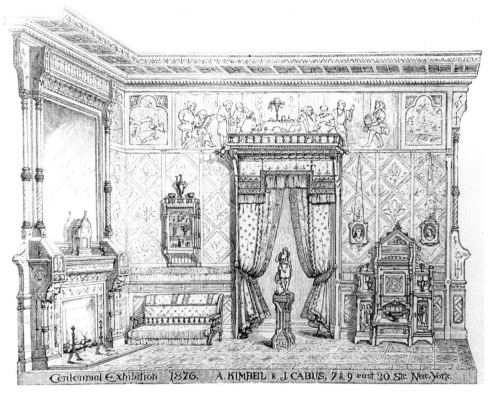

Centennial Exhibition 1876.　A. KIMBEL & J. CABUS, 7 & 9 east 20. Str. New York.

386

NOVEMBER 18, 1865.]　PUNCH, OR THE LONDON CHARIVARI.　195

GOTHIC FURNITURE.

Master George (on the arrival of the new cabinet). "OH, PA! DO LET ME HAVE IT FOR A RABBIT-HUTCH!"

384

383, 384

Punch comments on Eastlake　1865

This cartoon (left) appeared at the time when Charles Eastlake's *Hints on Household Taste* was being published as a series of articles in *Queen* (far left). 1865 was also the year Charles Bevan's Gothic furniture designs appeared in the *Building News*. Furniture in this robust Gothic style was very much an 1860s taste.

Charles Eastlake, 'A Library Bookcase' from *Hints on Household Taste*, 1865
Charles Keene, 'Gothic Furniture', *Punch*, 18.IX.1865

385, 386

Kimbel & Cabus of New York　1876

A trade card and a view of the Kimbel & Cabus stand from the Philadelphia Centennial Exhibition of 1876 give a very good idea of the distinctive style of furniture – derived from Charles Eastlake and Bruce Talbert – that they supplied.

Courtesy of The New-York Historical Society

387

387, 388, 389
Appropriate to the climate 1870s

In contrast to the cluttered and oppressively English-style Government House (plates 449–51), these rooms in a house in Freemantle (right) are furnished with the most insubstantial furniture that could be found, in consideration of the climate. The cane, wicker and bentwood chairs were obtainable from Foy & Gibson's furniture department, along with sideboards of a very common English design. In the accompanying photograph (left) the warehouse is shown fully stocked with a fashionable shipment of furniture. In distant settlements, where the supplies of such luxuries as English or French wallpaper might be very erratic, householders developed an aptitude for all kinds of home decorating. Stencilling was one of the most effective methods of embellishing a room and household magazines in the second half of the nineteenth century frequently carried patterns for cutting stencils. The Victorians had developed this art to a very high degree and patterns of great richness and complexity were achieved. It is possible that some of the decoration in the sitting room shown here, for example, the frieze, might have been made in this way.

Courtesy of The Battye Library, Perth

388

389

390

Holman Hunt in his studio 1865

The artist William Holman Hunt is shown here in his studio in Pimlico, shortly after he had returned from his epic journey to the East to seek out authentic settings for his biblical paintings. On the easel is the unfinished *Finding the Saviour in the Temple* which Hunt started work on in 1856. Scattered about the room are a number of useful and authentic accessories necessary to an artist engaged on an Eastern subject. However, the background of *Finding the Saviour* was painted from the Alhambra Court in the Crystal Palace at Sydenham, a sad comment on the value of his hazardous voyages in search of the true Holy Land.

J. Ballantyne, *William Holman Hunt in his Studio*
National Portrait Gallery, London

391

Beauty is Truth 1882

While beauty for William Morris was a practical necessity, for John Ruskin it was a moral issue. Ruskin's house at Brantwood, near Coniston in the Lake District, is a standard Victorian building that belies its role as one of

392

the great shrines of Victorian intellect. Ruskin's ideas – or lack of ideas – in matters of taste and home furnishings were commented on by friends and followers. Arthur Severn, for many years the *major domo* in Ruskin's household, claimed that Ruskin did not object to a room in 'execrable taste so long as there was a comfortable chair to sit in.' Nor did he seem to care 'what colours went together' (Arthur Severn, *The Professor, A Memoir of John Ruskin*, ed. James Dearden, 1967).

The study was situated in the original cottage part of Brantwood and faces Coniston Water. Apart from two comfortable chairs – one for writing and one for reading – and Ruskin's collection of watercolours by J. M. W. Turner (the painter whom he so ably championed), books and geological specimens dominate the room. The furniture came from Snells in Albermarle Street, London, the company that supplied Ruskin's parents' house in Denmark Hill; these were the furnishings he had grown up with.

W. G. Collingwood, *John Ruskin in his study at Brantwood Ruskin Museum, Coniston*

392

A young man in his College Room

1860s

Intellectual industry is apparent from the books on the table, yet the furniture and decoration in this college room is signally lacking in tell-tale signs of academic purpose. Indeed, the place of honour is given to riding crops. Though some undergraduates gained a reputation for avant-garde tastes in art and decoration, this room epitomizes the ruling taste of the upper-middle classes in the age after the pattern book and before the art-architect designs of the mid-1860s onwards. The room encapsulates everything that the Arts and Crafts movement resented. In the words of Walter Crane: 'furniture [was] afflicted with curvature of the spine . . . monstrosities of every kind [were] encouraged under glass shades.'

Formerly Hazlitt, Gooden & Fox Limited, London

Part Five

1880-1900

394

393, 394

Tile designs of the 1880s

The 'hastebeeste' design is reminiscent of similar exotic beast tiles by William De Morgan. The art of tile design, brought to such a degree of variety and perfection at this date, was one of the most readily available and cheap ways of bringing 'art' to the modest suburban home, and imitators of Morris and De Morgan abounded.

Michael Whiteway, London

Oscar Wilde, Whistler and the 'House Beautiful'

'Through a thick fog I found my way to Tite Street and looked for a white door – which being opened led me into a very ordinary hall passage painted white.' So began Adrian Hope's description of a visit to Oscar Wilde's house, No. 16 (now 34) Tite Street. Writing in March 1885, the first year of the Wildes' marriage, to Laura Troubridge to whom he was engaged, Hope gave a detailed account of all the main rooms in the house including the Wildes' bedroom (quoted in *Oscar Wilde*, by Montgomery Hyde, 1976). On the first floor:

The little manservant showed me into the room on the left looking out across Tite Street. . . . No fire and a look as if the furniture had been cleared for a dance for which the matting did not look inviting. The walls, all white, the ceiling like yours a little (gold) but with two lovely dragons painted in the opposite corners of it. On either side of the fireplace, filling up the corners of the room, were two three-cornered divans, very low, with cushions, one tiny sound Chippendale table, one armchair and three stiff other chairs, also covered with a sort of lacquer. . . . Effect on the whole better than it sounds. All the white paint (as indeed all the paint used about the house) was of a high polish like Japanese lacquerwork, which has great charm for one who hates paper on walls as much as I do.

The specifications for this decorating work survive in the papers of the architect, E. W. Godwin, who designed the scheme as well as much of the furniture for Wilde's house. For example, the entrance hall, which did not strike Mr Hope as being particularly out of the ordinary:

Dado 5' 6" Grey. Wall band white. Wall over and ceiling yellow. Woodwork white. Staircase: Walls and ceilings yellow. Dado grey continuing hall. Woodwork white and wall band to step with stair at intervals of 4 or 5 steps. Drawing room front: Woodwork ivory white walls distempered flesh pink from skirting to cornice. The cornice to be gilded dull flat lemon colour gold and also the ceiling margin to Japanese leather which latter will be provided by Mr Wilde and is to be properly fixed by Contractor. The wall band to be moulded wood as per sketch but ivory white. Drawing room back: Distemper pale green ceiling and cornice walls green darker.
Fireplace woodwork painted brown pink.

Adrian Hope was very taken with this drawing room:

The room at the back has a very distinctly Turkish note. No chairs at all. A divan on two sides of the room, very low, with those queer little Eastern tables in front. A dark dado, but of what colour I know not, as the window, looking on a slum, they have entirely covered with a wooden grating on the inside copied from a Cairo pattern which considerably reduced the little light there was today. A gorgeous ceiling and a fire quite made me fall in love with this room. . . .

The ceiling so much admired by Hope was designed by Whistler, and inlaid with peacocks' feathers.

Wilde's son, Vyvyan Holland, recalled the room as being 'lined with a peculiar embossed paper called lincrusta-walton, with a William Morris pattern of dark red and dull gold. The general decor was a mixture of the Far East and Morocco. . . .'

The dining room was perhaps the most unconventional of all. The specification gives little idea of a scheme that was far in advance of its time, especially as the dining room was the most unvaryingly equipped room of all, even in the houses of otherwise eccentric design.

For the dining room Godwin designed a suite of white furniture, the chairs in various Grecian forms, and around the walls an arrangement of shelving from which the meals were served. Adrian Hope continued:

Lunch was in the dining-room. . . . A cream coloured room with what Oscar assured me was the only sideboard in England, viz. a board running the whole length of the room and about nine inches wide at the height of the top of the wainscoting. Table of a dirty brown with a strange device: maroon napkins, like some rough bath towels, with deep fringes. Quaint glass and nice food made up a singularly picturesque table.

Wilde wrote ecstatically to Godwin about his designs: 'I enclose a cheque, and thank you very much for the beautiful designs of the furniture. Each chair is a sonnet in ivory, and the table is a masterpiece in pearl.'

Wilde's views on interior decoration, as embodied in his often repeated lecture on *The House Beautiful*, were a compound of ideas which he had heard discussed by Godwin and Whistler; not surprisingly, the decoration of Tite Street owed an overwhelming debt to Whistler's extraordinarily original schemes for his houses at 2 Lindsey Row (now 96 Cheyne Walk) and Tite Street (the White House at No. 13).

Whistler remarked to his friend Théodore Duret, 'For you know that I attach just as much importance to my interior decorations as to my painting' (letter of 1885); and he was credited with a number of decorating schemes for friends: Sir Thomas Sutherland, William Heinemann, Mortimer Menpes and Mrs D'Oyly Carte. The latter explained Whistler's intervention as follows:

It would not be quite correct to say that Mr Whistler designed the decorations of my house, because it is one of the old Adam houses in Adelphi Terrace, and it contained the original Adam ceiling in the drawing-room and a number of old Adam mantelpieces, which Mr Whistler much admired, as he did also some of the cornices, doors and other things. What he did do was to design a colour-scheme for the house, and he mixed the colours for distempering the walls in each

case, leaving only the painters to apply them. In this way he got the exact shade he wanted, which made all the difference, as I think the difficulty in getting any painting satisfactorily done is that painters simply have their stock shades which they show you to choose from, and none of these seem to be the kind of shades that Mr Whistler managed to achieve by the mixing of his ingredients. He distempered the whole of the staircase light pink; the dining room a different and deeper shade; the library he made one of those yellows he had in his drawing-room at The Vale [in Chelsea], a sort of primrose which seemed as if the sun was shining, however dark the day, and he painted the woodwork with it green, but not the ordinary painters' green at all. He followed the same scheme in the other rooms. His idea was to make the house gay and delicate in colour.
(Quoted in Pennell, *Recollections*, pp. 160–61.)

The passage above suggests a collaboration of perfect harmony and sensitivity, a contrast indeed with the scenes that attended the impetuous creation of the Peacock Room. In 1869 Whistler's Liverpool friend and patron Frederick Leyland bought a house in London, 49 Prince's Gate, and chose Richard Norman Shaw to reconstruct it in collaboration with Whistler and Thomas Jeckyll, who was to be responsible for installing Leyland's collection of porcelain on a specially designed scheme of shelves in the dining room.

The house is not particularly distinguished, and stands in a typical 1840s Victorian terrace, built to the design of H. L. Elmes. Inside, Norman Shaw helped to create an Italian palazzo, embellished with marble and mosaic, the wide staircase with its baluster of ormolu and bronze rescued from Northumberland House. This opulent setting provided the background for Leyland's collection of paintings, with Botticellis and Lippo Lippis among the works of Rossetti, Burne-Jones, Albert Moore and G. F. Watts. The limitations of Leyland's taste are well caught by Theodore Child in his description, 'A Pre-Raphaelite mansion', written for *Harper's Magazine* in 1890:

The morning-room is exceedingly cosy and comfortable, and at the same time every object in it is in good taste. The walls and ceilings are panelled with oak, inlaid with black and white woods in a simple geometrical design. The walls above the dado are covered with three large and six smaller pieces of Beauvais tapestry, with Teniers subjects, in perfect preservation and freshness of colour. On the floor is a bright Oriental carpet. The cabinets are Indian, Tyrolese and Italian work beautifully inlaid. The bibelots and ornaments are all choice, but discreetly arranged.

The focal point of the dining room was to be Whistler's painting *La Princesse du Pays de Porcelaine*. Whistler thought the colour scheme for the room, notably the pink flowers on the Spanish leather lining the walls and the red carpet border, conflicted with his painting. Leyland gave

Whistler permission to change the colour of the flowers; but he was not prepared for the elaborate peacock-feather decoration on the shutters, dado, ceiling and cornice, and he refused to pay the large sum demanded by Whistler for it. The alteration of his scheme literally drove Jekyll mad; but the Peacock Room is one of the most celebrated achievements of nineteenth-century decoration.

Murray Marks, who had reason to be bitter over the destruction of the planned background to a collection of blue-and-white porcelain, much of which had been bought by Leyland from his shop, recognized the room as a masterpiece. C. E. Williamson, Marks' biographer, wrote:

No one who has ever dined in the room or has ever seen it when closed and lit up, can say a word against the almost miraculous beauty of the decoration, which, by artificial light when the shutters which formed an integral part of the scheme were closed, was quite wonderful and entrancing, but it was complete of itself, not a background for porcelain or for anything else, a chef d'oeuvre doubtless, one of the great pieces of decoration in the world, but not what had been planned or proposed in view of the precious blue and white porcelain that was to have adorned its shelves.
(*Murray Marks and His Friends*, 1919, p. 95.)

395
Whistler's Peacock Room in Leyland's home at Prince's Gate, London 1869

Michael Whiteway, London

396

Whistler's Peacock Room in Leyland's home at Prince's Gate, London 1869

Michael Whiteway, London

Beautiful houses in the 1880s

Not everyone, even among those with artistic abilities and an interest in the 'house beautiful', adopted the Aesthetic style. Laura Troubridge described in her diary the decorating in 1880 of their new house at Hunstanton in Norfolk:

We were given a hundred pounds of our own money and went up to London with this in a bag. We began by seeing Irving at the Lyceum and fell in love with his wonderful flame colour velvet curtains, so decided we must have the like for the drawing-room. This, although not a large room, had a big bow window so needed an amount of curtain material. We found out where Irving's velvet came from and got some, quite undeterred by the fact that it was silk velvet and ten shillings a yard, only eighteen or twenty-two inches wide. We wanted a ceiling paper and saw one with gaily coloured humming birds but thought its white ground dull, so we had some made in Paris with a gold ground. The walls of the room were orange with a dark wooden dado and mottoes painted round the cornice. The carpet was plain brown

velvet pile. We also spent five pounds on a coffee set, but later decided we could not afford coffee after dinner! All this sounds rather silly, but we did not regret it for Hunstanton was a very bleak, dreary place, especially in winter, and our little room with its amazing ceiling and bright glowing walls and curtains was a great comfort.
(Laura Troubridge, *Life Amongst the Troubridges. Journals of a young Victorian 1873–1884*, ed. Jacqueline Hope-Nicholson, 1966, p. 155.)

Perhaps the charm of the Aesthetic style had palled for them by 1880. Some six years earlier the young Troubridges had experimented with a thoroughly artistic scheme for their 'den' in their grandparents' house:

Amy's present rage, which is shared by me, is to make her room pre-Raphaelite, with a border of P.R. bull rushes all round it. . . . The walls are pale yellow, with a rather wide pale blue-green border, the two doors and the window frame are black, with blue and gold panels – it is so pretty (p. 84).

One wall was hung with striped Moorish silk, with black shelves against it on which were displayed the fruits of 'china-hunting', a passion with the Troubridge girls. They also painted their own pots and tiles, a pastime that was later to be turned to good account when they sold tile designs to a London dealer, Mortlock, who had a shop in Oxford Street.

The colour scheme for the 'den' anticipated that of the drawing room in St John's Wood of a most celebrated arbiter of taste, Mrs Haweis. In 1878 Mary-Eliza Haweis moved with her husband and family to a house in St John's Wood Road, where she proceeded to decorate her drawing-room in shades of amber, cream, gold, yellow and blue. The house became known as the Amber House. Not long after moving in, Mrs Haweis started work on her influential publication *The Art of Decoration*, which appeared in the summer of 1881. In the last section of the book Mrs Haweis makes a plea for the architect of a house to interest himself in the details of its decoration and furnishing, in the design of the fireplaces, the doors, even the furniture. It seems like an echo of Charles Eastlake's words written nearly fifteen years earlier; in the introduction to *Hints on Household Taste* he had remarked:

Fifty years ago an architect would have perhaps considered it beneath his dignity to give attention to the details of cabinet work, upholstery and decorative painting. But I believe that there are many now, especially among the younger members of the profession, who would readily accept commissions for such supervision if they were adequately remunerated. . . .

Eastlake was probably aware of straws in the wind. The age of the architect-designer had already dawned by the time those words appeared in print. Mrs Haweis must have known that architects were actively involved in the interior adornment and arrangement of the houses that

397
Rossetti's bedroom at 16 Cheyne Walk 1882

H. Treffry Dunn, who painted many of the rooms in the house including this view of the bedroom, recorded his impressions in *Recollections* (1904):

I thought it a most unhealthy place to sleep in. Thick curtains, heavy with crewel work in the 17th century designs of fruit and flowers (which he had bought out of an old furnishing shop somewhere in the slums of Lambeth), hung closely drawn round an antiquated four poster bedstead. A massive panelled oak mantelpiece reached from floor to ceiling, fitted up with numerous shelves and cupboard-like recesses all filled up with a medley of brass repoussé dishes, blue china vases filled with peacock feathers, oddly fashioned early English and foreign candlesticks, Chinese monstrosities in bronze, and various other curiosities, the whole surmounted by an ebony and ivory crucifix. The only modern thing I could see anywhere in the room was a Bryant and May match box! On the other side of the bed was an old Italian inlaid chest of drawers, which supported a large Victorian mirror in a deeply carved oak frame. Two or three very uninviting chairs, that were said to have belonged to Chang the Giant – and their dimensions seemed to warrant that statement as they took up a considerable amount of space – an old fashioned sofa, with three little panels let into the back, whereupon Rossetti had painted the figures of Amor, Amans and Amata, completed the furniture of the room. With its rich, dark green velvet seats and luxurious pillows, this sofa looked very pretty and formed the only comfortable piece of furniture visible.

H. Treffry Dunn, watercolour
Private collection

397

398

398
'My Aesthetic love' 1881

Once widely accepted, the Aesthetic movement became an easy target for cartoonists and satirists of the 1880s. China, Japanese fans and peacock feathers were instantly recognizable motifs. As with most long-running fashions, Aesthetic accessories become relatively cheap. Unlike the 'bamboo' furniture of the 1820s which was of beech made to look like bamboo, mass-market japonaiserie and chinoiserie pieces were actually made of bamboo. Godwin had originally designed his furniture with an eye to cost, making it accessible to a wider market once it was plagiarized by the big firms. The year 1881 was also when F.C. Burnand's play *The Colonel* opened, a skit on the Aesthetic movement. Godwin attended a performance and observed that the sets were too well designed to serve satire well. And, he noted, the leading lady's dress was ridiculed on stage, but one very similar was unremarkable when she wore it leaving the stage door.

A. Concanen, *My Aesthetic love*, pictorial music cover

they were designing. With the new publication which followed *The Decoration of Houses* she demonstrated the extent of her acquaintance with some of the most highly evolved examples of the work of the architect-designer. *Beautiful Houses* was published in 1883; it contains descriptions of such notable artistic achievements as Leighton's house in Holland Park Road designed by George Aitchison, Alma-Tadema's remarkable Roman villa in St John's Wood (not far from the Amber House) and G. H. Boughton's house in Kensington.

Not long after the publication of *Beautiful Houses* Mrs Haweis was at last able to occupy the most quintessentially artistic house of them all, Rossetti's Tudor House on the river at Chelsea. Although this had been sadly neglected, much remained as it had been in Rossetti's day and some things Mrs Haweis left untouched; not surprisingly the beautiful faded yellow of the walls in the long first-floor drawing room were retained.

Mrs Haweis was at heart a Pre-Raphaelite. She had experimented when she was first married with a white-painted room, but had regretted it as a failure because she believed it to be unflattering to the complexion. She would have been startled to find herself behind the times in decorating taste, but by the time *Beautiful Houses* appeared Wilde's dining room was only a year into the future. The idea caught on and became widely accepted as 'artistic', a sign of sensibility and exquisite taste.

One debatable result of the effect on taste of the 'Exhibition' style was the prominence given to ingenuity and intricacy in manufacture. The highly ornamented curvilinear furniture and decorative pieces in the enduringly popular rococo style were made possible by machine production. The very antithesis of the 'Eastlake' style, it is first and foremost a commercial decorator's style, lacking the relationship between functional structure and surface ornament that is the most important characteristic of architect-designed furniture. The designs of Bruce Talbert, for example, a considerable influence on American taste in the second half of the nineteenth century, are based on straight lines ornamented with architectonic detail, such as dentil friezes and moulded cornices, or pointed-arch and cusped-arch panels. This produced a very satisfying harmony between the decoration of the shell of the room and the design of the contents.

This is the path that led to the Arts and Crafts Movement: the Renaissance palaces of the Vanderbilts were going in another direction. There are two strands of American taste for this neo-Renaissance style, just as there were in England. In her reminiscences Consuelo Vanderbilt Balson described the house in New York in which she spent her childhood:

Choosing Richard Morris Hunt as her architect, my mother built a large ornate white stone house in the French Renaissance style at the north-west corner of Fifth Avenue and Fifty-second Street. . . . The dining-room was enormous and had at one end twin Renaissance mantelpieces and on one side a huge stained-glass window, depicting the Field of the Cloth of Gold on which the Kings of England and France were surrounded with the knights, all not more magnificently arrayed than the ladies a-glitter with jewels seated on high-backed tapestry chairs behind which stood footmen in knee-breeches.
(*The Glitter and the Gold*, 1953, p. 8.)

The Vanderbilt houses in New York were legendary. The interiors were fabulously ornate. The house of William H. Vanderbilt, built between 51st and 52nd Streets, was decorated by the celebrated firm of Herter Brothers. It was their largest commission, using six or seven hundred craftsmen for a year and a half on the furniture, carpets, marquetry and mosaics. With the third Vanderbilt house, that of Cornelius Vanderbilt II at 1 West 57th Street, the Tiffany House on Madison Avenue at 72nd Street, the Havermeyer House, and the famous Villard Houses built round three sides of a courtyard on Madison Avenue, New York acquired in a very short space of time in the early 1880s a nucleus of Renaissance-style houses of a grandeur that cumulatively was never equalled at any other time in the nineteenth century.

In spite of Consuelo Vanderbilt's reservations, these French inspired neo-Renaissance interiors achieved for the Villard and Vanderbilt Houses in New York, the Pitman House in Cincinatti, and the Ames-Webster House in Boston, make an impressive and individual contribution to the art of interior decoration. Those described and illustrated in *Artistic Houses* (1882–4), a lavish publication celebrating the work of the most fashionable decorators of the day (for example Herter Brothers, Tiffany's Associated Artists and Calvert Vaux) are mainly in New York, but the Oliver Ames House in Boston was no less splendidly ornate. The mosaic-encrusted ceiling of the drawing room is as intricate as that in W. H. Vanderbilt's New York palace, and the easily recognizable fabrics from Herter Brothers are used for the upholstery.

However, Consuelo Vanderbilt's distaste for her childhood home proved to be a straw in the wind of the reaction to come. The tremendous amount of artistic impedimenta cluttering up the neo-Renaissance interior was seen as being long overdue for reassessment. Inevitably, since the framework, wall decoration, carved panelling, ornamented friezes and elaborately moulded architraves were not appropriate to a more austere approach, much highly evolved and beautifully crafted work was jettisoned along with the meretricious jugs, bowls, fans, photograph frames and bunches of pampas grass.

The book in which the new purist approach is outlined appeared in 1897. *The Decoration of Houses* by Edith Wharton and Ogden Codman has been described as the

THE CIMABUE BROWNS. ("TRAIN UP A CHILD," &c.)

Antiquated Grandpapa (fresh from Ceylon). "Now, my Darlings, we're going to make a regular day of it. First we'll go to the Zoo. Then we'll have a jolly good blow-out at the Langham Hotel. And then we'll go and see the Pantomime at Drury Lane!"

Master Cimabue. "Thanks awfully, Grandpapa! But we prefer the National Gallery to the Zoological Gardens!"

Miss Monna Givronda. "Yes, Grandpapa!—And we would soonah heah Handel's *Judas Maccabæus*, or Sebastian Bach's glorious 'Passions-Musik,' than any Pantomime, thank you!"

399

399

'The Cimabue Browns'

This cartoon by George du Maurier appeared in *Punch*, 3.I.1880.

starting point for 'interior decoration as we know it today' (John Fowler and John Cornforth, *English Decoration in the Eighteenth Century*, 1974, p. 15). This charming book, with its emphasis on the superiority of French taste and on the importance of good proportion based on architectural principles, brings to mind a whole different spectrum of light and colour in rooms, an atmosphere of soft blues and yellows sparkling with the reflections from gilt-framed mirrors, as epitomized in the paintings of Edith Wharton's great friend Walter Gay. A reviewer wrote of the book:

When the rich man demands good architecture his neighbours will get it too. The vulgarity of current decoration has its source in the indifference of the wealthy to architectural fitness. Every good moulding, every careful detail, exacted by those who can afford to indulge their taste, will in time find its way to the carpenter-built cottage. Once the right precedent is established, it costs less to follow than to oppose it.

(From the anonymous review in *Architect and Building News*, 22 January 1898.)

The Wharton-Codman influence spelt the demise of a long-lived nineteenth-century obsession with re-creating styles of past ages or of alien cultures – notably of the East. Houses with suites of rooms running the gamut of Gothic, Renaissance, Rococo, Louis Seize, Egyptian, Japanese and Indian styles became old-fashioned almost overnight. The first twentieth-century generation of decorators were Wharton-Codman converts, and the fundamental message of the book – that the best way to decorate involved a simple, uncluttered and coherent scheme based on the finest classical examples of French and Italian architecture – was to prevail with traditionalists (as opposed to modernists) for a very long time.

400
The French château of an American aesthete *c.*1900

Walter Gay was a friend of Edith Wharton, and the eighteenth-century scheme in his painting would have come close to the ideal offered in Wharton and Codman's *The Decoration of Houses* (1898). Refinement is apparent in every detail: the blue mounts and gold frames of the Old Master drawings follow the example of the eighteenth-century collector Mariette. The white-painted chairs were a feature of the eighteenth-century revival that was taking place in the avant-garde Paris of the 1890s. Translated into the language of the American rich, this style – which had attracted Parisians because of its simplicity and relatively low cost – becomes coarse and oppressive. Forsyth Wickes, the Boston collector, understood the delicacy of the eighteenth-century style, and his donation of furniture and *objets d'art* to the Museum of Fine Arts in Boston is an example of this taste correctly interpreted.

Interior at the Château de Breau. Seine-et Marne, oil
Private collection

400

401

401, 402
The clutter disappears 1881–1908

In the 1880s 'artistic' rooms were still full of clutter, but it was artistic clutter. More austere rooms arrived with the fashion for antique furniture and watercolours. These two rooms span a period of more than twenty years. The Clausen painting of 1881 (above) shows an early example of the plainly decorated and sparsely furnished style. The semi-circular side table with inlaid banding *à la* Sheraton has an early eighteenth-century mirror hung above. In the reflection is an arrangement of autumn leaves and dried grasses stuck unceremoniously into an oriental pot. The watercolours have plain gold frames and wide white mounts. The Rothenstein picture of a room in Hampstead (right) exhibits many similar features. The simplicity is enhanced by the good furniture; likewise, the furniture has no competition. Such rooms, by virtue of their lack of pretensions, have a timeless charm. This is perhaps possible only when the furniture – which constitutes the main feature of the room – is both loved and admired.

George Clausen, *Interior*, 1881
Private collection
William Rothenstein, *Hampstead Interior*, 1903
Courtesy of the Fine Art Society, London

402

403

403, 404, 405
'The house of taste' 1888

We have a record of Menpes's interiors in the photographs taken to illustrate the auctioneer's catalogue when his house in Chelsea was put up for sale in 1909. Few Japanese schemes were carried out so ambitiously or with such indifference to the conventional contemporary standards of comfort. Menpes himself had started off more tentatively and his previous house in Fulham, which had been decorated with Whistler's help, was furnished with elegant Sheraton-style chairs and tables, the rooms being merely embellished with some ornamental Japanese fans and embroideries. In 1888 Menpes stated his own views on interior decorating in a description of the scheme to a reporter from the *Pall Mall Gazette*, and the following note appeared on 13 December 1888:

THE HOUSE OF TASTE – THE IDEAS OF MR MORTIMER MENPES ON HOME DECORATION.

Imagine walls and ceiling of a lovely lilac hue, from which hangs a weird Japanese lantern. On your left standing under the screened window, is a round table clothed with a rich Japanese cover with dragons and strange fish and birds woven into the fabric. Upon this cover lie a Japanese card-tray and a Japanese box. The floor is covered with a simple cloth of black and white squares, upon which a huge Japanese frog keeps guard over the gong. This is only a panel of the picture, for the completion of which you must look through an open door into a luminous little chamber covered with a soft wash of lemon yellow, which is relieved by a trio of sombre etchings, gems by Whistler, by Menpes and by Short. . . . From the antechamber we passed through the open door into a large drawing-room, of the same soft lemon-yellow hue. The blinds were down, the fog reigned without, and yet you would have thought that the sun was in the room.

Menpes is quoted as finding the yellow scheme to be immensely flattering to the complexions of his visitors. On taking over the house he had found it papered with sage-green 'diaper' paper by Morris – one of the most popular patterns, much in evidence at the Linley Sambourne House and in Ionides's house in Holland Park – which he had instantly replaced with the colour washes described above. He presented his views on decorating as his own, though they were taken directly from Whistler's friends and supporters. They were possibly also surprised that this style of decoration should seem to the writer of the *Pall Mall Gazette* to be so startingly original at this date. Only with the Mackmurdo house did Menpes move into realms completely beyond even the extravagance of the 'Peacock Room'. The kind of complete scheme that Menpes achieved was rarely successful in the hands of less analytical Japanese fanatics.

Royal Borough of Kensington and Chelsea, London

404

405

Theatrical orientalism   1890s

C.J. Phipps designed this room at 7 Chesterfield Gardens, London W1 (below) for Rachel and Frederick Beer. Phipps was the leading architect of theatres in the 1880s and '90s; Frederick Beer was the son of Julius Beer, who had owned the *Observer*. Frederick became proprietor in 1880. He had travelled widely before returning to London to edit the *Sunday Times*, a post that he relinquished to his wife, Rachel Sassoon, when he became editor of the *Observer* in 1894. Indicative of the clutter in this room is the fact that the camera appears in the mirror, a rare occurrence in the Lemere *oeuvre*. Chesterfield Gardens is an example of what amateur orientalism could be in the hands of the rich. With advice and guidance from

406

'Eunice', the home decorations column in *The Lady*, and purchases from Liberty's, most middle-class homes could have their oriental cosy corners, with bamboo chairs, Japanese fans and more or less Far Eastern wallpapers and textiles.

In the Edward Lauterbach house at 2 East 78th Street, a magnificent mansion sited near the newly built Metropolitan Museum of Art (1894), each of the reception rooms was devoted to the arts of a different culture. The hall and stairway were decorated in the Islamic style with embroidered hangings, mosque lamps, ewers and furniture inlaid with ivory and mother-of-pearl imported from the Near East. The dining room was Romanesque European, a riotous mixture combining medieval and Renaissance motifs. The drawing room was rococo of a most debased kind with carved Belter-style seat furniture, Chinese, Japanese and Turkish embroidered silks and a tiger skin on the geometric parquet floor. The billiard room (above right) in the Japanese style is uncharacteristically restrained. Although it owes nothing to the refined Japanese of Whistler and Godwin, it is by no means the most overdone of the Japanese-style rooms of its day. The applied bamboo fret on the walls recalls the best of the Brighton Pavilion decoration. The embroidered cover to the billiard table, a pair to one used most jarringly in the drawing room, is perfectly appropriate here.

The taste for japonaiserie varied in thoroughness and authenticity. It was largely metropolitan taste and fulfilled a need that Arts and Crafts satisfied in a suburban setting. This London house (below right) belonged to John Hatchard Smith, and was in De Vere Gardens, Kensington. The chair in the background in front of the folding screen was advertised by P. Bastendorff & Co. in *The Cabinet Maker and Art Furnisher* for September 1886. Other firms specialized in split and varnished bamboo: W.F. Needhams of Birmingham advertised bamboo lengths for appliqué-work dados, ceilings and friezes as well as the openwork screen that is used as a divider between these two rooms.

Photographs by H. Bedford Lemere (plates 406, 408)
National Monuments Record, London
Photograph by Joseph Byron
Byron Collection, Museum of the City of New York

407
408

409

409, 410

Belle Vue House, Chelsea 1882

William Bell Scott, who had clearly felt little enthusiasm for Morris's 'Palace of Art', lived from 1876 in an elegant eighteenth-century house on the river in Chelsea. However, without making any very radical changes but by mixing antique furniture and rugs amongst practical pieces for daily use, Bell Scott achieved a very refined version of the 'Aesthetic' manner for himself. The touches of Queen Anne and Japonisme were discreetly applied; in the sitting room the ceiling was picked out in blue and white, like Wedgwood ware. An overmantel with brackets

was contrived to house a display of oriental plates. It resembles the rather more carefully designed overmantel in the China Room of J.VL. Pruyn (plate 411). In the library the distinctive frieze was formed of panels very sparsely decorated with birds, which also fly across the blue ceiling. The dado and walls beneath the frieze were painted, respectively, Indian red and green; the ceiling very faint blue in the centre with darker blue meeting the cornice. The result is a charming setting with a very individual character.

From Moncure Conway, *Travels in South Kensington*, 1882

411

The China Room of J.V.L. Pruyn, Albany, New York 1876

As American Ambassador in Peking, Mr Pruyn availed himself of the opportunities for collecting Oriental porcelain and lacquers. These he interspersed with fine examples of European wares, for example Sèvres – both contemporary and eighteenth-century pieces – Meissen and Dresden, as well as old majolica and delftware. This is a collector's room, the decoration of white and crimson being conceived entirely as a background to the display. In the centre of the parquet floor a massive dark blue Sèvres vase stands on a crimson Indian rug; the overmantel mirror is framed with a border of crimson velvet on which velvet-covered brackets support small and exquisite items of rare porcelain. The velvet mantel pelmet is also crimson, less of a fire hazard than usual as the grate contains 'a gas-fire imitation of soft-coal'.

From C.W. Elliott, *American Interiors*

411

410

412, 413

Dining Room and Drawing Room of the Grand Ducal Palace, Darmstadt 1906

In 1897 M.H. Baillie Scott was commissioned by Ernst Ludwig, Grand Duke of Hesse, to redecorate the Drawing Room and Dining Room in the palace at Darmstadt. The two rooms were designed to present a contrast, the Dining Room dark and rather heavy as a foil for the light and delicate Drawing Room. However, contemporary photographs, the only surviving evidence for the appearance of these rooms, suggest that they looked almost uniform with pale panelling and a much darker frieze. As well as the Arts and Crafts furniture, supplied by Ashbee's Guild of Handicraft and including one of the singular chairs derived from Burne-Jones's *Holy Grail* tapestries, the Drawing Room was soon furnished with other odd bits and pieces very detrimental to the effect intended by the designer.

From M.H. Baillie Scott, *Houses and Gardens*, 1906

414

414, 415
Old English and Art Nouveau combined *c.* 1900

In this scheme for the decoration of the dining room (below) at Glen Falcon, Douglas, Isle of Man, Baillie Scott has taken the Old English style as his starting point for a scheme incorporating some Art Nouveau features, such as the very obtrusive frieze and the leaf-and-branch capitals to the supporting piers of the inglenook and the top of the sideboard. This scheme was exhibited in 1900 at the Royal Academy; the critic in *The Studio* remarked on the source, commenting: 'Mr Baillie Scott with his discreet and his early methods of decoration, is well represented' (vol. 20, July 1900, p. 94). The source for the bedroom (left) is clearly the same, though the architectural elements are less obtrusive. The very shallow fireplace surround echoes the Queen Anne style, and was a favourite device with Baillie Scott for rooms where an inglenook was not appropriate. This design was also published in *The Studio*.

From M. H. Baillie Scott, *Houses and Gardens*, 1906

415

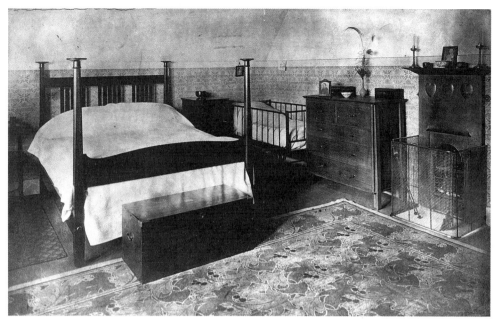

421

422

421

Richness out of simplicity 1899

The Orchard, Chorleywood was C.F.A. Voysey's own house which he built for himself in 1899, at the mid-point of his two decades of successful practice before the Great War. Though devoted to the vernacular style, he rejected a historicist approach; he saw himself developing a tradition. It is not always easy to trace in his designs everything that he claimed in his writings. In designing interiors, cleanliness was a priority: he avoided dust-traps even on his own clothes, which he designed for himself without lapels or trouser turn-ups. He insisted that a house was a friendly place: 'light, bright, cheerful rooms, easily cleaned and inexpensive to keep. Not mocking the abodes of the wealthy, but sincerely sufficient for our use' ('The Aims and conditions of the modern decorator', *Journal of Decorative Art*, xv). Rooms are usually low-ceilinged in Voysey's houses, as he considered them cheaper to heat; the surfaces are usually hard, easily cleaned tiles or enamel-painted woodwork. The richness of his furniture designs stems from well-proportioned pieces, usually of oak, that are set off by a carefully chosen decorative feature, more often than not employing a heart motif. It is the recurring heart motif and the delicately tapering forms that mark Voysey's furniture. Because Voysey himself designed all the details of a house down to door latches and hinges, the rooms, though filled with strong individual decorative features – furniture, fire-place, wallpaper and frieze – still have a sense of wholeness. Like Morris & Co., Voysey was later absorbed into suburbia and his idiosyncratic art has been watered down and tainted by bad copies and careless borrowings. His simple forms lent themselves to mass production, but once out of Voysey's hands they lost his 'sense of grace, proportion, dignity, delicacy or greater fitness' (Voysey, 'Ideas in Things' from *The Arts Connected with Building*, ed. T.R. Davidson, 1909). This picture shows the bedroom at The Orchard, Chorleywood, Hertfordshire.

National Monuments Record, London

422

Ashbee at home *c.* 1900

C.R. Ashbee's Magpie and Stump, the architect's own house on the Chelsea Embankment, London, had the distinction of a mural decoration by the young artist and critic, Roger Fry.

From *The Studio*

423

424
A ducal commission 1890s

Most Arts and Crafts architects used designs that were but variations on a simple theme that had developed from the vernacular and sophisticated Gothic forms. The cottage – in fact or fiction – was the chosen ideal. The reconstruction of Welbeck Abbey, near Nottingham, called for a richness rarely seen in the secular buildings of the Arts and Crafts era. In 1889 Henry Wilson was asked to complete work at Welbeck left unfinished at the death of J.D. Sedding, the designer originally commissioned. Wilson was Sedding's assistant. He produced schemes for the library and chapel which were rejected by the Duke of Portland as far too dear even for a peer of his means. This is a design for the screen for the approach to the Chapel.

The British Architectural Library, RIBA, London

423
A Scottish architect's own house

c. 1904

The Pleasance, Gullane, Muirfield was designed by the architect Sydney Mitchell for his own occupation. Shown here is the living room, an interesting amalgam of Arts and Crafts, Old English and Art Nouveau, furnished in the revived eighteenth-century manner. The exposed beams of the ceiling, although painted white, bear down oppressively on the space. It is curious how the architect has employed every conceivable visual trick to reduce the apparent height of this not very lofty space, a device in the tradition of Nash's attempts to make Prinny's cottage at Windsor seem smaller than it really was. The other rooms in the house also have very noticeable decorative features at frieze height, giving an oddly cramped appearance to the proportions of the wall between the skirting and the frieze. Hermann Muthesius thought this house of sufficient interest to merit inclusion in his *Das englische Haus*, 1904.

Photograph by H. Bedford Lemere
Private collection

424

425

425, 426

A French artist at home   Early 1900s

The dining room of Jacques-Emile Blanche's house near Dieppe is done up in the true 'artistic' style, which is self-consciously unstylish, or even anti-style. The ensemble is arranged to suit personal whim and habit. Like Sarah Bernhardt, Blanche was ahead of his time in admiring French provincial furniture and toile de Jouy. The advantage of being ahead of your time is, of course, in the price.

Photographs by J. Walter Barnett
Victoria and Albert Museum, London

427

Madame Bernhardt chez elle   1894

Shown here rehearsing a play, the actress was both a lionized celebrity and an artist. She had a talent for sculpture, and the room has much of an artist's taste in the toile de Jouy and white-painted eighteenth-century style chairs. The ailing palm in its ribbon-decked basket supplies an actressy glamour appropriate to her professional fame.

Photograph from the *Picture Magazine*, January–June 1894

427

426

428

428, 429
Scandinavian Arts and Crafts 1890s

Carl Larsson was an early subscriber to *The Studio* (first issued in 1893), and was familiar with the wider European trends of Japonisme and Arts and Crafts; in his own house he introduces elements of traditional Swedish folk art as well as eighteenth-century revival and his own personal touches. Larsson's wife's contribution to the decoration was the hand-woven embroidered textiles. Larsson's series of twenty-six watercolours, *Ett Hem*, recorded these sophisticated interiors. Published in 1899, it established the Scandinavian style of Arts and Crafts interior.

'Atel jen, ena Hälften' and 'Lathörnet', watercolours
Nationalmuseum, Stockholm (Statens Konstmuseer)

429

430

430

An American artist's country studio 1894

The scene of this painting is the artist William Merrit Chase's summer studio at Shinnecock, Long Island. When it was exhibited it was quite well received by the critics, although one commented on the subsidiary role allotted to the two figures, remarking that the furnishings, the silks and cushions seemed to assume a greater importance in the composition. This can hardly have displeased the artist, since it was what he had intended. Now, at a distance of nearly a century, the environment in which the action is depicted takes place has a social and historical interest of its own. Merrit Chase frequently used his studios as settings for his pictures. The New York studio building on 10th Street, which had become the focus for a group of artists including Winslow Homer and Edward Lamson Henry, features in many of his works in the 1880s; in the 1890s he concentrated on the summer studio at Shinnecock. The difference in tone cannot be explained simply by the different phases in his work: the colours, rich and dark with gold ornament, deemed appropriate to the city would have been quite out of place in the bright sunlit rooms at Shinnecock, where light, clear colours prevail. The chair in the foreground, Japanese and of bamboo, still very fashionable in the 1890s, stamps this as a rural retreat.

W. Merrit Chase, *The Friendly Visit*
National Gallery of Art, Washington DC (Bridgeman Art Library)

435

436

435, 436, 437
Light and air in Denmark *c.1890*

Larsson's *Ett Hem* provided the popular landmark for a style of 'artistic' interior that had been developing in Scandinavian artistic circles since the 1860s. The Arts and Crafts ideal was often a vehicle for chauvinism, the re-assertion of values peculiar to a nation and culture. The vaunting of the vernacular against the academic was one of the attractions of Arts and Crafts. Scandinavia as a whole began to break with the dominant Continental academicism in the 1860s. Most notable were the group of artists who gathered for summers at Skagens, a seaside village in northern Denmark. Their usual subject matter was their own simple daily life, with a strong and conscious rediscovery of Nordic values. This celebration of an artistic – and Nordic – milieu made simple folk life fashionable. Apart from the inexpensive life, Skagens' attraction was the northern light. The new emphasis on the bright, creamy luminosity went hand in hand with the rediscovery of eighteenth-century neo-classicism: Danish art and interiors of the years from 1800 to 1870s had been dominated by a musty, Kierkegaardian gloom. The composition of the Bindesbøll portrait emphasizes the ceramic pot almost at the expense of the subject, a reference to Bindesbøll's leading role in Danish decorative arts; pottery design was one of his interests.

Ludwig Find, *Thorwald Bindesbøll in his Workroom*, 1890
Statens Museum for Kunst, Copenhagen
Viggo Pedersen, *Woman and Child in an Interior*, 1888
Statens Museum for Kunst, Copenhagen
L. Tuxen, *Coffee is Poured, Skagens, c.1890*
Private collection (Bridgeman Art Library)

437

438, 439, 400
The Indian tradition 1870s

The great achievements of Moghul decoration fascinated British travellers. Paintings, and later photographs, were sought by visitors. The fine tracery of the floral ornament found its way into both furniture and interior designs. Alfred Morrison's London house at 16 Carlton House Terrace was decorated by Owen Jones, whose refined classical ornament fades into the trailing stylized flowers of Indian inlay. Jones's interior was dominated by the Moorish style, and the jump to Moghul from Moorish was not great. George Aitchison employed formal floral devices very close to Indian prototypes in his design for an inlaid serving table for Frederick Lehmann.

Lockwood Kipling, brother-in-law of artists Edward Burne-Jones and Edward Poynter, was responsible for the Indian billiard room (below right) added in about 1886 to Bagshot Park, in Surrey, home of the Duke and Duchess of Connaught. Queen Victoria must have been

179. Saman Burj or the Princess' Boudoir, Delhi

439

440

favourably impressed by what she saw when she visited the house in 1890, for it was at this date that she conceived the idea of her own Indian Room (above) at Osborne House, her maritime residence on the Isle of Wight. Lockwood Kipling was applied to, and he recommended that a colleague at the Lahore School of Art, Ram Singh, should come to England to execute the woodwork and supervise installation. For this room, the mouldings were cast in plaster from carved wood details by Messrs. Jackson & Co. The ornament is again very intricate, but resplendent rather than meretricious, as was much of the Indian work that found its way here.

Photograph of the Princess's boudoir, Moti Masjid, Agra
Victoria and Albert Museum, London
Photographs of the Indian Room at Osborne, Isle of Wight, and the Billiard Room at Bagshot Park, Surrey
National Monuments Record, London

357

The Indian Merchandise at Liberty's
c. 1900

Trade and the *va-et-vient* of travellers, visitors and architects to the sub-continent ensured an increasingly scholarly regard for Indian culture which culminated in exhibitions that were held in the second half of the century at South Kensington. These exhibitions gave important exposure to the work of Indian craftsmanship and renewed interests in Indian ornamentation. Chauvinism helped, too, when in 1876 Disraeli gave Queen Victoria the title Empress of India.

Private collection

441

442

443

LA CHASSE AUX LIONS.

Mrs. Ponsonby de Tomkyns (bursting into her husband's smoking-room). "PONSONBY! QUICK!! PEN, INK, AND PAPER!!!—AND WRITE IMMEDIATELY!!!!

Mr. Ponsonby de Tomkyns. "WHAT IS IT NOW, MY LOVE?"

Mrs. Ponsonby de Tomkyns. "WHY, MONSIEUR DE PARIS IS COMING OVER WITH HIS FAMILY TO VISIT ENGLAND. WRITE AND SECURE THEM FOR THURSDAY WEEK. WE SHALL HAVE CROWDS—ALL LONDON!"

Mr. Ponsonby de Tomkyns. "MY LOVE, HIS ROYAL HIGHNESS WILL NEVER COME TO THE LIKES OF US!"

Mrs. Ponsonby de Tomkyns. "YOU GOOSE! IT'S NOT THE COMTE DE PARIS! IT'S MONSIEUR DE PARIS, AS THEY CALL HIM—THE PUBLIC EXECUTIONER, YOU KNOW. DO AS I TELL YOU!"

[*Ponsonby did as he was told. All London came to Mrs. Ponsonby de Tomkyns's Thursday Afternoon—but Monsieur de Paris DIDN'T. He took his Wife and Children to Madame Tussaud's instead, to see the Guillotine! Faithless Monsieur de Paris!! Poor Mrs. P. T.!!!*

444

442, 443, 444

Smoking rooms   1879, 1900

George du Maurier's vision of the Ponsonby de Tomkyns' smoking room (left) has a rather theatrical, contrived look. The heraldic window, however, would have implied big investment, and would not necessarily disappear when fashion turned against the Turkish divan and caned chairs. The other rooms (above) are much less expensive. Many Japanese schemes were realized very cheaply from readily available bamboo furniture and fitments manufactured from imported lengths of bamboo and small lacquer panels. A few ornaments, fans and prints and the effect was complete. The widely popular dado was made of Japanese *tatami* matting. Even Morris was known to approve of this idea.

'Pretty rooms and what they cost', *The House*, 1900 (plates 442, 443)
From *Punch*, 12 July 1879 (plate 444)

445, 446, 447

An Indian scheme by H. & J. Cooper 1893

The Indian Room at Osborne seems restrained in comparison with a scheme carried out for Mrs Wallace Carpenter in 1893 by H. & J. Cooper at Ashley Place, Westminster. Such a thorough-going scheme was presumably rare. Cooper's are known to have done several rooms akin to Ashley Place; an Indian scheme for exhibition by them (below) later appeared in *The Magazine of Art*, 1904. However, most people who were attracted to Indian furnishings stopped at a few curiosities such as pierced metal lights, trays, rugs and embroideries. Cooper's 'Indianization' looks from photographs to have been flimsy in execution, and the popular charm of such eye-catching rooms may well have been their low cost. Complete, and greater, Indian schemes do survive, for example, the Durbar Room assembled in Lord Brassey's Grosvenor Square House (now in the Hastings Museum) and the rooms at Bagshot Park.

Photographs by H. Bedford Lemere
National Monuments Record, London

445

446

447

448

The drawing room at Hallmore 1887

This is a modest and typical example of artistic taste. The Japonisme is not overdone; there is a renewed respect for the Sheraton style of furniture. This kind of room would not have been particularly fashionable when first arranged, and might have stayed almost unaltered well into the present century. One feature that would have changed was the treatment of the furniture. The heavy mahogany and ebonized surfaces of the typical Victorian piece had encouraged the use of french polish, and this bad habit had carried over into the eighteenth-century revival of the 1890s, when many Sheraton pieces were scraped, filled and 'French polished' with shellac. This was contrary to the eighteenth-century practise of waxing wood. The flat and uniform high finish of french polishing was preferred into the first decades of the twentieth century. Fashionable antique-hunters were slow to appreciate that something old should show signs of its age in the colour and texture of the wood.

From a family album
Private collection

448

449, 450, 451

Government House, Perth, Western Australia *c.*1885

These photographs show the Gothic-style mansion, in about 1885, when Sir Frederick Broome was Governor. He is shown standing by the fireplace, reading. It was observed that throughout much of the nineteenth century the Australian settlers remained faithful to the conventions of furnishing that were in fashion in Britain, even though this was absurd in view of the very different climate.

The flowery carpets and heavy solid chairs of England's cold and foggy climate reign supreme beneath the Austral sun. The Exhibitions have done something towards reforming our domestic interiors, but it will be a long time before the renaissance of art as applied to households, which appears to be taking place in England, makes its way her in any considerable force.
(R. Twopenny, *Town Life in Australia*, 1883, p. 40.)

The rooms in Government House are indistinguishable from a rather commonplace English town house of the same date.

Courtesy of The Battye Library, Perth

449

450

451

452
The dining room of
George W. Wales 1876

A Boston Back Bay house of a more modest kind than the great Commonwealth Avenue town mansions, this is the ambiance of a dedicated china collector. The many devices adopted for the display of collections in an age of china-mania are fascinating. Mr Wales reputedly had the largest china collection in Boston, and this room is put forward by Elliott as an example of the effective use of the 'few fine old china dishes' that exist in most households. The colour scheme for the room was crimson for the walls, widely held to be an ideal background for a display of china, and green, the furniture and woodwork being of oak.

From C.W. Elliott, *American Interiors*

452

453

453–456
The Ames-Webster House,
Boston 1890s

It is difficult to imagine a more different approach to room arrangement in two houses of the same date in the same city and even the same neighbourhood as these magnificently appointed rooms and Mrs Gardner's heterogeneous assemblage of superlatively rare and valuable works of art (plate 42). The Ames-Webster mansion stands on the corner of Commonwealth Avenue in the Back Bay area of Boston. Immensely elaborate in conception, with a romantic profusion of mansard roofs and pavilions, turret-like chimneys and lines of dormer windows, the house was started in 1872 for Frederick L. Ames by the firm of Peabody & Pearce. Additions were made in 1882. The interiors shown here are by Herter Brothers. The most remarkable thing about the scheme of the drawing room (overleaf, plate 456) is how closely it resembles that of the drawing room decorated by the same firm for J. Pierpont Morgan in his vast Madison Avenue house in New York (see Thornton, *Authentic Decor*, 1984, plate 441). The room has the same deep cove with painted 'mosaic' decoration, the same moulded frieze, the same ceiling, the same dado and many of the same pieces of furniture.

The Bostonian Society, Boston

455

456

457

457

Dining Room, Tudor House, Hampstead 1890s

Tudor House was built in 1883 for William James Goode (1831–92), the son of Thomas Goode, founder of the chinaware emporium in South Audley Street, London. He employed George & Peto who created the 'Aesthetic Rooms' in the Goode shop.

Photograph by H. Bedford Lemere, *Intérieures anglais*
Private collection

458

Curling Hall, Largs 1890s

Curling Hall, built by the Paisley architect T.G. Abercrombie (1862–1926), was situated in the seaside town of Largs. The glass of the doors, with its bevelled edges and pitted surface, was experimental and new in 1893, but was later to become a common feature.

Photograph by H. Bedford Lemere, *Intérieures anglais*
Private collection

459

The Smoking Room, 34 Alexandra Drive, Liverpool 1890s

Designed and installed by S.J. Waring & Sons for R. R. Lockett. The tiles of the fireplace surround are Craven Dunnill.

Photograph by H. Bedford Lemere, *Intérieures anglais*
Private collection

458

459

460, 461, 462

Three grand dining rooms   1880s–90s

The painting below shows a dinner at Haddo House nearing its end. The dessert has been served and the piper is walking up and down the room playing to the guests. Lord and Lady Aberdeen are entertaining Gladstone in their newly renovated dining room. Decorated in the revived eighteenth-century style by firms from Edinburgh and London in 1880, it was still quite an advanced taste for that date. The choice of the pale bluish green for the walls is characteristic and the lamp on the delicate, tall, gilt torchère is of eighteenth-century neo-classical inspiration. The colour scheme is reminiscent of an eighteenth-century painting – the delicate gold screen in particular, with its swags and flying birds. Just such a screen, also decorated with birds, is a prominent feature of Boucher's *La Toilette* (Thyssen Collection). The furniture throughout the house is eighteenth-century style reproduction and was installed with the carpets, curtains and wall hangings during the renovations. The table decoration of autumn leaves is very unusual, quite unlike the elaborate formal arrangements recommended by household manuals of the period. The editions of Mrs Beeton at this date and well into the Edwardian period have colour plates showing garlands of smilax edging the table cloth, and graduated trumpet-shaped silver vases with cut flowers at each place setting, as well as in the centre of the table. The fern-like plants in the silver wine cooler mirror the table decorations at Sandringham which, though

460

more profuse, also feature plants in silver containers – wine coolers and cisterns, beakers and goblets. The many-branched candelabra with the individually shaded candles are a conventional feature of both these arrangements, but it is curious to notice the napkins on the table at Sandringham: at a time when the taste for elaborate, tortured folding of starched linen was at its height, they are simply folded to lie conveniently at each place. In contrast, even the unlaid table at Ranfurlie, in Australia (above right), suggests the elaboration of the table setting. The profusion of vases with their cut-flower arrangements would have been matched by decorative silver baskets and individual chafing dishes with spirit burners. As at Haddo, a large screen masks the serving door, but in this more modest household a gasolier with five lamps replaces the candelabra. The Sandringham dining room (below right), of course, has works from the incomparable royal collections on the walls – at Haddo an elegant arrangement of portraits forms the only ornament on the plainly decorated green walls. At Ranfurlie, however, patterns proliferate. On the walls the filling and frieze are separated by a formal border and the ceiling is papered with another pattern within the plasterwork cornice. Ranfurlie is not exceptionally over-decorated, in fact it is even quite restrained for the date; but the contrast with the cool eighteenth-century revival taste at Haddo is marked.

Alfred Emslie, *Dinner at Haddo House*, 1884
National Portrait Gallery, London
The dining room at Ranfurlie, 1890s
La Trobe Collection, State Library of Victoria, Melbourne
The dining room at Sandringham, from an album of the 1890s
Victoria and Albert Museum, London

461

462

463

464

463

Rothesay Terrace, Edinburgh 1890s

Sydney Mitchell built this house for John R. Findlay (1859–98) who was the proprietor of *The Scotsman*, an antiquary and one of the major benefactors of the Scottish Portrait Gallery. The plates inserted in the dado rail were secured with brass rings; this rare device is also to be found in Alma-Tadema's designs for Henry Marquand's house in New York.

Photograph by H. Bedford Lemere, *Intérieures anglais*
Private collection

464

Billiard Room, Byfleet Lodge, Weybridge 1890s

This photograph was taken for the decorators Trollope & Sons in 1883. The Moyr Smith illustrative panels supply a sense of lavishness to a very common detail in English houses of this date. Bannister Fletcher, in the *Architectural Record* of 1895–96, wrote: 'A very pretty and useful feature in a billiard room is an extra space at one end, where may be planned the fireplace, and which can be fitted up with a card table and raised lounges for watching the game itself. Sociability is certainly a feature of the end of this century, and ladies do not separate themselves nearly so much from gentlemen as was formerly the custom. This space or nook, then, can be used by the ladies when doing their work, while the gentlemen are enjoying a game at billiards without losing the pleasure of each other's society.' Bannister Fletcher, 'Smaller Houses of the English Suburbs and Provinces', *Architectural Record*, vol. v, 1895–96, p. 321.

Photograph by H. Bedford Lemere, *Intérieures anglais*
Private collection

465

Monkhams, Woodford, Essex 1890s

Woodford was a respectable London suburb of the 1890s. Monkhams was decorated for Arnold Hill by George T. Robinson, who was chief in-house designer with Trollope & Sons. Robinson also write on art and decoration for *The Manchester Guardian* as well as the *Magazine of Art*; he had trained as an architect, but in the 1880s devoted himself to interior design, much of his work being done for ocean liners.

Photograph by H. Bedford Lemere, *Intérieures anglais*
Private collection

466

467

466, 467
Princess Mathilde's hôtel in the rue de Berry, Paris 1882

In the rue de Berry house an *enfilade* of reception rooms culminated in the great sixty-foot long *jardin d'hiver* roofed with glass (plate 121). The *salons* were furnished sumptuously and with a view to the evenings of conversation for which the Princess was celebrated. These two sketches by François Schommer show the intimate groups of chairs that would have formed the setting for the literary and political discussions that she enjoyed. These rapidly executed brush and wash sketches are reminiscent of an oriental painting style, possibly influenced by the great interest in Japanese art of this period.

F. Schommer, *Interior views of the hôtel in the rue de Berry*, brush and wash
Musée des Arts Décoratifs, Paris (Sully-Jaulmes)

468
A staircase hall at the turn of the century 1882

By the end of the century the purist approach to historical revival styles had been abandoned. The eclecticism which is the hallmark of the nineteenth century lost all its pretensions to order or system. The accumulation of *objets* and curiosities here has no obvious relationship to the architecture, which is a version of the reformed Gothic with unusually delicate coloured stained glass windows. The collecting follows no particular programme: it is a personal accumulation of a kind that can only survive as a 'time capsule'. The experience of such celebrated examples as Calke Abbey in Derbyshire and Erdigg in Wales suggest that the arrangement of possessions is so tuned to one individual's taste that rationalization and reconstructions fail to create an atmosphere in which the whole becomes more than simply the sum of its uneven parts.

Jonathan Pratt, oil
Christopher Wood Gallery (Bridgeman Art Library)

475

475, 476

The Gardner sitting room in Boston and the house of a London architect 1890s

The taste in evidence in this scheme for the house of an architect (right) has something in common with Jack and Isabella Stewart Gardner's in their Beacon Street house (above). Tapestries, bronzes, cabinets and rare early wooden sculptures might all have been found in the Gardner house. This room is in 7 Collingham Gardens, photographed while occupied by Harold Peto, partner in the architectural firm of Peto and George, who were responsible for the development of Collingham and Har-

rington Gardens in London. The collection of *objets d'art* and bric-à-brac has none of the breadth and connoisseurship that distinguishes the Gardner collection, with the result that this Aesthetic interior has a more self-conscious air than the artlessly overcrowded treasure house in Boston. Peto's predilection for the Northern Renaissance was entirely suited to the style of the house with its rather dark and heavy Jacobethan detailing, historicist panelling and coffered ceilings. In 1897 Ogden Codman and Edith Wharton wrote in *The Decoration of Houses* (p. 187):

Good objects of art give to a room its crowning touch of distinction. Their intrinsic beauty is hardly more valuable than their suggestion of a mellower civilisation – of days

476

when rich men were patrons of 'the arts of elegance', and when collecting beautiful objects was one of the obligations of a noble leisure. The qualities implied in the ownership of such bibelots are the mark of their unattainableness. The man who wishes to possess objects of art must have not only the means to acquire them, but the skill to choose them – a skill made up of cultivation and judgement, combined with that feeling for beauty that no amount of study can give, but that study alone can quicken and render profitable.

Photograph Isabella Stewart Gardner Museum, Boston
Photograph by H. Bedford Lemere, *Intérieurs anglais*
Private collection

477

478

479

477, 478
C'est Bing *c.* 1900

The *Salon Bleu* created by Georges de Feure and the dining room from the Atelier de l'Art Nouveau exemplify the taste that was emerging in turn-of-the-century Paris. The exhibit mounted by Siegfried Bing was widely publicized and the shapely furniture designs were rather insensitively plagiarized in Britain by commercial firms such as Liberty's and Warings. The purer forms of Art Nouveau remained the preserve of Continental designers, finding particularly powerful expression in Milan and Brussels.

Drawings, heightened with gouache
Musée des Arts Decoratifs, Paris (Sully-Jaulmes)

479
A room in the Dijsselhof, The Hague 1890

Although this ambitiously figured woodwork has a strong Art Nouveau flavour, the actual proportions are conventional. Only the most outstanding designers were able to dictate the actual structure so that the elongated or curving forms could be carried through to the very walls of the building itself. Most Art Nouveau decoration is merely surface ornament supported by furniture with 'whiplash' lines. Once these superficial decorative elements were removed, a new 'Modern' effect was easy to impose on the bare shell.

Gemeente Museum, The Hague

480
An American dressing room 1890s

This very completely realized example of the highly ornamented and detailed style of interior decoration is from the Rockefeller House at 4 West 54th Street in New York. Such built-in schemes with the carved surrounds and the finest inlay in the woodwork, all made to match the specially designed free-standing furniture, are rare and very expensive to execute. Aitchison and Owen Jones made similar schemes for their wealthy patrons, for example Frederick Lehmann and Alfred Morrison; intricately carved woodwork was a feature of Rothschild taste, notably at Halton and Mentmore. The repeating motif in the door and window surrounds, in the form of a 'trophy' of toilet implements, a cut throat razor, scissors and hand-mirror, is a delightful touch, if inappropriate to the 'Saracenism' that inspired the scheme as a whole.

Museum of the City of New York

480

481, 482
A château in Denmark 1911, 1916

Liselund is a small neo-classical château in a 'rustic' idiom situated on the island of Mons, Denmark. It was built in 1795 by Baron de la Calmette as a present for his wife, Lisa. The château was set in an English-style parkland, and has been preserved along with the colourful *trompe l'oeil* interiors. Liselund fascinated the artist Peter Ilsted (1861–1933), who often painted the château. The pale, cool colours of the interior caught the mood of the younger Danish artists at the turn of the century. Liselund had remained untouched throughout the nineteenth century, and when the widow of the second owner died in 1877 the château was unveiled in its pristine beauty. Its lightness and colour reappeared at the very time when Denmark was beginning to shake off its dark and sombre decorative phase. Shown in Ilsted's painting

482

is a view of the Garden Salon seen from the doorway of the Monkey Room; it is decorated in a simplified Louis Seize style with the painted wood furniture ranged around the room in the eighteenth-century manner. The Monkey Room itself, with the eponymous monkey on a tall pier glass, is in pale pink with Wedgwood-style medallions. This range of pinks, mauve-greys, ivory woodwork and lime-whitened floorboards is characteristic of Ilsted's work. Other Danish artists, Vilhelm Hammershøi (1864–1916) and Carl Holsøe (1863–1935), also painted interiors that exploited the same neo-classical, simply furnished rooms with walls and woodwork in luminous, creamy blues. Ilsted was obviously conscious of the Dutch interior genre, but the colour schemes that form the backdrop to his interiors are assuredly *after* Liselund. The revived eighteenth-century taste forms the background to the two girls playing, and the chairs closely echo the chairs in the Liselund dining room. The silhouettes on the wall complete the effect.

Interior at Liselund, oil, 1916; *Interior with Two Girls Playing*, mezzotint, 1911
Bury Street Gallery, London

481

483

Josephine and Mercie 1908

Tarbell's domestic scene has a background which is constructed around elegant antique pieces. The room served as an all-purpose sitting room in a household that did not possess a whole suite of dressing room, boudoir and morning room. It has a lived-in ease that belonged to a degree of wealth, but without the social constraints and expectations that dominated the plan and purpose of the Victorian home.

Edmund Tarbell, *Josephine and Mercie*, oil, 1908
Corcoran Gallery, Washington DC

483

484

485

484, 485
The sitting room at
179 Queen's Gate *c.* 1892

One of two adjacent houses designed by William Emerson (1843–1924) for two returning Anglo-Indian nabobs. No. 179 was built for G. W. Allen (1831–1900), a business-man who made his fortune in newspapers in British India. No. 178 was built for James Walker who had been a banker and one of the proprietors of Allen's *Allahabad Pioneer*. The choice of Emerson was presumably decided by his Anglo-Indian connections: he had built Lucknow Cathedral and the university at Allahabad. That two old Anglo-Indian hands between them should have created such a Western interior is something of a disappointment. Emerson's designs return some way to his professional beginnings in the office of William Burges, as the ornate Gothic fireplace in the sitting room suggests. For the rest, Arts and Crafts style is mixed freely with Elizabethan revival.

Photographs by H. Bedford Lemere, *Intérieurs anglais*
Private collection

The library of William Cullen Bryant, Roslyn, Long Island 1876

The library of the poet Bryant (1794–1878) is furnished with pieces of traditional
American manufacture made to suit the modest late eighteenth-century house. Bryant himself
provides the description of the room:

*The shelves of the library are of wood of the tulip tree, rather neatly made and varnished.
They contain from three to four thousand volumes. There is a fireplace in the room which was
once of the ample dimensions common a hundred years ago, about the time that the house was built,
but is now reduced to such dimensions as to receive a Franklin stove or open fireplace.
This has been surrounded by Dutch tiles of ancient pattern, representing events in Scripture history.
The room has bay-windows, one on the North side looking out upon a cluster of huge pear trees,
supposed to be more than a hundred years old, between the trunks and branches of which
we caught glimpses of Hampstead Harbour and white gleams of gliding sails.*

From C.W. Elliott, *American Interiors*

THE WORKING LIBRARY OF A NINETEENTH-CENTURY ARCHITECT AND DESIGNER

James O'Byrne (1835-97)

The libraries owned by the men and women – artists, architects, designers and critics – who formed the dominant tastes of their time are of great interest, and it is rare to find such collections catalogued intact. This ignorance about book-collecting also extends to the secondary figures in art and architecture. The library of James O'Byrne is a happy exception. From its catalogue we can pinpoint the works of reference that would be to hand for a Victorian architect working in the Gothic-revival style.

In July 1987 the library of the Liverpool-based architect was dispersed at Christie's, London in a sale comprising 235 lots. Much of the material is predictable, the standard periodicals and reports that any architect would acquire in the course of his professional career. Many of the volumes carry not only O'Byrne's own bookplate, but also the stamp of his drawing office in Liverpool.

To an extent the catalogue simply serves to confirm what can be easily deduced; that the architects of the period had access to a varied range of illustrated publications. Historicism in architecture and decoration requires that practitioners should be well informed of precedents and ancient models. Some of this working knowledge would have been acquired first-hand by sketching. The rest would probably have been drawn from illustrated publications which made available structures and ornaments from all civilizations and historic periods. Some of the forms of nineteenth-century architecture and decoration can be traced back directly to the influence of this or that publication. The eclectic nature of nineteenth-century design is understandable given the wide choice of material illustrated in these publications, and the date when certain key studies appeared is very relevant to a perception of its development.

As a pupil of Pugin, a Catholic and an architect of numerous ecclesiastical buildings, O'Byrne would naturally have had a strong interest in this strain of architectural scholarship. He possessed works by Pugin; he also owned Batty and Thomas Langley's *Gothic Architecture* (1747), the great inspiration for eighteenth-century Gothic design as Pugin would be for the neo-Gothic of the nineteenth century. He had several of Henry Shaw's highly illustrated works: *Details of Elizabethan Architecture* (1835), *The Encyclopedia of Ornament* (1842) and *Specimens of Tiled Pavements* (1859), as well as *Specimens of Ancient Furniture* (1866 edition), which was probably the most influential of Shaw's publications, all of which were widely copied. So were James Colling's two works, *Gothic Ornament* (1846–50) and *Art Foliage for Sculpture and Decoration* (1865).

Works of equal interest to antiquarians and architects included R. Billing's *Baronial and Ecclesiastical Antiquities of Scotland* (1845–52), Edward Blores' *Monumental Remains of Noble and Eminent Persons* (1826) and J. Britton's *Architectural Antiquities* (1807–26) and *Fonthill Abbey* (1833). There was the standard work on the Old English style, Joseph Nash's *The Mansions of England in the Olden Time* (1839–49), and also John Clayton's *Collection of Ancient Timber Edifices of England* (1846).

He had Burges's *Architectural Drawings* (1870), but books by other leading figures of High Victorian Gothic must be considered under-represented: Sir George Gilbert Scott's *Personal and Private Recollections* is noted, but nothing by Edmund Street or John Sedding except for a folio collection of photographs, prints and cuttings entitled 'Gothic Architecture'. This may have been assembled by O'Byrne himself, and features his more celebrated contemporaries, including Street, Norman Shaw and Alfred Waterhouse. French contemporary architecture is covered in the handsomely illustrated eight volumes of César Daly's *L'Architecture privée du XIXe siècle* (1872–77) and also his historical survey *Motifs historiques d'Architecture*, which covered architecture in France from the Renaissance to Louis XVI.

As might be expected, Eugène Viollet-le-Duc is strongly represented, with six works including the highly influential ten-volume *Dictionnaire raisonné de l'Architecture française du XIe au XVIe siècle* (1858–68). John Ruskin, the guru of art and morals for many in High Victorian England, has comprehensive coverage with seventy-seven volumes.

The library also included James Stuart and Nicholas Revett's *Antiquities of Athens* (1762–1816), Robert Adam's *Ruins of the Palace of the Emperor Diocletian at Spalato in Dalmatia* (1763) and Isaac Ware's *Designs of Inigo Jones*, which were the most important English sources for classical architecture. Palladio, Scamozzi and Piranesi and William Watkin's edition of Vitruvius (1812) give good coverage of Roman and Italian buildings, while rare French works such as d'Hancarville's *Collection of Etruscan, Greek and Roman Antiquities* (1766–7) and Monfaucon's *L'Antiquité Expliquée* (1722, supplement 1757) also figure in the library.

O'Byrne had books on the less mainstream styles of the day: J. Bourgoin's *Les Arts arabes: Architecture* (1873). Parvillée's *Architecture et décoration turques au XVe siècle* (1874). He seems to have kept abreast of fashion with S. Bing's *Artistic Japan*, Thomas Cutler's *Grammar of Japanese Ornament and Design* (1880) and a collection of Japanese picture books. His interest in Japan did not extend to Christopher Dresser, none of whose writings seem to have been in his possession, though Owen Jones was represented by both *The Grammar of Ornament* and the *Alhambra*.

As to the gaps in what might be expected of a Victorian library, it is hard to say whether they are later losses or signs of lack of interest on O'Byrne's part. However, this was the great age of the periodical, and *The Builder* and *Building News* and *The Architect* would have supplied most of the information and ideas required by the practising architect. Other periodicals he absorbed were J.C. Loudon's *The Architectural Magazine* (1834–38) and the *Art-Union*, later to become *The Art Journal*. He, or his office, took *The Church Builder*, *The Magazine of Art* and *The Studio*, and the French monthly *Le Moniteur des Architectes*.

Plainly, evidence that an architect or designer had a book in his possession does not constitute proof he plagiarised from it; however, it must be assumed that the busy practice had little time for the painstaking invention of ornament. Clients and critics who were also fellow architects often rewarded archaeological exactitude in Gothic-revival buildings more highly than original invention, and since a great deal of an architect's work consisted of restoring medieval churches, textbooks may be called essential tools of the trade.

In the case of William Morris, the relationship between his book collecting and his sources of inspiration is now becoming clearer. Morris's library contained a greater percentage of antiquarian books; he held no good opinion of modern works, even if many illustrated books of the nineteenth-century were of a very high standard (*William Morris and the Art of the Book*, exhibition catalogue, Pierpont Morgan Library, New York, 1976).

O'Byrne's library is a rare survival. Although we still have the sketchbooks of many eighteenth- and nineteenth-century architects from which it is possible to trace the evolution of many of their decorative schemes, the clues provided by the catalogue of such a professional library are an invaluable addition.

A bibliography of nineteenth- and early twentieth-century works

The list that follows does not claim to be exhaustive. It will, however, give an indication of the nature and variety of published source material on decoration available to the nineteenth-century architect and decorator.

1801
PERCIER, C. and FONTAINE, P.F.L.
Recueil de décorations intérieures, Paris
Influential neo-classical source book of interiors showing details of decoration and furnishings by these French designers.

1802
DENON, DOMINIQUE-VIVANT
Voyage dans la Basse et la Haute Egypte, Paris
Reflected the interest in Napoleon's discoveries in Egypt and provided Thomas Hope with inspiration for his Egyptian decoration and furniture.

1803
REPTON, HUMPHRY
Observations of the Theory and Practice of Landscape Gardening, including some remarks on Grecian and Gothic architecture, London
The 'remarks' on architecture are still relevant to the sensible planning of a modest house for the use of a family rather than for a display of grandeur.

1804
BEAUVALLET, PIERRE-NICHOLAS
Fragment d'Architecture, Sculpture et Peinture dans le style antique, Paris (reissued 1820)
An inexpensive and practical pattern book of motifs for a variety of craftsmen including, according to the author, carpenters, manufacturers of chintz, mousseline and printed calico, japanned ware, enamel and glass.

1807
BUSBY, C.A.
A Collection of Designs of Modern Embellishments suitable to parlours, dining and drawing rooms, folding doors, chimney pieces, verandas, friezes, etc., London (date approximate)
Busby studied at the Academy Schools and commenced his career in England, but in 1815 he departed to America in order to avoid his creditors. When he returned he entered into partnership with Amon Wilds and was responsible for much of the Regency-style terraced housing in Brighton.

HOPE, THOMAS
Household Furniture and Interior Decoration, executed from designs by Thomas Hope, London
The impact of this book was considerable, although there is little evidence of direct copying of the designs.

WILKINS, WILLIAM
The Antiquities of Magna Graecia, Cambridge
Illustrations and descriptions of the important sites of antiquity visited by Wilkins during his four-year tour of the Greek and Roman antique world, 1801–5. The Grecian sites yielded material of more relevance to architects than to decorators, though Thomas Hope attempted to arrive at an authenticity of the spirit of Greek ornament in his suggestions for Grecian interiors and furniture. Later Greek-revival decoration tended to rely on the application of ornamental details culled from a somewhat limited vocabulary of conventional motifs.

1808
DANIELL, THOMAS & WILLIAM
Oriental Scenery, London (6 vols, completed 1808)
The illustrations to this publication and the subsequent *Picturesque Voyage to India* (1810) provided inspiration for the Indian style in the early nineteenth century.

REPTON, HUMPHRY
Designs for the Pavilion at Brighton, London

SMITH, GEORGE
A Collection of Designs for Household Furniture and Interior Decoration, London
A more approachable, and thus more influential, collection than Hope's of the previous year, this book of designs comprises 158 coloured plates of predominantly Grecian inspiration but with some Gothic, Egyptian and Chinese examples.

1809
ACKERMANN, RUDOLF
Repository of Arts, London (to 1828)
A monthly magazine with ideas for 'fashionable furniture', drapery and decoration reproduced in colour. Included were designs by G. Smith, George Bullock, A.C. Pugin and J. Taylor.

1810
LANDI, GAETANO
Architectural Decorations, London

OSMONT and DEZON
Recueil de Draperies d'Hallavant mis an jour et augmenté par Osmond et Dezon, Paris
Hand-coloured plates of draperies, curtains, beds etc. in the Empire style.

1812
SMITH, GEORGE
A Collection of Ornamental Designs, after the antique, London
Forty-three engraved plates in a linear style reminiscent of Percier and Fontaine.

1813
BEUNAT, JOSEPH
Recueil des dessins d'Ornements d'architecture de la manufacture de Joseph Beunat, à Sarresbourg et à Paris, Sarresbourg and Paris
Trade catalogue of designs in the Empire style of

Percier and Fontaine containing decorative details of every description as well as complete room schemes with ground plans. The material used for the manufacture of these decorative accessories may possibly have been *carton-pierre*, a substance closely related to papier-mâché. This firm was subsequently acquired by Heiligenthal of Strasbourg, a large firm that handled the distribution of Percier and Fontaine's decorations throughout Europe.

1814
MOSES, HENRY
A Collection of Antique Vases, Altars, Paterae, Tripods, Candelabra, Sarcophagi, etc. from various museums and collections, London
One hundred and fifty-one plates, some hand-coloured, by Thomas Hope's collaborator on *The Costume of the Ancients*; much used by students and designers.

1817
GELL, SIR WILLIAM and GANDY, JOHN P.
Pompeiana. The Topography, Edifices and Ornaments of Pompeii, London (to 1819)
Gell rightly claimed that this was the first publication in English on the finds at Pompeii, which first came to light in 1748, but were only systematically excavated from 1755. An edition of *Pompeiana* appeared in French in 1827.

PYNE, W.H.
The History of the Royal Residences of Windsor Castle, St James's Palace, Carlton House, Kensington Palace, Hampton Court, Buckingham House and Frogmore, London (to 1819)
Most of the hand-coloured aquatint plates in the three volumes of this beautiful production are of interiors.

1820
AGLIO, AGOSTINO
Architectural Ornaments, London

1822
BORSATO, GIUSEPPE and VALLARDI, GIUSEPPE
Opera ornamentale di Giuseppe Borsato, Venice
Illustrated with sixty plates of designs for furniture and interiors in the manner of Percier and Fontaine. Borsato (1771–1849) was Professor of Ornament at the Accademia in Venice.

1823
RUTTER, JOHN
Delineations of Fonthill and its Abbey, Shaftesbury
An illustrated guide to Beckford's Gothic fantasy with descriptions of the furnishings, colour schemes and notable works of art.

1824
MEYRICK, SAMUEL RUSH
A Critical Inquiry into Ancient Armour as it existed in Europe, but particularly in England, from the Norman Conquest to the reign of King

Charles II. Illustrated with a series of richly coloured engravings, London

The plates for this important early study of the history of armour were engraved from the author's drawings by Richard Bridgens. The book was greatly admired by Sir Walter Scott, whose taste for ancient arms and armour was shared by many of his contemporaries.

1826

SMITH, GEORGE

The Cabinet-maker's and Upholsterer's Guide, being a complete drawing book. . . . To which is added a complete series of new and original designs for household furniture and interior decoration, London

1827

BASOLI, ANTONIO

Compartimenti di camere, Bologna

1830

BEUTH, PETER

Vorbilder für Fabrikanten und Handwerker

The earlier part of Beuth's book, dealing with architecture and designs for interiors, was largely the work of Karl Friedrich Schinkel, the important architect and designer.

1831

ZAHN, JOHANN WILHELM

Ornamente aller klassichen Kunstepochen, Berlin (to 1843)

A handsomely illustrated collection of Pompeian, Egyptian and antique vase motifs which was admired by the London decorator Morant.

1833

CHENAVARD, CLAUDE-AIMÉ

Nouveau Recueil des dessins de Tapis, Tapisseries et autre objets d'ameublement exécutés dans la manufacture de MM Chenavard à Paris, Paris (to 1835)

This is an expanded version of Chenavard's *Recueil* of 1828, which had only thirty plates compared to the forty-two of the later publication. Among many designs for objects and furniture there are also schemes for complete interiors in the Egyptian, Chinese and Turkish styles.

LOUDON, J.C.

An Encyclopaedia of Cottage, Farm and Villa Architecture and Furniture, London (new edition: 1839)

Massively illustrated work, which had a considerable influence both in Britain and, through admirers such as A.J. Downing, in the United States.

1834

BÖTTICHER, C.G.W.

Ornamenten-Buch, zum praktischen Gebrauche für Architectur, Berlin (to 1844)

With Zahn, Bötticher was one of the earliest authors to exploit the possibilities of lithographic illustrations for ornament books of this type. The

designs are unusually simple and bold for this date, and foreshadow the strikingly original work of Owen Jones and Albert-Charles-Auguste Racinet.

1835

Journal für Möbelschreiner und Tapezierer (founded; to 1853)

Published in Mainz and Frankfurt. Delicate late neo-classical or Biedermeier schemes by Wilhelm Kimbel of the kind seen in many modest family portraits of the date, particularly in Northern Europe.

PUGIN, A.W.N.

Gothic Furniture in the Style of the Fifteenth Century, London

1836

JONES, OWEN

Plans, Elevations, Sections and Details of the Alhambra, London (to 1845)

SHAW, HENRY

Specimens of Ancient Furniture drawn from existing authorities by Henry Shaw, FSA, with descriptions by Sir Samuel Meyrick, London

Seventy-four engraved plates with twelve hand-coloured. This book being the first to investigate antique furniture history was very influential.

1837

THIOLLET and ROUX

Recueil de Menuiserie et de Décorations intérieures, Paris

Contains very interesting details from celebrated houses with the names of the architects, and sometimes even the decorators, supplied.

1838

BRAYLEY, EDWARD WEDLAKE

Illustrations of Her Majesty's Palace at Brighton; formerly the Pavilion: executed by the command of King George the Fourth, under the superintendence of John Nash Esq. architect, London

Sumptuous hand-coloured plates provide a detailed record of one of the most exotic royal residences ever built.

BRIDGENS, RICHARD

Furniture with candelabra and interior decoration, London

An associate of George Bullock, Bridgens worked at Abbotsford for Sir Walter Scott. His friend Henry Shaw etched and aquatinted the fifty-eight plates for this book, which were then hand-coloured. Although his strongest predilection was for the Regency Grecian style favoured by Bullock, Bridgens has included here twenty-seven plates in the currently popularized Elizabethan style.

PHILLIPS, GEORGE

Rudiments of Curvilinear Design, London (to 1840)

Early publication of Japanese and Indian designs presumably taken from the few available published sources.

1839

Art Union (later *Art Journal*) (founded; to 1911)

Acquired the highest reputation in the mid-century for publishing catalogues of the London International Exhibitions of 1851, 1862 etc., and for the extensive reporting of design matters. Prince Albert was a valued patron.

1840

ARROWSMITH, H., W. and A.

The House Decorator and Painter's Guide; containing a series of designs for decorating apartments suited to various styles of architecture, London

The sixty-one plates in this collection show mainly wall schemes. Of interest are the Elizabethan rooms and furnishings that were just coming into general use.

CLERGET, CHARLES-ERNEST and MARTEL, CHARLES (?)

Encyclopédie universelle d'Ornements antiques, Paris (date approximate)

The first collection of ornamental designs to be described as an encyclopaedia, it includes examples of Greek, Roman, Egyptian, Islamic, Indian, Chinese, Japanese, medieval and Renaissance decoration.

CONDY, NICHOLAS

Cothele, on the banks of the Tamar, the ancient seat of the Rt. Honble the Earl of Mount Edgcumbe. With a descriptive account by the Rev. F.V.J. Arundell, London

A fine set of interior views of a completely intact Tudor ensemble of house and furnishings.

ROUX, H. and BARRÉ, M.L.

Herculaneum et Pompéii. Recueil général des peintures, bronzes, mosaïques, etc., Paris

The French excavations at Pompeii popularized the style for architecture and interior decoration, and this seven-volume work was intended for the use of artists and decorators. The subject matter is conveniently classified and the format modest.

1841

HIGGINS, W. MULLINGAR

The House Painter, or Decorator's Companion: being a complete treatise on the origin of colour, the laws of harmonious colouring, the manufacture of pigments, oils and varnishes; the art of house painting, graining, and marbling, London

An important aspect of Victorian interior decoration explained by an obscure architect.

1842

BIELEFELD, CHARLES FREDERICK

On the Use of the Improved Papier-mâché in furniture in the interior decoration of buildings and in works of art, London

Papier-mâché was widely used in decoration as an alternative to plasterwork. It could be mass-produced in a great variety of intricate patterns. Bielefelds of the Strand were one of the most successful manufacturers.

TEXIER, CHARLES
Description de l'Arménie, la Perse et la Mésopotamie, Paris

1843
The Builder: an illustrated magazine for the drawing-room, the studio, the office, the workshop and the cottage (founded; still in print)
The most important English architectural paper in the mid-nineteenth century, edited from 1844 to 1883 by George Godwin.

1844
Annales archéologiques (founded; to 1870)
Started by A.-N. Didron, this learned French journal contained propaganda for the Gothic revival in architecture and design. After Didron's death in 1864 his son continued the journal until 1870.

GRUNER, LEWIS (LUDWIG)
Fresco Decorations and Stuccoes of Churches & Palaces, in Italy, during the 15th and 16th centuries . . . and a comparison between the ancient arabesques and those of the 16th century by Mr A. Hittorff, London
The Italian Renaissance interior, with particular emphasis on Raphael and his school, exhaustively explained by Prince Albert's mentor and adviser Ludwig Gruner. Some copies with hand-coloured plates were produced, but the intention was that the purchasers should colour their own copies and a final plate, with a numbered key as a colour guide, is provided for reference.

HAY, DAVID RAMSAY
Original Geometrical Diaper Designs, London
These designs suggest that Hay, an eminent Edinburgh decorator and theorist, had made a study of Islamic geometric decoration.

1846
GRUNER, LEWIS (LUDWIG)
The Decorations of the Garden Pavilion in the Grounds of Buckingham Palace, London
Prince Albert's decorated pavilion of frescoed rooms illustrated in colour.

1847
BALLANTINE, JAMES
Tradesman's Book of Ornamental Designs, Edinburgh

1848
COLLING, JAMES K.
Gothic Ornaments, being a series of examples of enriched details and accessories of the architecture of Great Britain. Drawn from existing Authorities by James K. Colling, Architect, London
An important source book for neo-Gothic decoration of the period.

1849
CLARKE, WILLIAM
Pompeii: its past and present state; its public and private buildings etc., London

This is in essence a summary of a number of earlier pioneering works by M. Mazois, Sir William Gell and T.L. Donaldson, but with additional notes and drawings by Clarke himself. The two volumes have nearly three hundred text illustrations in all, presenting the contemporary state of knowledge about Pompeii.

GEORGE JACKSON & SONS
Part of the Collection of Relief Decorations as executed in papier-mâché & carton pierre, by George Jackson & Sons, Rathbone Place, London
Trade catalogue with an impressive range of designs from contemporary competitors of Bielefelds of the Strand (see p. 391).

Journal of Design and Manufactures (founded; to 1852)
Cole was the moving spirit behind this journal, and the Great Exhibition was its main focus. Illustrated; also contains textile samples and wallpapers.

LAYARD, SIR AUSTEN H.
Nineveh and its Remains, London

1850
DOWNING, A.J.
The Architecture of Country Houses; including designs for cottages, farm-houses, and villas, with remarks on interiors, furniture, and the best modes of warming and ventilating, New York
The last and fullest work by Downing, including two well illustrated and perceptive chapters on interiors which were widely influential in the United States.

GRUNER, LEWIS (LUDWIG) and BRAUN, EMIL
Specimens of Ornamental Art selected from the best models of classical epochs. Illustrated by eighty plates . . . with descriptive text by Emil Braun, London
One of the finest and earliest of the large chromolithographic albums, with examples of Italian decorative art from Pompeian frescoes to Raphael and Giulio Romano, and including illustrations of Cardinal Bibiena's frescoed bathroom in the Vatican.

1851
HITTORFF, JAKOB IGNATIUS
L'Architecture polychrome chez les Grecs, Paris
A pupil of Percier, Hittorff was one of the most influential of Victorian architects experimenting with colour. This publication appeared in the same year as Semper's *Über Polychromie*, and preceded by five years Owen Jones's celebrated *Grammar of Ornament*.

RUSKIN, JOHN
The Stones of Venice . . . with illustrations drawn by the author, London (to 1853)
The engraved and lithographed plates with their hand colouring have lost almost none of the delicacy, sensitivity and fine detail of Ruskin's drawing style. A work of profound scholarship

and passionate feeling, like all his publications, it had enormous impact and contributed to Ruskin's unassailable position as the most influential critic of his day.

WYATT, M. DIGBY
The Industrial Arts of the Nineteenth Century, London (to 1853)
A record, in the finest chromolithographic illustrations, of the arts and manufacturers of the Great Exhibition of 1851.

1852
LEIGHTON, JOHN
Suggestions in Design, being a comprehensive series of original sketches in various styles of ornament. Arranged for application in the decorative and constructive arts. With descriptive letterpress by James K. Colling, London (to 1853)
This book went into later editions and also appeared in New York. Leighton was an early enthusiast for Japanese art and published a book on the subject in 1863.

1853
LAYARD, SIR AUSTEN H.
Nineveh and Babylon, London

1855
Building News. A weekly illustrated record of the progress of architecture (to 1926)

1856
JONES, OWEN
The Grammar of Ornament. Illustrated by examples from various styles of ornament, London
The importance of this handsome production, with its one hundred richly coloured chromolithographic plates, can hardly be overstressed.

WORNUM, RALPH NICHOLSON
Analysis of Ornament. The characteristics of styles, London
Based on a series of lectures given to students of the Government School of Design in 1848, this is a concise guide to the history of ornament from Egyptian to eighteenth-century designs.

1858
The Universal Decorator (to 1859)
Edited by Francis Benjamin Thompson. Fortnightly partwork of collected articles from journals, periodicals and standard works on all aspects of the applied arts and decoration. Notable contributors included Eastlake, Sydney Smirke and Westmacott.

VIOLLET-LE-DUC, EUGÈNE
Dictionnaire raisonnée de l'Architecture française du XIe au XVIe siècle, Paris (to 1868)
The most influential architectural dictionary of the century. Viollet's work was remorselessly mined for ideas by his contemporaries and successors.

1859
BEAUMONT, ADALBERT DE and COLLINOT, EUGÈNE-VICTOR

Recueil de dessins pour l'Art et l'Industrie
Greatly expanded in the 1880s, after de
Beaumont's death, and issued as *Encylopédie des
Arts décoratifs de l'Orient*, beginning with
Ornaments de la Perse (1880), *de la Chine* (1882),
Arabes (1883), *du Japon* (1883) etc.

1860
Berliner Möbel-Journal (to 1861)
Lithographic plates of designs for furniture and
upholstery of revived rococo inspiration, giving
an excellent idea of commercial German
production in the mid-century.

GRUZ. H.
*Motifs de peintures décoratifs pour Appartements
modernes*, Paris, Berlin and Liège
The colour schemes illustrated here confirm the
impression given by contemporary descriptions
and depictions of rooms of sombre, rather impure
colours and richly inlaid woodwork.

GUILMARD, D.
*La Décoration au XIXe siècle. Décor intérieur des
habitations. Composé, dessiné et exécuté par les
principaux artistes décorateurs de Paris*, Paris
(approximate date)
A collection of designs presented as forty-eight
tinted plates by Prignot, Sauvestre etc.

1861
*L'Art pour tous. Encyclopédie de l'art industriel et
décoratif* (founded; to 1906)
Its fine illustrations served as a source for designs
in the historical revival style.

1863
VIOLLET-LE-DUC, EUGÈNE
Entretiens sur l'Architecture, Paris
Viollet's theory of architecture, highly influential
for later generations of architects including
Guimard and Gaudi. It was translated into
English and appeared in 1877.

1864
KERR, ROBERT
*The Gentleman's House: or how to plan English
residences, from the parsonage to the palace; with
tables of accommodation and cost, and a series of
selected plans*, London
The classic publication on the subject of
planning, with minutely detailed analysis of the
functions of the house.

1867
GRUNER, LEWIS (LUDWIG)
*The Terra-cotta Architecture of North Italy,
XIIth–XVth centuries. Portrayed as examples for
imitation in other countries. From careful drawings
and restorations by Federigo Lose. Edited by Lewis
Gruner*, London
The influence of this study can be seen in Godfrey
Sykes's work in this medium at the South
Kensington Museum.

TALBERT, BRUCE. J.
Gothic Forms applied to furniture, metalwork and

decoration for domestic purposes, London
Talbert's book was repeatedly plundered for
illustrations by later authors. His influence in
America was considerable, as can be seen from
the rooms illustrated by Charles Wyllys Elliott in
American Interiors (1875).

1868
EASTLAKE, C.L.
Hints on Household Taste, London
The most carefully thought-out treatise on
furnishing of the period, this book was so
influential in America, where it was published in
1872, that the American neo-Gothic became
known as the Eastlake style.

1869
The Architect (founded; still in print)
This important late-Victorian journal,
containing much information on design, has
become a trade journal in the present century.

PRISSE d'AVENNES, A.-C.-T.-E.
*L'Art arabe d'après les monuments du Caire depuis
le VIIe siècle jusqu'à la fin du XVIIIe*, Paris
(to 1877)
The buildings are examined in great detail
including the decoration and furnishings.

1870
DALY, CÉSAR
*L'Architecture privée au XIXe siècle. Nouvelles
maisons de Paris et des environs*, Paris (3 series
to 1877)
These three volumes from the editor of the *Revue
générale de l'Architecture*, a leading architectural
theorist, provide an unsurpassed record of
Haussmann-style Parisian architecture. The
illustrations include coloured interior views.

1872
Blätter für Kunstgewerbe, Vienna (to 1898)
Illustrations of new designs and historic
examples, with an emphasis on the Renaissance
revival.

Furniture Gazette (founded)
Trade magazine which merged in 1894 with
Furniture and Decoration.

1873
*The Art-Workman. A monthly journal of design
for the artist, artificer and manufacturer* (founded;
to 1883)
With fine illustrations, some in colour.

DRESSER, CHRISTOPHER
The Principles of Decorative Design, London
Dresser's scientific and functional approach to
design had a great impact on his contemporaries
and successors. He was himself a prolific designer
with a strongly marked personality using linear
and angular forms with great effect in both
surface and integral ornamentation.

RACINET, AUGUSTE
*Polychromatic Ornament. One hundred plates in
gold, silver and colours, comprising upwards of two*

thousand specimens of the various styles of ancient,
oriental and mediaeval art, and including the
Renaissance and the seventeenth and eighteenth
centuries*, London (first English edition of book
published in Paris 1869)
A worthy successor to Owen Jones.

1874
DRESSER, CHRISTOPHER
Studies in Design, London (to 1876)

SULLIVAN, EDWARD
Facsimiles of National Manuscripts of Ireland (to
1884)
Influential in the development of the revived
Celtic style which is the basis of much Arts and
Crafts decoration.

1876
American Architect and Building News (founded;
to 1938)
First issued in Boston in the year of the
Philadelphia Centennial Exhibition; the
acknowledged models were the English *Building
News* and *The Architect*, the first being some
twenty years older. Contains much information
on design and decoration.

ELLIOTT, CHARLES WYLLYS
*The Book of American Interiors, prepared from
existing houses, with preliminary essays and
letterpress descriptions*, Boston
An early and exceedingly interesting series of
illustrations showing contemporary American
middle-class taste, from an author who was
himself an interior designer.

1877
L'Art et l'Industrie (founded; to 1888)
Illustrations of designs for the decorative arts,
with an emphasis on Renaissance revival.

WATT, W.
*Art Furniture from designs by E. W. Godwin with
hints and suggestions on domestic furniture*,
London
Illustrated examples of Godwin's Anglo-
Japanese and Jacobean furniture designs, as well
as suggestions for decoration with panelled dados
and wallpapers.

1878
Magazine of Art (founded; to 1904)
Had a strong team of writers and decorative
artists as contributors.

ALCOCK, RUTHERFORD
Art and Industries of Japan, London

The Art Interchange. A household journal
(founded; to 1904)
A New York magazine with the emphasis mainly
on interior and home decoration.

AUDSLEY, G.A.
Outlines of Ornament, London

1879
The Art Amateur. A monthly journal devoted to the

cultivation of art in the household, (founded; to 1890)
Includes Japanese-inspired designs.

JONQUET, A.
Original Sketches for Art Furniture, in the Jacobean, Queen Anne, Adam and other styles, London

1880
The Artist. Journal of home culture (founded; to 1902)
In 1885 adopted large format and new title, *The Artist, Photographer and Decorator*; clearly hoped to rival *The Studio*. Another change of title in 1896: *The Artist, An illustrated monthly record of arts, crafts and industries*.

Cabinet Maker and Art Furnisher. A monthly budget of designs and information (founded; still in print)

Cassell's Household Guide. Being a complete encyclopaedia of domestic and social economy and forming a guide to every department of practical life, London
Cassell's guide contains comprehensive suggestions for the embellishment of every corner of the house with complete instructions for the making of even quite substantial pieces of furniture.

CUTLER, THOMAS. W.
Grammar of Japanese Ornament and Design, London

MOSER, D.H.
Book of Japanese Ornamentation, London

1881
AUDSLEY, G. and W.
Outlines of Ornament in the Leading Styles, London
Serving as both historical survey and practical guide, this book appeared in America in 1882.

Decoration (founded; to 1889)
The decorative designer J. Moyr Smith was editor.

COOK, CLARENCE
The House Beautiful. Essays on beds and tables, stools and candlesticks, New York
The frontispiece by Walter Crane is one of the key documents of the Aesthetic style in house decoration.

EDIS, R.W.
Decoration and Furniture of Town Houses, London
This book came out of a series of lectures delivered to the Society of Arts, 'Decoration Applied to Modern Houses', in 1880. The illustrations, drawn by Maurice B. Adams, include Edis's own drawing room.

1882
AUDSLEY W. and G.
Polychromatic Decoration as Applied to Buildings in the Medieval Style, London and Paris

A detailed examination of thirteenth-century geometric ornament.

CONWAY, MONCURE DANIEL
Travels in South Kensington with notes on decorative art and architecture in England, London
As well as including the most detailed account at that date of the genesis and the collections of the South Kensington Museum, this book is full of information on contemporary interior decoration. Included are Alfred Morrison's London house, George Aitchison's work for Lehmann and Leighton, an account of Alma-Tadema's house and a whole chapter on Bedford Park.

DAY, LEWIS F.
Everyday Art, London
A book of modest and practical advice on the ornament of the interior.

Decorator and Furnisher (founded; to 1894)
A New York magazine.

DRESSER, CHRISTOPHER
Japan, its architecture, art and art manufactures, London
Dresser was concerned to reach the working man with his publications, and placed a great deal of emphasis on manufacturing processes in this careful account of Japan and Japanese art.

1883
ADAMS, MAURICE B.
Artists' Homes, London
Beautifully drawn in delicate and highly detailed line, this collection serves as a celebration of the Queen Anne style.

Artistic Houses, being a series of interior views of a number of the most beautiful and celebrated homes in the United States with a description of the art treasures contained therein, New York
The American millionaire taste of the 1880s is comprehensively celebrated in this handsome volume.

BATLEY, H.W.
Series of Studies for Domestic Furniture Etc., London
Batley included very elegant Japanese schemes in this collection.

PULLAN, RICHARD POPPLEWELL
The Architectural Designs of William Burges, London
Drawn in detailed and delicate line, these plates have the effect of making Burges's designs seem approachable even in a domestic context.

1884
HAVARD, HENRI
L'Art dans la maison (Grammaire de l'ameublement), Paris
A handbook with 260 engravings on interiors and their furnishings, in a conventional style accurately reflecting the current state of French middle-class taste.

1885
Art and Decoration. An illustrated monthly devoted to interior and exterior decoration (founded; to 1886)
A New York magazine.

1886
PULLAN, RICHARD POPPLEWELL
The House of William Burges, London
An invaluable photographic record of the contents of the Tower House in Kensington.

1887
DAY, LEWIS F.
The Planning of Ornament, London
Another example of simple, practical advice on patterning.

SMITH, J. MOYR
Ornamental interiors, London

1888
Artistic Japan. A monthly illustrated journal of arts and industries (founded; to 1891)
Edited by Bing, and including illustrations of Japanese arts and crafts, textiles, prints, masks, ceramics, etc., many of them in colour.
The French edition was entitled *Le Japon artistique* and the German, *Japanischer Formenschatz*.

1889
Dekorative Vorbilder (founded; to 1929)
Published in Stuttgart by Julius Hoffmann and copiously illustrated, mainly in colour, this magazine had an English edition entitled *The Art Decorator*.

1890
De Architect (founded; to 1907)
A luxuriously produced journal published by the Amsterdam association Architectura et Amicitia, it contains designs by the Dutch avant-garde designers such as Berlage.

Art Decorator. A periodical publication of selected samples of decorative art, old and new (founded; to 1929)
The English version of *Dekorative Vorbilder*.

Arte italiana decorative ed industriale (founded; to 1911)
Mainly dealing with the history of decorative design but including some modern ideas. Excellent plates, some printed in colour.

Furniture and Decoration (founded; to 1898)
A trade magazine; incorporated *Furniture Gazette* in 1894.

Nouveau Journal d'Ameublement (founded; approximate date)
Sumptuous interiors with a suggestion of Art Nouveau. A collection of forty coloured plates from this publication was issued in Turin in the 1890s.

1892
ABBOT, THOMAS K.
Celtic Ornaments from the Book of Kells (to 1895)

AUDSLEY, G. and M.
The Practical Decorator and Ornamentist, London
Handsomely illustrated wth large chromo-lithographic plates, this was, however, an expanded version of the earlier work *Outlines of Ornament in the Leading Styles* (1881) and much of the material was no longer very fashionable.

1893
The Studio (founded)
Carried articles on all aspects of fine and decorative arts. The illustrations were striking, though the text tended to be uncritical. Ernest George, Voysey and Baillie Scott all received enthusiastic coverage.

1895
BINET, RENÉ
Esquisses décoratives, Paris

BING, S.
Artistic America, London

1896
Architectural Review (founded; still in print)
First issued under the editorship of Henry Wilson, this is now the leading architectural journal. In the early years there was a great emphasis on the art of design and decoration.

Architecture d'aujourd'hui (founded; to 1966)

1897
Art et Décoration (founded)
Published by the Librarie Centrale des Beaux-Arts, and committed to design reform, with articles on Horta and Alphonse Mucha in the first issue.

CODMAN, OGDEN and WHARTON, EDITH
The Decoration of Houses, New York

VERNEUIL, M.P.
L'Animal dans la décoration, Paris

1898
L'Art décoratif (founded)
Started by Julius Meier Graefe as the French counterpart to *Dekorative Kunst*. Meier Graefe was an admirer of C.R. Mackintosh and the Glasgow School.

1900
CROUCHE, JOSEPH and BUTLER, EDMUND
The Apartments of the House. Their arrangements, furnishing and decoration, London
Suggestions for interiors in an Arts and Crafts version of the neo-Jacobean manner from a Birmingham architectural partnership.

REMON, GEORGES
Intérieurs modernes, Paris (approximate date)

Designed by an architect, sumptuously reproduced in a facsimile of watercolour, showing strong influence of the Aesthetic movement and of Art Nouveau.

1904
SHAW SPARROW, W.
The British Home of Today. A book of modern domestic architecture and the applied arts, London
Illustrated, with ten plates in colour. Contributions from leading contemporary architects and designers, including Lorimer, Walton and Brierley.

1906
MAKOWSKY, SERGE
Talachkino. L'art décoratif des ateliers de la Princesse Tenichef, St Petersburg
An illustrated account of the art colony that was set up to express the native Russian idiom in the context of the Arts and Crafts movement.

1907
SHAW SPARROW, W.
Flats, Urban Houses and Cottage Homes, London
Illustrated, with nineteen plates in colour. Contributors include Benson, Hoffmann, Norman Shaw, Ashbee, Lutyens and Baillie Scott.

BIOGRAPHICAL INDEX OF ARTISTS, DESIGNERS, DECORATORS AND ARCHITECTS

including their principal societies and firms

ABILDGAARD, Nicolai Abraham (1743–1809)
Danish neo-classical painter, architect, designer. Travelled in Italy in 1770s. From mid-1790s designed interiors for the Danish court. For his own 'Klismos' chairs he collected specially curved pieces of wood.

ADAMS, Maurice Bingham (1849–1933)
Architect, draughtsman and furniture designer. Norman Shaw's *Sketches for Cottages* (1878) and Godwin's *Artistic Conservatories* (1880) carried his drawings; his *Artist's Homes* (1883) was more a series of advertisements for the Queen Anne revival. His journalism for the *Building News* and his furniture designs show the influence of the style. He took over the building of the idealistic artists' colony of Bedford Park from Shaw.

AGLIO, Agostino (1777–1857)
Landscape painter. Active in Rome in 1790s, where he met William Wilkins; they travelled to Greece together. Settled in London in 1803, practising as a decorative painter. Painted Pompeian Room in the Garden Pavilion at Buckingham House. His *Architectural Ornaments* (1820) carried neo-classical designs for capitals, friezes, silver etc.

AITCHISON, George (1825–1910)
Architect, interior designer. Apprenticed to his father, who had been as much an engineer as architect, he was an early advocate of cast iron. The main body of his work was interiors and alterations for London society, where his elegant handling of opulent and complex schemes became his stock-in-trade.

ALBERT, Prince Consort (1819–61)
Amateur architect, patron of the arts, reformer. His great coup was to set up the 1851 London Exhibition, which highlighted the bad as well as the good in industrial manufacture. Instrumental in setting up the South Kensington Museums. Professional and princely interest in all aspects of art and manufactures.

ALMA-TADEMA, Sir Lawrence (1836–1912)
Decorative painter. Trained under Baron Wappers at Antwerp Academy. Moved to London in 1870. His Byzantine decorations for his own house were widely admired. Commissioned by Henry Marquand to design furniture and interiors for his New York mansion.

ARROWSMITH BROTHERS (founded late 1830s)
'Decorators to Her Majesty'. Published their catalogue, *House Decorator and Painter's Guide*, in 1840; it contained colour plates in Gothic, Elizabethan, Louis Quatorze, Moorish and Pompeian styles.

L'ART NOUVEAU (founded 1895)
Gallery in rue de Provence, Paris, opened by Siegfried Bing. The gallery showed work of designers who were working in a strong curvilinear tradition stemming from William Blake, Viollet-le-Duc's cast-iron designs and the ideas of the Aesthetic movement. The shop gave its name to the style which dominated official art in Paris after 1900, when Bing's displays at the Paris Centennial Exposition received acceptance by the general public.

ARTS AND CRAFTS EXHIBITION SOCIETY (1888–1914)
A showcase for the new decorative arts founded under the aegis of the Art-Workers' Guild. Its first two exhibitions in 1888 and 1889 at the New Gallery were commercial and artistic successes. In 1890 it made a loss. Exhibitions were subsequently mounted at three-yearly intervals. It brought out *Arts and Crafts Essays* in 1893, and continued to represent British Arts and Crafts at home and abroad until the Great War.

ART-WORKERS' GUILD (founded 1884)
Formed by combining the St George's Art Society and The Fifteen. The former, founded in 1883, was entirely composed of Norman Shaw's pupils; The Fifteen were headed by Lewis F. Day and had been founded in 1882. The Guild's members included all workers in the decorative arts, not exclusively architects. Its foundation is a reflection on the debate which raged in the 1880s as to whether architecture was a profession or an art. The Art-Workers took the latter view.

ASHBEE, Charles Robert (1863–1942)
Architect, designer, visionary. Trained under G.F. Bodley. Founded his Guild of Handicraft in London's East End in 1888, a craftsmen's co-operative in the decorative arts. His architectural commissions were few but widely influential. For his house, the Magpie and Stump in Chelsea, the Guild executed the interiors and furniture. They also made Baillie Scott's designs for the Grand Duke of Hesse at Darmstadt.

AUDSLEY, George Ashdown (1838–1925)
Produced in collaboration with his brother William, an architect, some of the finest chromolithographic books of the late nineteenth century: *Cottage, Lodge and Villa Architecture* (1868), *The Keramic Art of Japan* (1875), *The Ornamental Arts of Japan* (1882–4), *Outlines of Ornament* (1878), which deals with flat patterning in a range of styles, and in collaboration with Maurice Ashdown Audsley *The Practical Decorator and Ornamentalist* (1892). By reason of the quality of their illustrations, the Audsleys' books reached a wide audience.

BAILLIE SCOTT, Mackay Hugh (1865–1945)
Architect and designer. His furniture and interior designs straddled Arts and Crafts and Art Nouveau. *The Studio* first covered his work in 1895 with 'The Decoration of Suburban Homes'; thereafter his elegant designs and illustrations were perennially popular. His reputation on the Continent was assured with the Darmstadt interiors designed for the Duke of Hesse in 1897.

BALLANTINE, James (1808–77)
House-painter, stained-glass designer. His *Treatise on Painted Glass* (1845) featured designs in varied historical styles. The *Tradesman's Book of Ornamental Designs* followed in 1847. A close friend of David Hay, he also wrote a life of the painter David Roberts.

BASILE, Ernesto (1857–1932)
Architect. Moved from Palermo to Rome, where he designed furniture in the Art Nouveau style, acclaimed at the Turin Exhibition of 1902.

BASOLI, Antonio (1774–1843)
Decorative painter. His *Compartimenti di camere* (1827) featured some of his own work, which was usually neo-classical, though he did also use an attenuated Gothic style.

BATLEY, Henry W.
Architect and etcher, furniture and textile designer. Pupil of Talbert. His *Series of Studies for Domestic Furniture Etc.* (1883) shows Godwin and Jeckyll's influence. Trained Arthur Silver and towards the end of his career went to work in the Silver Studio.

BEAUMONT, Adalbert de (d. 1869)
Designer and scholar. Interested primarily in eastern ornament and design; worked as designer in the ceramic firm of Collinot, mainly in a Persian idiom. His designs, ranging from Turkish to Japanese, were published posthumously.

BECKFORD, William (1760–1844)
Antiquarian, author, collector, gardener. Creator of Fonthill, one of the first neo-Gothic 'abbeys'. From his Moorish Smoking Room in his house in Lisbon in the 1790s to his Italianate Lansdowne Tower in the 1840s, Beckford showed tastes which were advanced and often influential.

BENSON, William Arthur Smith (1854–1924)
Under the aegis of William Morris, set up a metalware workshop. In 1896 became chairman of Morris & Co. Leading promoter of Arts and Crafts Exhibition Society. His own designs, light fittings in particular, were exhibited at Bing's shop, Art Nouveau.

BENTLEY, John Francis (1839–1902)
Architect, designer of wallpaper, furniture and textiles. His rebuilding of Carlton Towers included innovative furniture designs.

BERTHAULT, Louis-Martin (1771–1823)
Architect, trained under Percier; a protégé of the Empress Josephine. Decorated her apartments at Compiègne before her divorce in 1809.

BERTHON, Paul-Emile (1872–1909)
Pupil and follower of Eugène Grasset. Designed furniture in the Art Nouveau style; best known for his posters and decorative panels.

BEUTH, Peter Christian Wilhelm (1781–1853)
Prussian bureaucrat, a friend of Schinkel. Headed a committee to improve design in Prussia, whose publications *Vorbilder für Fabrikanten und Handwerker* (1821, 1830, 1837; reissued 1863) comprised designs in the applied arts and remained influential in Berlin. Beuth also founded the technical school movement in Prussia.

BEVAN, Charles (fl. 1865–1883)
Furniture designer and manufacturer, active in 1860s and '70s. Worked in the 'Modern Gothic' style after J.P. Seddon. Described himself as 'Medieval Art Designer'; created the furniture for the house of Titus Salt.

BINDESBØLL, Thorvald (1846–1908)
Architect, designer of pottery and furniture in a style that moved from neo-classical to Art Nouveau.

BINET, René (1866–1911)
Watercolourist and designer. His *Esquisses décoratives* (1895), with sixty plates, covered various styles of interiors.

BODLEY, George Frederick (1827–1907)
Architect. With Thomas Garner, a leading High Church Gothic-revival partnership. founded the church-furnishing firm of Watts & Co.

BRACQUEMOND, Félix (1833–1914)
An early devotee of Japonisme; designed ceramics using decorations from *ukiyo-e* albums, notably the *Mangwa* of Hokusai. A talented etcher; his work was shown at the first Impressionist exhibition in 1874.

BRADLEY, Will (1868–1962)
Graphic artist associated with Chicago Arts and Crafts school. His designs for furniture and rooms appeared in the *Ladies' Home Journal* at the turn of the century. Influenced by Baillie Scott and Mackintosh.

BRIDGENS, Richard (fl. 1820s to 1840s)
Designer. Associated with George Bullock. Designed furniture for Battle Abbey and for Abbotsford. Elizabethan furniture was his speciality. *Furniture with Candelabra* (1833, 1838) was the most influential pattern book of the Elizabethan revival in England.

BROWN, Ford Madox (1821–93)
Painter; associated with members of the Pre-Raphaelites, an advocate of F.D. Maurice's workers' education movement. Founder member of Morris & Co, for whom he designed furniture and textiles. Painted furniture for Seddon and Rossetti.

BULLOCK, George (d. 1818)
Trained as sculptor, but made his living as general furnisher. In partnership with the architect and draughtsman Joseph Gandy, they called themselves 'Architects, Modellers, Sculptors, Marble Masons, Cabinet Makers & Upholsterers'. As a furniture designer, Bullock adapted neo-classical forms into a heavier, more massive idiom that developed naturally into Gothic- and Elizabethan-revival styles. His furniture employs inlay work close to boulle, and decorative play of the natural grain of different woods.

BURGES, William (1827–81)
Architect, designer. Made an idiosyncratic rendering of thirteenth-century Gothic his own. His attractive character as much as his designs influenced a generation of architects in the 1860s. Cardiff Castle, Castell Coch, and his own house in Melbury Road are complete Burges *oeuvres* from the architecture down to the smallest detail of decoration and furnishings.

BURNE-JONES, Sir Edward (1833–98)
Painter, pupil of Rossetti. Designed textiles and stained glass for Morris & Co. Also did decorative painting work for the firm's furniture and interiors. Associated with all activities of the Arts and Crafts movement.

BUTTERFIELD, Lindsay Philip (1869–1948)
Designer of textiles and wallpapers. Created tapestry designs for the firms of Mortons, Libertys; wallpapers for Essex & Co, Arthur Sanderson.

CARRIER-BELLEUSE, Albert-Ernest (1824–87)
Metalwork designer. In 1850 moved to England and designed ceramic ware for Mintons, Wedgwood and Brownfields. Returned to France in 1855 and continued as metalwork designer; but also designed furniture including several pieces for La Païva. Designed decorations for Grande Galerie in the Louvre; in 1876 became the reforming artistic director at Sèvres.

CHEVREUL, Michel-Eugène (1786–1889)
Trained as a chemist, invented modern wax candles. Director of dyeing at Gobelins from 1824. His researches into colour and subsequent book *The Principles of Harmony and Contrast of Colours* (France 1839, England 1854) put colour theory on to a scientific footing.

CLERGET, Charles-Ernest (b. 1812)
Designer of porcelain for the Sèvres factory, and tapestry for the Gobelins. His books on ornamental designs include *Nouveaux Ornements* (1840) and *Ornements Teintés* (1841), each with eighteen plates; more ambitious, with eighty-four plates, was *Encyclopédie universelle d'Ornements* which carried illustrations by other designers.

CODMAN, Ogden (1863–1951)
Architect and interior designer. Co-author with Edith Wharton of *The Decoration of Houses* (1897). His own decoration and furniture were in the simplified eighteenth-century taste that was the central message of their book.

COLE, Sir Henry (1808–82)
Designer and reformer. With Prince Albert, one of the prime supporters of 1851 Great Exhibition. Took a reforming stand on schools of design, out of which grew the Victoria and Albert Museum. The Felix Summerly Art-Manufactures venture of 1847–8 introduced a new concept to British design; perhaps his greatest influence, since he had no followers.

COLLCUTT, Thomas Edward (1840–1924)
Architect and furniture designer. A leading figure in Queen Anne revival. Designed furniture for Collison & Lock, Gillows and Maples.

COLLING, James Kellaway (1816–1905)
Architect and draughtsman whose publications on Gothic architecture and ornament were standard cribbing material for much of the Victorian Gothic movement.

COLONNA, Edouard (1862–1948)
Worked for Associated Artists in 1880s. His famous 'Broom Corn' designs were widely influential in the United States. Returned to Europe in late 1890s and designed jewellery, furniture and fabrics for Bing's Art Nouveau.

COOPER, H. & J. (fl. 1870s to 1890s)
Firm of interior decorators based in London. Award-winning exhibitors at the 1878 Paris Exposition, they maintained their high reputation for interior design into the 1890s.

COTTINGHAM, Lewis Nockalls (1787–1847)
Architect, furniture and metalwork designer. Designed Gothic furniture; collected fragments of architectural ornaments (this collection became basis of the Architectural Museum in London.) His *Working Drawings of Gothic Ornament* (1822–9) had great impact on the Gothic revival.

CRACE (until 1917)
Family firm of decorators which began with Edward Crace (d. 1799) in the second half of the eighteenth century. His son, John (1754–1819), worked at Carlton House and Althorp. Frederick

(1779–1859) was responsible for the interiors of the Royal Pavilion at Brighton. His son, John Gregory, was associated with A.W.N Pugin both at the New Palace of Westminster and later as a designer for the firm; Pugin later became unhappy at Crace's debasement of his ideals in furniture and decoration. John Diblee Crace (1838–1917) continued the family tradition as designer and manager of the firm.

CRANE, Walter (1845–1915)
Painter, illustrator, designer, socialist. He admired Morris & Co.; his work developed all aspects of the Arts and Crafts movement in unofficial tandem with Morris. His European reputation began in the 1890s and his work was shown at Bing's shop; Art Nouveau. Honorary Member of Vienna *Seccession* in 1897.

DANHAUSER, Joseph Ulrich (1780–1829)
The Danhauser factory was founded in 1804; it was awarded the imperial licence in 1808, at which time 130 workers were employed in making furniture and other domestic decorative items. His drapery designs show a degree of fantasy, while the furniture is the simplest and most elegant expression of the Biedermeier taste of Vienna. After his death his son took over the running of the firm, but fashion had turned away from Danhauser's sophistication and the manufactory closed in 1842.

DAVIS, Alexander Jackson (1803–92)
Architect. At the centre of the New York literary and artistic world from the late 1820s. Early influences were English: Thomas Hope, Pugin and Loudon, on whom he based his own publication *Rural Residences* (1838). With Ithiel Town, Davis designed many of the most important buildings of mid-century America.

DAY, Lewis Foreman (1845–1910)
Designer of stained glass, textiles, tiles and wallpapers for the major manufacturers. His journalism and writings were his most important influence. *Everyday Art* (1882), written for a popular audience, consolidated lay interest in domestic decoration.

DE MORGAN, William Frend (1839–1917)
His pottery works opened in the 1870s. His successful experiments with Persian colours and new glazes established him as the leading Arts and Crafts tile manufacturer. He worked closely with Morris & Co., then later in partnership (1888–98) with Halsey Ricardo, who decorated his interiors with De Morgan tiles.

DENIS, Maurice (1870–1943)
Founder member of Les Nabis group, with Paul Sérusier as leader; Pierre Bonnard was a member in the 1890s, as was Edouard Vuillard. Print, posters, stained glass, furniture and interior decoration, were the Nabis' main concerns.

DENON, Dominique-Vivant, Baron (1747–1825)
His *Voyage dans la Basse et la Haute Egypte* of 1802 became a standard source for Egyptian-revival architecture and furniture design. Later he was the aide-de-camp on artistic matters to Napoleon. Designed the Sèvres Egyptian service.

DESTAILLEUR, Hippolyte-Alexandre (1822–93)
Architect, designer of furniture and interiors. Worked for the Rothschilds and the European plutocracy. Adept in eighteenth-century French styles. He was a collector of drawings and prints; edited Du Cerceau's *Les plus excellens Batiments* (1577). His own work is recorded in *Recueil d'estampes relatives à l'Ornementation des appartements* (1863, 1871).

DOWNING, Andrew Jackson (1815–52)
Architect, gardener. Introduced the work of J.C. Loudon into the Unites States. Loudon's influence is strongly marked in his own *The Architecture of Country Houses* (1850). His own house in New York State was an early example of Tudor revival in America.

DRESSER, Dr Christopher (1834–1904)
Designer and botanist. Studied at Somerset House School of Design. His main mentor was Owen Jones, whose influence was marked throughout Dresser's career. Britain's first industrial designer for mass manufacture, he exploited all the advantages of contemporary technology. His insistence on abstraction from natural forms and his thoughtful functionalism provides the link between Pugin and the Modern Movement. His works include *The Principles of Decorative Design* (1873), *Modern Ornamentation* (1886), *Japan, its Architecture, Arts and Art Manufacture* was the result of his tour of Japan from 1876 to 1877; its writing was delayed by illness and it was only published in 1882.

DYCE, William (1806–64)
Through his teaching at the Schools of Design and textbooks on design, Dyce encouraged a tendency to adorn objects rather than design them. A leading figure in the fresco revival, especially at the New Palace of Westminster and in work for Prince Albert at Osborne House.

EASTLAKE, Charles Locke (1836–1906)
Trained as an architect. His impact on the nineteenth century was principally through his writings. *A History of the Gothic Revival* (1872) remains the classic study. His articles of the 1860s in *The Queen* were re-issued as *Hints on Household Taste* in 1868. *Hints* summed up avant-garde trends in British furniture design and decoration. When published in the United States, the book and its simple line illustrations had instant and lasting impact. The revived Gothic style in America was dubbed the 'Eastlake style' – somewhat to Eastlake's embarrassment when later developments moved away from his ideas and advice.

EDIS, Robert William (1839–1927)
Architect and writer. An exponent of the Queen Anne style. He was a publicist for Morris & Co., Godwin, Burges and furniture designers of the 1870s. *Decoration and Furniture of Town Houses* (1881) concentrates on the middle-market Queen Anne house; the decoration favoured is by Crane, Talbert and Morris & Co., and the furniture is by Godwin or plainly designed after Godwin.

FEUCHÈRE, Léon (1804–57)
'Architecte Décorateur'. His eclectic and virtuoso designs in *L'Art Industriel* (1842) include an early example of a Moorish smoking room, as well as rooms in other nineteenth-century styles.

FEURE, Georges de (1868–1928)
Poster designer. He also created two interiors for the Pavillon de L'Art Nouveau at the Paris 1900 Centennial Exposition.

FONTAINE, Pierre-François-Léonard (1762–1853)
Architect, draughtsman; studied under A.F. Peyre, later worked in the office of Heurtier. Went into partnership with Percier in 1794. Published *Palais, Maisons, et autres Edifices modernes dessinés à Rome* in 1798; this introduced Renaissance ideas into the Percier and Fontaine *oeuvre* which otherwise was strictly neo-classical. Fontaine's career survived the Empire and he worked for the Bourbons and Louis-Philippe; this work was recorded in his *Palais Royal* (1829) and *Résidences de Souverains (1833)*.

GIMSON, Ernest (1864–1919)
Plasterworker and furniture designer. He had trained as an architect, but abandoned it for chair-making. In 1893 he went into partnership with the brothers Ernest and Sidney Barnsley designing and making furniture in the Cotswolds. After 1900 Gimson abandoned plasterwork for furniture design, again in a style that he had developed in the 1880s while at the Leicester School of Art and afterwards in London. He self-consciously shunned machine manufacture, though ironically it was the Modernists who most appreciated his plain and angular style.

GODWIN, Edward William (1833–86)
Architect; writer; furniture, clothes and theatre designer. The most flamboyant and brilliant figure of the 1870s and '80s, Godwin left his mark on furniture design and helped create a radically simplified interior that was adapted from Japanese traditions, Greek, Egyptian and English Renaissance forms. His attempt to market his own designs in his 'Art Furniture Company' failed. However, ten years later in 1877, in conjunction with William Watt, Godwin's designs were once more sold under his own name and this time successfully. His later furniture was in the Anglo-Japanese style. More than anyone he popularized the Japanese aesthetic. His work with such celebrated figures as Wilde and Whistler ensured public recognition.

GRASSET, Eugène (1841–1917)
Architect; textile, stained-glass, poster, book and ceramic designer. His early influences, Viollet-le-Duc and Japan, contributed to his successful Art Nouveau poster and graphic designs of the late 1880s. His teaching and his writings on the decorative arts displayed reforming zeal; he was a founder member of the Société des Artistes Décorateurs in 1897. His publications included the didactic *La Plante et ses applications ornementales* (1897).

GREENAWAY, Kate (1846–1901)
Primarily an illustrator of children's books; her simple and naive pictures of children defined an ideal of nursery culture to a whole generation. The illustrations were reproduced as tiles and wallpapers.

GREENE, Charles Sumner (1868–1957)
With his brother Henry Mather, Greene developed a fusion of Arts and Crafts with Japanese and Chinese styles. They took this to California, where the brothers set up a successful architectural practice and furniture workshop.

HAWEIS, Mary Eliza (1848–98)
Through her books, including *The Art of Beauty* (1878) and *The Art of Decoration* (1881; this was in the 'Art in the Home' series, along with Mrs Orrinsmith's *The Drawing Room* and Lady Barker's *The Boudoir*), and especially *Beautiful Houses* (1882) she popularized an ideal of the artistic interior. She herself moved into Rossetti's house after his death.

HAY, David Ramsay (1798–1866)
Hay first began his house-painting career at Abbotsford; he soon established himself as Edinburgh's leading decorator. His book on colour, *The Laws of Harmonious Colouring* (1828), was an essential vademecum for the applied arts. His work on geometric patterning, *Original Geometrical Diaper Designs* (1844), likewise played an important role in Victorian decorative art.

HOLLAND, Henry (1745–1806)
Architect; he made a close study of French sources and employed a French assistant, J.-P. Trécourt, as well as French craftsmen to produce a style of great elegance and sophistication that was popular with the aristocracy. Designed Carlton House Terrace for the Prince Regent.

HOPE, Thomas (1769–1831)
Amateur architect, collector of sculpture, apostle of the Greek revival. His two houses, Duchess Street and The Deepdene, which he designed for himself, were curiosities of the age. Hope adapted Greek forms to decoration and furniture. He reached a wider audience with his *Household Furniture and Interior Decoration* (1807), illustrating Duchess Street interiors and his furniture designs.

HUBBARD, Elbert (1856–1915)
In 1894 visited England and admired William Morris's Kelmscott Press and the Morrisian ethos in general, which he re-created in an artistic community in New York State. He bought a press, The Roycroft Press, and soon started up a furniture workshop selling bulky Arts and Crafts designs as 'Aurora Colonial Furniture'.

JACK, George Washington Henry (1855–1932)
Assistant, then successor, to Philip Webb. Worked closely with Morris as chief designer of furniture in 1890s; also of tapestries and stained glass. Worked in LCC Architect's Department.

JECKYLL, Thomas (1827–81)
Architect; designer of furniture and cast iron. His fireplaces for Barnard, Bishop & Barnard were enduringly popular. His furniture mixed Jacobean, Japanese and Chinese forms with varying success. Designed cast-iron Japanese Pavilion at Philadelphia Exposition of 1876.

JONES, Owen (1809–74)
Trained as an architect; worked as designer. Achieved prominence with *Plans, Details and Sections of the Alhambra* (1836–45); his name became synonymous with Moorish forms of decoration. He was enthusiastic about the new material, cast iron. Commissioned by Cole to decorate the interior of Paxton's Crystal Palace. His arrangement of colours was controversial, but the scheme's popular success silenced his critics. His experiments with colour and geometric design were given authoritative shape in *The Grammar of Ornament* (1856), which set the pace for decorative arts for much of the nineteenth century. Jones designed cast-iron buildings and decorated interiors, usually for public buildings. His geometric designs were employed on most decorative materials – tiles, silks etc. – and were a ubiquitous Victorian taste.

KLENZE, Leo von (1784–1864)
Architect; studied in Empire Paris, notably with Percier and Fontaine. Court architect to Jerome Bonaparte, King of Westphalia. After 1815 moved to Munich and worked for Ludwig of Bavaria. His style was a Germanic court neo-classicism. Also designed The New Hermitage for the Romanovs.

LA FARGE, John (1835–1910)
Stained glass designer; mural painter. Heavily influenced by Japanese forms, the Pre-Raphaelites and William Blake, he had a successful career on the American East Coast; among his works in stained glass are the windows for H. H. Richardson's Holy Trinity, Boston (1878). His stained-glass work was taken up by Bing's shop, Art Nouveau.

LARSSON, Carl Olof (1853–1919)
Painter in watercolour and fresco; illustrator. His watercolours of an idealized home life in an airy neo-classical interior, collected in *Ett Hem* ('A Home') of 1899, succeeded in their reforming intentions and made a simple, peasant-style home the fashion in Scandinavia.

LATROBE, Benjamin Henry (1764–1820)
Architect, trained in England; emigrated to America. Leading Greek-revival and neo-classical architect; also designed furniture, notably for the Capitol and White House, Washington DC.

LETHABY, William Richard (1857–1931)
Architect, writer, designer. Worked for Richard Norman Shaw. Founder member of Art-Workers' Guild. His architectural work – in style akin to Philip Webb – was limited, but of the highest quality. His design work covered furniture (with Gimson he had set up the unsuccessful furniture workshop, Kenton & Co.), stained glass, cast iron, printing and interior decoration; he worked closely with Morris & Co, on Stanmore Hall. His book *Architecture, Mysticism and Myth* (1892), an attempt to find a modern architectural style from amid the contemporary so-called 'free style', was influential at the time. Principal of LCC Central School of Arts and Crafts 1900–12.

LIBERTY, Sir Arthur Lasenby (1843–1917)
Opened Liberty & Co. in Regent's Street, London, 1875; 1881 catalogue, *Eastern Art Manufactures and Decorative Objects*, catered for the Aesthetic movement's needs. A furniture and decoration showroom opened in 1883, and Libertys employed the best of British designers for their products. Libertys was the medium through which many avant-garde tastes were popularized.

LORIMER, Sir Robert Stodart (1864–1929)
Architect. An admirer of Morris & Co., he was an Arts and Crafts architect who designed his own furniture for his houses, as well as other decorative details. He also worked in Gothic and eighteenth-century styles.

LOUDON, John Claudius (1783–1843)
A Scottish gardener with a strong Enlightenment urge for improvement. His *Encyclopedia of Cottage, Farm and Villa Architecture* (1833) was a pattern book *raisonné* that established the Italianate villa and conservatory in the heart of the nineteenth-century suburb. Although Italianate was his recommended style, the *Encyclopedia* covers all historic styles and all conceivable buildings and details with earnest didactic purpose. Through A.J. Downing, Loudon's message spread to the United States.

MACKMURDO, Arthur Heygate (1851–1942)
Architect, draughtsman, designer. Founder of the short-lived Century Guild, which was an Arts and Crafts-inspired club for the younger generation of artist-designer-craftsmen. His frontispiece to *Wren's City Churches* (1883) is conventionally counted as the starting point for Art Nouveau.

MASRELIEZ, Louis-Adrien (1748–1810)
Sculptor; interior designer at the Swedish court.
He travelled in southern Europe during the 1770s
and '80s and evolved his own neo-classical style
of decoration, which he took back to Stockholm
in 1784, establishing himself as Sweden's leading
designer.

MORRIS, William (1834–96)
The presiding genius of the Arts and Crafts
movement. His Red House (1859–60) was
designed by Philip Webb and furnished and
decorated by Morris and his friends with
handmade items from their own designs in a
Gothic-vernacular idiom. From the
revolutionary Red House grew the firm of Morris
& Co. Morris's particular talent was pattern
design, but it was his personality, energy and
socialist idealism that gave direction to three
generations of artists, architects and designers.

MUTHESIUS, Hermann (1861–1927)
Architect. Worked in Tokyo, then employed as
architect by the Prussian state. His admiration
for the British Arts and Crafts movement began
when he was sent *en poste* to London in the 1890s.
His three-volume *Das englische Haus* (1904) was
the definitive survey of Arts and Crafts
architecture and interiors.

NESFIELD, William Eden (1835–88)
Architect. His early works are usually Gothic;
however, in the 1860s and '70s he was associated
with Norman Shaw and the Old English revival.

OLBRICH, Joseph Maria (1867–1908)
Architect; worked in the office of Otto Wagner.
Designed wallpapers and interiors in an Art
Nouveau style. Involved from the beginning in
the Vienna Secession of 1897. He moved to
Darmstadt Artists' Colony, where he played a
leading role in the design of the Darmstadt
stands at the Paris Exposition of 1900. His style
moved towards a plainer neo-classical idiom.

PERCIER, Charles (1764–1838)
Architect; studied under A.-F. Peyre. In
partnership with Fontaine. With *Recueil de
décorations intérieures* (1801), a manifesto folio of
neo-classical designs, they became the court
architects of the Empire.

PRIGNOT, Alexandre-Eugène (b. 1822)
Interior designer. He worked in London and
Paris from late 1840s to 1880s. Proficient in Louis
Seize and neo-classical styles. His *Les
Ornementistes du XIXe siècle* (1851) included his
own designs and *La Marbrerie moderne* (1879)
was entirely devoted to his work.

PUGIN, Augustus Charles (1769–1832)
Draughtsman, architect, furniture designer.
Began work in England in Nash's office. His
illustrations and designs of Gothic furniture
appeared in Ackermann's *Repository of Arts*
(1825–7) and were later published in book form
as *Gothic Furniture in the Style of the Fifteenth

Century (1835). His other books include
Specimens of Gothic Architecture (1821, 1823) and
Gothic Ornaments (1831), all cribbable source
material for the early Gothic revivalists. His
Examples of Gothic Architecture (1831, 1836) was
completed in its second volume posthumously by
his son A.W.N. Pugin.

PUGIN, Augustus Welby Northmore (1812–52)
Architect, designer, polemicist. Revolutionized
Gothic for the nineteenth century. Continued his
father's experimentation with Gothic, which
became increasingly archaeological and was then
transformed into a personal crusade when he
converted to Catholicism in 1835. Pugin's
activities included the lion's share of the design
of Barry's New Palace of Westminster; he
designed the Medieval Court of the 1851 Great
Exhibition as well as tile designs for Mintons and
metalwork design for Hardman & Co. Although
Pugin's mastery of medieval forms was complete,
his best designs were a new and personal
development of Gothic. His functionalist
approach, though dressed in a Gothic idiom,
provided lasting inspiration.

REDGRAVE, Richard (1804–88)
Painter and designer; associated with Henry
Cole, first as a designer of glassware for Cole's
unsuccessful Summerly enterprise. Edited Cole's
Journal of Design and Manufacture; involved
with 1851 Exhibition, where he attacked the
applied ornamentation of many of its exhibits. A
leading figure with the South Kensington
Museums, and in 1874 made Director of Art with
the Department of Education.

REIBER, Emile-Auguste (1826–93)
Architect, designer, founding editor of *L'Art pour
tous* (from 1861). Proficient designer in the
revival styles, as well as Arabic and Chinese; in
1870s moved heavily into the Japanese style.

RICARDO, Halsey Ralph (1854–1928)
Architect. In partnership with De Morgan, for
whom he designed tiles and vases. His motto of
'colour as comfort' was wedded to the idiom of a
late Arts and Crafts designer.

ROBINSON, George Thomas (*c.* 1828–1897)
Architect, interior designer, journalist. Art
director for decorating firm Trollopes from the
late 1870s onwards. His articles in *The Guardian*
and *The Magazine of Art* covered all aspects of
the decorative arts.

RUSKIN, John (1819–1900)
Writer, geologist, draughtsman, amateur
designer. As a prolific writer on art, architecture,
design and morality, his influence on Victorian
sensibilities is hard to overestimate. His *Stones of
Venice* (1851) solved the crisis of the Gothic
revival by introducing the essentially urban,
classical, Gothic style of Venice into British
architecture. His geological knowledge gave
authority to polychromatic architecture.

Alongside Carlyle and F.D. Maurice, Ruskin is
one of the Victorian prophets who wished to see
nineteenth-century society move away from
manufacturing and capitalism.

SCHINKEL, Karl Friedrich (1781–1841)
Architect. Worked in the office of the Gillys,
father and son. Inherited Friedrich Gilly's
mantle in 1790. Perfected an elegant neo-classical
idiom. Architect to the Prussian court in 1815.
The Gothic style, which had featured in Gilly's
monument to Frederick the Great, was
developed in his architecture and furniture
designs. Although he was fascinated with Gothic
forms in his designs, they never achieved the
elegance of his neo-classical work. Through his
association with the Prussian state, his designs
and architectural ideas received wide and lasting
currency.

SCHULTZ, Robert Weir (1860–1951)
Architect. Worked in Norman Shaw's office;
strongly influenced by Lethaby. Worked for
Lord Bute, for whom he designed furniture.

SEDDING, John Dando (1838–91)
Architect. Trained under Street; in practice on
his own in London 1874. Worked in Gothic style
for buildings; his interiors and furniture
employed Jacobean style but shifted towards
Arts and Crafts manner later on.

SEDDON, John Pollard (1827–1906)
Architect. Son of a cabinet-maker (who actually
made many of his designs), he worked closely
with Morris & Co. and adapted his designs to
include painted panels by Burne-Jones, Brown
etc. He also designed pottery and stained glass.

SEMPER, Gottfried (1803–79)
Architect; porcelain and furniture designer.
Designed sections of 1851 Great Exhibition,
including Canadian and Egyptian. Taught
furniture and metalwork at Malborough House
School of Design 1852–5. Wrote a theoretical
work, *Der Stil* (1861–3). Took up a teaching post
in Zurich (1855), from where he dominated Swiss
thinking on architecture and design.

SHAW, Richard Norman (1831–1912)
Architect, designer. Pupil of William Burn,
assistant to G.E. Street, he set up in practice
with W.E. Nesfield in 1862. Designed houses for
the Bedford Park garden suburb 1877–8, after
Godwin's designs had been rejected. Designed
furniture and wallpapers. Style of his furniture
stands between Morris's most massive Gothic
designs and Burges's decorative panache.

SILVER, Arthur (1853–96)
The Silver Studio, opened in 1880, was one of the
more successful Arts and Crafts ventures. Silver
was a proficient designer of textiles and
wallpapers, and became the leading commercial
designer of the 1890s.

SMITH, George (fl. 1801–1828)
Furniture designer and maker. He produced a range of pieces in the fashionable styles of the Regency which were illustrated in several catalogue-pattern books: *A Collection of Designs for Household Furniture and Interior Decoration* (1808), *Cabinet-maker's and Upholsterer's Guide, Drawing Book and Repository* (1826). His designs were also carried in Ackermann's *Repository*.

SMITH, J. Moyr (fl. 1868–1887)
'Decorative artist'. Trained in Dresser's studio; limited but proficient draughtsman and designer. Editor of *Decoration* from 1881.

SOANE, Sir John (1753–1837)
Architect; pupil of George Dance the Younger, whose style Soane took over and adapted to his own romantic temperament. Designed furniture in neo-classical and Gothic idioms. His interiors ranged from the neo-classical to an idiosyncratic Gothic and neo-classical hybrid in his own house-cum-museum, which included a 'Monk's Cell' complete with fragments of Gothic stonework.

STEVENS, Alfred (1817–75)
Sculptor, decorative painter. The head of the 'Renaissance' style in the applied arts in nineteenth-century Britain. Studied in Italy; taught at London and Sheffield Schools of Design. Chief designer for Hoole & Co., ironfounders. Designed vases for Minton. Decoration work included Dorchester House, and his own studio and house for which also did the furniture; designed and executed spandrel panels for St Paul's Cathedral in mosaic.

STICKLEY, Gustav (1857–1946)
Trained as stonemason; worked as chair-maker. Visited Europe in 1898 and fell under the influence of Arts and Crafts designers. Returned to United States, designed and made 'Craftsman' chairs. Founded 'United Crafts', originally a guild-based workshop that soon became a successful commercial enterprise; founded journal *The Craftsman* (1901–16).

STREET, George Edmund (1824–81)
Architect. Leading exponent of Gothic revival. Furniture designs are solidly Gothic. Most of his decorative work was done for church restoration.

SUMNER, George Heywood Maunoir (1856–1940)
Painter and designer. Closely involved with Art-Workers' Guild and Arts and Crafts Exhibition Society. Expert in sgraffito decoration.

SYKES, Godfrey (1824–66)
A follower of Alfred Stevens, who developed the 'Renaissance' style when working on the decoration of the Museums complex at South Kensington. The memory of Stevens perpetuated through Sykes dominates the internal adornment of these museums and also the decorative friezes on the Albert Hall.

TALBERT, Bruce J. (1838–81)
Wood-carver, furniture designer. Commercial designer of wallpapers, cast iron. Produced a massive Gothic style of furniture for many of the leading furniture manufacturers. *Gothic Forms applied to furniture, metalwork and decoration for domestic purposes* was published in 1868 (though dated 1867 on the title page), the same year as Eastlake's *Hints*, which it echoes in advocating weighty, well-built forms.

THONET, Michael (1796–1871)
Furniture designer and manufacturer. Pioneer of the bentwood chair, which exploited his own patented invention of laminated wood. His furniture was exhibited in London in 1851 to high acclaim.

TIFFANY, Louis Comfort (1848–1933)
Painter, decorative artist. Second generation of the Tiffany jewellery business. In 1879 started the commercial decorating firm of Associated Artists. From wallpapers, turned to designing stained glass. Tiffany Glass Co. founded in 1885; its products, exhibited by Bing, became an Art Nouveau staple. Succeeded as artistic director to the family business on his father's death in 1902.

VAN DE VELDE, Henri (1863–1957)
Painter, decorative designer, writer. After being close to Post-Impressionists, espoused Morris's ideas on the decorative arts. Thereafter, in writings and design work, was in the forefront of late nineteenth- and early twentieth-century trends in design and decoration. Designed interiors for Bing's Art Nouveau Gallery. He began his own company to produce his furniture and metalwork designs.

VIOLLET-LE-DUC, Eugène (1814–79)
Pre-eminent architect and writer of the Gothic revival in France. Responsible for a huge volume of restoration work on medieval religious and secular buildings. *Dictionnaire raisonné de l'Architecture* (1859–68) was the essential vademecum of all nineteenth-century Gothicists. His studies of furniture and dress of the Middle Ages are likewise detailed and authoritative. *Entretiens sur l'architecture* (1863–72) are essays towards a rational architecture that would meet contemporary and future materials and forms.

VOYSEY, Charles Francis Annesley (1857–1941)
Architect, designer. His distinctive style of architecture and design was very influential from the death of William Morris to the outbreak of war in 1914. Designed wallpapers, fabrics, tiles and metalwork for commercial manufacturers; his furniture designs he supervised himself. They followed a basic formula with varying details which were repeated for each commission. Insisted on designing a house right down the last detail. Unlike those of most Arts and Crafts designers, his social ideals were limited to a simple aesthetic that was individual and conservative.

WALTON, George (1867–1933)
'Ecclesiastical and house decorator'. Worked with C.R. Mackintosh in Glasgow. Influenced by Voysey's art and design. Furniture contained Glasgow Arts and Crafts influences. For his redecoration of the Kodak premises in London, and work in Glasgow, Brussels, Milan and Vienna, he used a sturdy Secession style.

WEBB, Philip (1831–1915)
Architect, furniture designer. Pupil of Street. Founder member of Morris & Co. for whom he was chief furniture designer. He also created stained-glass designs, and animal designs for tapestries etc. Webb believed that architecture and designs should be 'commonplace' – a view of the vernacular tradition that shunned showiness or anything that went beyond a simple functional directness. Much of his architecture was done in conjuction with Morris.

WHEELER, Candace (1827–1923)
Member of Tiffany's and Associated Artists. Designed textiles and wallpapers which showed Japanese influence. Also created designs for furniture and for her first love, embroidery. Her books include *Principles of Home Decoration* (1903).

WILLEMENT, Thomas (1786–1871)
Heraldic stained-glass designer. Also designed tiles, woodwork and 'Elizabethan' wallpapers.

WILSON, Henry (1864–1934)
Architect. Assistant to J.D. Sedding. Designer of metalwork that uses late Gothic-revival and Byzantine-revival motifs. Also designed commercial wallpapers and some furniture.

WYATT, Benjamin Dean (c. 1775–1852)
Architect, a specialist in theatre design. Interior design work, developed through theatre interiors, was of an opulent neo-classical style. Reconstructed authentic Louis Quatorze rococo designs for a series of prestigious London addresses.

WYATT, Sir Matthew Digby (1820–77)
Architect; a member of the Wyatt dynasty of architects. His book *The Geometrical Mosaics of the Middle Ages* (1848) led to him doing tile designs for Maw & Co. Associated with the circle of Henry Cole. Commissioner of 1851 Exhibition. Aided by Burges, produced *Metalwork and Artistic Design* (1852); went on to design the ironwork at Brunel's Paddington Station.

ZAHN, Johann Karl Wilhelm (1800–71)
Architect and archaeologist. Studied in France and Italy. His *Die schönsten Ornamente und merkwürdigsten Gemälde aus Pompeii, Herkulaneum und Stabiae* (1829 onwards) was the first book to use colour lithography. His *Ornamente aller klassichen Kunstepochen* (1831) includes Pompeian wall treatments and antique vases, and also features the decorations of Giulio Romano's Palazzo del Te in Mantua.

BIBLIOGRAPHY

The decorative arts of the nineteenth century are a comparatively recent subject for research. The revolt against Victorianism begun by the Bloomsbury movement continues to permeate popular ideas about the nineteenth century in Britain. Until very recently France maintained an ambiguous attitude to the very existence of the nineteenth century after Napoleon.

AMES, WINSLOW
Prince Albert and Victorian Taste, London, 1968

ARTS COUNCIL OF GREAT BRITAIN
The Age of Neo-Classicism, London, 1972
The best survey of the arts in Europe from 1780 to 1820.

ASLIN, ELIZABETH
E. W. Godwin, Furniture and Interior Decoration, London, 1986
Readable and sensitively illustrated study by an authority on Godwin's decorative work.

BIRMINGHAM MUSEUM
By Hammer and Hand; The Arts & Crafts Movement in Birmingham (Ed. Alan Crawford), 1984

BRIGHTON MUSEUM
Catalogue *C. F. A. Voysey: Architect & Designer*, London, 1978

CENTRAL SCHOOL OF ART AND DESIGN
Catalogue *W. R. Lethaby; Architect, Design and Education*, London. 1984

CLEMMENSEN, TOVE
Skaebner og Interiorer (Danish Drawings from Baroque to Arts & Crafts) 1984

COLLARD, FRANCES
Regency Furniture, London, 1985
Scholarly survey of furniture and allied decoration from the 1790s onwards.

COOPER, JEREMY
Victorian and Edwardian Interiors and Furniture: From Gothic Revival to Art Nouveau, London, 1987
Important work that gathers together under one heading the previously neglected furniture and interiors of Victorian designers and craftsmen.

COOPER, NICHOLAS
The Opulent Eye, London, 1976
Contains a selection of Bedford Lemere's photographs, mainly of the Edwardian era.

CORNFORTH, JOHN
English Interiors 1790–1848; The Quest for Comfort, London, 1978
Useful *catalogue raisonnée* of upper- and middle-class interiors.

CRAWFORD, ALAN
C. R. Ashbee: Architect, Designer, Romantic Visionary, 1981

DAVIDSON, CAROLINE
The World of Mary Ellen Best, London, 1986

FORGE, SUZANNE
Victorian Splendour in Australian Interior Decoration 1837–1901, Sydney, 1981

GIEDION, SIGFRIED
Mechanization takes Command, Oxford, 1948
One of the earliest and still the best study of the 'ruling taste' in applied arts and design from factory to the home.

GIROUARD, MARK
Sweetness and Light: the 'Queen Anne' Movement, 1860–1900, Oxford, 1977
Chapter VI deals with the artistic interior; the book gives a good account of the Queen Anne ethos as well as its architecture.

GRAND PALAIS, PARIS
L'Art en France sous le Second Empire, Paris, 1979
A well documented coverage of the decorative arts together with chapters on furniture and architecture.

HÔTEL DE ROHAN, PARIS
Les Parisiens chez eux au 19e siècle, Paris, 1977
The influence of Paris – 'the capital of the nineteenth century' – in the arts and the art of living was perhaps the greatest of any individual city in the late eighteenth and nineteenth century.

JERVIS, SIMON
High Victorian Design, London, 1983
Survey of the main strands of design theory and pratice with illustrations covering all aspects of decorative arts and architecture.

LYNN, CATHERINE
Wallpaper in America; From Seventeenth Century to World War I, New York, 1980
Meticulous and readable monograph on wallpaper that *inter alia* charts Americans' attitudes to the home and its décor.

MAYHEW, E. M. and MYERS, M.
A Documentary History of American Interiors, New York, 1980

METROPOLITAN MUSEUM OF ART, NEW YORK
In Pursuit of Beauty; Americans and the Aesthetic Movement, New York, 1986
Complete and thorough coverage of the development of the decorative arts in America from the Philadelphia Exposition of 1876 to the 1930s.

MORLEY, JOHN
The Making of the Royal Pavilion Brighton, London, 1984
Detailed account of the building and design of the Pavilion provides insights into the decorative arts of the Regency and beyond.

NATIONAL MUSEUM OF WALES, CARDIFF
Catalogue *William Burges; Art-Architect*, Cardiff, 1981

NAYLOR, GILLIAN
William Morris by himself, London, 1988

NAYLOR, GILLIAN
The Arts & Crafts Movement, London, 1971

PARRY, LINDA
William Morris Textiles, London, 1983

PRAZ, MARIO
An illustrated history of Interior Decoration, from Pompeii to Art Nouveau, London, 1964 (translation of *La filosofia dell' arredamento*)
Classic work that brought interior decoration within the ambit of scholarly art history.

ROYAL ACADEMY OF ARTS, LONDON
Victorian & Edwardian Decorative Art: The Handley-Read Collection, London, 1972
The Handley-Reads were scholars and pioneer collectors of Victorian furniture, the designs of William Burges in particular.

SUDLEY ART GALLERY/H. BLAIRMAN & SONS
Catalogue *George Bullock 1783–1818*, 1988
Clive Wainwright's Introduction establishes both the context of Bullock's art and his importance.

SWEETMAN, JOHN
The Oriental Obsession, Cambridge, 1988
This important strand of nineteenth-century sensibility is charted through both the decorative and fine arts.

THORNTON, PETER
Authentic Decor; The Domestic Interior 1620–1920, London, 1984
Scholarly and precisely illustrated; both a general survey and a detailed study of European and American ideas on interior decoration.

VORONICHINA, A.N.
Views of the Hermitage and Winter Palace, Moscow, 1983

WATKIN, DAVID
Thomas Hope and the Neo-Classical Idea, 1968
An important study of Hope and the ideas and tastes current between 1780 and 1820.

WATSON-GUPTILL INC.
Nineteenth-Century Furniture, New York, 1982
Important for its coverage of American furniture in the first half of the nineteenth century.

WEDGWOOD, A.
Pugin Family Catalogue of the Drawings Collection of the R. I. B. A., London, 1977
The introduction to each section and the catalogue entries for the drawings provide a guide to A. W. N. Pugin's decorative work as well as his architecture.

WEISBERG, GABRIEL P.
Art Nouveau Bing, New York, 1986

INDEX